To Sharon,
with best wishes
Alexandra Costa

STEPPING DOWN FROM THE STAR

STEPPING DOWN FROM THE STAR

A SOVIET DEFECTOR'S STORY

Alexandra Costa

G. P. PUTNAM'S SONS *New York*

G. P. Putnam's Sons
Publishers Since 1838
200 Madison Avenue
New York, NY 10016

Library of Congress Cataloging-in-Publication Data

Costa, Alexandra, date.
Stepping down from the star.

1. Costa, Alexandra, date. 2. Russians—United
States—Biography. 3. Defectors—United States—
Biography. I. Title.
E184.R9C67 1986   973.92′092′4   86-9472
ISBN 0-399-13195-7

Printed in the United States of America
1 2 3 4 5 6 7 8 9 10

FOREWORD
AND ACKNOWLEDGMENTS

This is a book about the shadowy world of defection—an emotionally difficult decision for those who contemplate it, an often frustrating process for those who follow it. There have been many books and memoirs on the subject, but the motivations and feelings of the people on both sides—those defecting, those receiving—are still all too often misunderstood.

I had been thinking of writing the story of my own defection for some time when an incident in November of 1985—the defection to the United States of KGB officer Vitaly S. Yurchenko, followed by his highly controversial redefection to the Soviet Union—convinced me it was time to come out into the open. After seven years of living under an assumed name, I wanted to speak out about the problems that bring people to the painful decision to leave their own country and seek refuge in the free world, and about the problems they still must face when "safe."

Like many such people, I loved Russia. I still do. I hope that Americans who read this book will understand at least one thing—how fortunate they are to live in a free country, in a political system that does not force its citizens to choose between their love for their country and their desire to be free and to exert control over their own lives. Being free is the greatest gift a country can give to its citizens.

I also hope that this book will give people a glimpse of life in Russia, and will bring a better understanding of the Russians as people—people who are all too human, and who cope with the problems of everyday life just like Americans do, only in their own and very different ways. The Soviet Union is here to stay; I have no hope that it will change its ways any time soon, and Americans will have to live with it—or die with it. During my time in the United States, I have encountered many emotions concerning Russians, and one of them is fear, simply because Russians are such an enigma to many people here. I sincerely hope that this book will make a small dent in the wall of incomprehension.

This book was not intended to be an exposé; neither do I intend to point fingers at anyone. I especially do not want to hurt any of my former friends who were at the Soviet Embassy in Washington at the time I was there. Therefore, although most of the embassy people described in this book are real people, and their names have not been changed, there is one composite character in the book. All statements that the Soviet authorities might regard as too candid, though they came from various people in the embassy, are attributed to this character, named "Peter." The names of my friends in the Soviet Union have also been changed, except for my relatives, who are already known to the Soviet authorities. For obvious reasons, all names of the FBI and CIA personnel involved in my case have been changed, too.

There are so many people to whom I owe a debt of gratitude for bringing this book into existence that I do not know where to begin, so I will start chronologically.

My sincere thanks and appreciation go to Tara Sonenshine, executive producer of *ABC Nightline* and Patrick Tyler of the *Washington Post*. Not only were they the first people to bring my story to the public, but they also encouraged me to take it one step further and write a book, read the first draft chapters, and gave me suggestions on the direction the book should take.

Next, I would like to thank my agent, Esther Newberg, of International Creative Management, for her belief in me, her encouragement, and for making an idea of a book a reality.

I would like to thank Tom Ferraro of UPI and my friends Jill Cornish, and Heather Evans for reading the draft of the manuscript and making suggestions on what aspects of Soviet life might be interesting to the American public.

My greatest thanks go to my editor, Neil Nyren, for his patience in working with someone who was not only a first-time author, but whose native language was not English. Blessed is the author who has an editor who makes him (or her) rewrite entire chapters until a collection of reminiscences and notes becomes what it is supposed to be—a book.

I wish I could thank separately many other people—my "white knights" in the Federal Bureau of Investigation and the people in the Central Intelligence Agency—who have made it possible for me to become a part of this country in the first place, but I cannot mention them by name. To all of them who read this book—you will always remain a part of my fondest memories.

And, finally, my thanks to my children, Kristina and Konstantin, who became experts in opening cans of Spaghetti-Os and following the instructions on TV dinners in those three months when I was trying to juggle my manuscript and my regular work. Their presence in my life has governed many decisions I have taken in the past ten years; their love got me through many difficult moments, and it is to them that I dedicate this book.

ALEXANDRA COSTA
March 1986

Anastasia, tell me who you are
Are you someone from another star?

"Anastasia"

CHAPTER 1

On the morning of August 2, 1978, my husband
Lev Mitrokhin left for work around nine, as usual. The office of
the Soviet Copyright Agency was on K Street, but first he planned
to stop briefly at the embassy one and a half blocks away. The
weekly Aeroflot flight from Moscow had arrived the night before,
and there would be mail for us there—both from our Moscow
office and from our relatives. I asked him to call me as soon as he
got to the office to let me know if there'd been a letter from my
mother. I figured he'd get there by about ten o'clock.

There was nothing unusual about my request—letters from home
were treasured and eagerly awaited. Nor was it unusual for me to
ask him to come home for lunch—I said I needed the car to run
errands in the afternoon, and since we were the only people in
our small office, nobody checked on his whereabouts or absences.
Although we were formally attached to the embassy, where Lev
held the diplomatic rank of first secretary, we ran the agency more
or less independently.

For me, however, that morning was anything but usual. The day
had been carefully planned weeks in advance, and it was crucial
to my plan that I receive that call—to make sure that he was finally

in the office, at least twenty minutes' driving time away, and that he would indeed return home for lunch. Today was the day that would change my entire life forever—I was defecting from my country and asking for asylum in the United States. The operation had been in preparation for months, and now only a few hours separated me from that final step. It also meant that I had less than three hours to change my mind if I wanted to—the action I was contemplating was irreversible. There would be no way back later.

Most of my belongings were already packed. We had been scheduled to return to Moscow in September, and I'd been gradually sorting things out and putting nonessentials in boxes in preparation for our departure. Actually, I hadn't been packing for me, but for Lev. Whether he decided to stay with me or not, he would not have much time for packing. If he stayed, we would have to act fast; if he did not, he would be sent home on the first available plane—most likely the flight from New York the next day. For myself, I had only a couple of suitcases with my clothing and my children's clothing, a box with a few of my favorite records and tapes, and some memorabilia from home.

The final packing did not take long, and I settled down to wait for Lev's call. Time moved so slowly. I picked up the newspaper, then put it down—I could hardly comprehend what I was reading. The children played quietly. They were mere toddlers—Kitty was three and one-half and Konstantin one and one-half—and I wished I had more adult company to help me pass the time.

There was a knock on the door. My heart leaped. No one was supposed to come here—who could that be?

The FBI had been renting an apartment upstairs for the past several months to make our meetings easier, and I was supposed to go there after I got "the call," but no one was supposed to take the risk of coming to my apartment. What if it was the KGB? What if they had found out after all, despite all the secrecy, despite all the planning?

Trembling, I opened the door—and saw Jim's smiling face.

"Moving company, ma'am," he said. "Ready?"

"Yes," I said, sighing with relief.

He read my face and smiled again. "He is parking his car," he said casually. "Won't be long now. Thought you'd like some company. Have any coffee?"

His cheerful mood made me feel better. Of course they were leaving nothing to chance. All Lev's comings and goings would be carefully monitored that day. I was certain that the phones were tapped as well. As I had discovered long before, these people knew their job.

We spent another half an hour drinking coffee and smoking. Despite Jim's cheerfulness, I felt that he was nervous, probably as much as I was, which was unusual. Jim always appeared to be easygoing; he had a way of making people comfortable with him. It was at least partly due to his appearance; with his medium height, sort of homely looks, soft brown eyes and slightly receding hairline, he was the kind of guy you could meet on the street every day without paying much attention. He was slightly tense now, though. After all, nobody had ever defected from the Soviet Embassy in Washington before. It was a major operation for the FBI.

Finally the phone rang. It was Lev.

"No letters," he said. "Not much from the office, either."

"OK. I'll be leaving now," I answered, trying to sound as casual as possible. I'd told him the night before that I'd been invited to have tea with our neighbor, an elderly lady with whom I'd become friendly, so that he wouldn't be surprised if I did not answer the phone later. "And try not to be late for lunch," I added.

"One o'clock," he said. "See you later."

I took a last glance at the apartment. It was clean and neat, everything in place. On an empty dining table, two white envelopes leaned against a flower vase, strategically positioned to catch Lev's eye as soon as he came in through the patio door. One was a letter to the embassy with the formal announcement of my intention to stay in the United States for personal reasons; another was for Lev, explaining my motives in more detail and asking him to stay with me.

My heart was pounding and I began to feel slightly faint. "Let's go," I told Jim. I picked up my son and took my daughter's hand;

Jim picked up a basket containing the children's toys, baby food, and diapers. We took the staircase to the second floor, avoiding the elevator that faced the front desk. Jim would get the rest of the things later.

The door to the other apartment opened the moment Jim knocked—we'd obviously been expected. Several men were there. I knew one of them, John, my very first contact. Over the past few months I had met with him and Jim quite a few times. He was also the one I'd been supposed to call in case of emergency, and I felt reassured by his presence. It was comfortable to see a friendly face. In the beginning I'd been a little scared of him. He was over six feet tall, and his round face with dark penetrating eyes, closely cropped dark hair, slightly crooked nose, and normally stern expression, gave him a rather hawkish look. In time, however, I'd learned that those dark eyes that seemed to notice everything could also be filled with warmth and laughter, and I'd come to trust him completely.

The other two men sitting at the dining room table I had not met before. They were introduced as Larry and Craig; Larry was concentrating on something that looked like a portable radio and barely gave me a glance. He was very tall, with reddish-blond hair and very pale blue eyes, and looked almost menacing. If he had been the one who had met with me the very first time, instead of John, I thought, I probably never would have decided to do what I was doing now. He fit the image of FBI agents exactly—unsmiling, deadly efficient, and dangerous.

I sat at the table, and John brought me a cup of coffee. He knew I needed it, as well as a cigarette. "You look pale," he said quietly.

"I don't feel well," I said. "I've got this terrible heartbeat, and I don't know what to do with it. I hope I won't faint."

"That's all we need," Larry said. "Why don't you take a sedative?"

"I don't have any," I said. Then I remembered I had some sleeping pills in the apartment—they probably contained a mild sedative. Jim was going downstairs to pick up the rest of my things, and I told him where to find the medicine. He was back in a few minutes, and I took the pills. Gradually the heartbeat subsided. By then Larry had finished his radio conversations and raised his head. He smiled, and suddenly there was nothing menacing about him.

"Feel better?" he said. "Now, for the last time—are you sure?"

"Yes."

Was I sure? At that moment I felt that I was.

The reasons for my defection were so many, so complex, that even then it was difficult to sort them out and decide which was the most important. My marriage had been steadily deteriorating, my concern for my children's future back in the Soviet Union had been steadily growing—yes, those had both been important factors. But the primary factor had been that after almost three years of living and working in the United States I'd begun to appreciate the opportunities that people had here for taking control of their own lives. I was thirty-four, well educated, and had a good job back in the Soviet Union, but for several years before coming to the United States I had experienced a vague feeling that my life was following a predetermined pattern that was being laid out by somebody else. I could not define it exactly except for the realization that I did not particularly like what I was doing but could not see any alternative. It was not until I came to the United States and started dealing with American businesses that the perception finally took shape. What was missing in my life was the ability to make choices, to make my own decisions. It was simply not possible in the highly regulated, bureaucratic Soviet society. I wanted to become a part of that business world I had seen here, to try things on my own, and maybe make mistakes, but at least to achieve something on my own merit and abilities rather than having my life controlled by restrictions and dogmas. In the Soviet Union there was always somebody else who decided how I should live my life. Now, I had a choice.

My thoughts were interrupted by Larry's voice.

"I'm still not sure about the letters." He was talking to Jim now. "It would be better if she just left a note asking him to meet her outside and then gave him the letter to the embassy. What if he calls the embassy first?"

"I know my husband better than you do," I said. "He is not going to call anywhere until he talks to me, and he will also need time to think, even if it's just a few minutes. I will ask him to destroy the personal letter later."

"While we're on the subject," Larry said, "are there any weapons in the house?"

"Only kitchen knives. Besides, if you think he will try to kill me, that's ridiculous."

"You never know," he said. "People can do strange things under stress. Well, if you think he'll behave, we'll have to trust your judgment, but we are not going to take any chances. And now, let's go—we don't have much time."

We all went downstairs, this time to the main entrance. In front of the door was a taxicab. To my surprise we went straight to it.

"It's less conspicuous this way," John said, intercepting my puzzled look. Larry, Jim, John, and I got into the car. Craig stayed behind.

"Sorry, no air," said the driver as we were getting in. The car windows were open, but the hot August air inside the car was suffocating.

"Where are we going?" I asked Jim. It was eleven o'clock. I knew we would be back by one o'clock to meet with Lev, but that's where my knowledge of the plan ended.

"It's not far," he said. "We'll just take the children to a safe place and then we'll bring you back."

The drive was indeed short. Several miles west on Route 50, we pulled over to a motel. In the motel room were three people—two men and a blond girl dressed in what looked like a light blue nurse's uniform. I assumed she was a babysitter to take care of the children. The men were probably agents.

It turned out that one of the men was from the Immigration and Naturalization Service. He had the papers with him that I had filled out a couple of months before: a request for asylum for myself and my children and an application for citizenship—John had told me that paperwork could take a couple of months, and he'd wanted to have everything ready by the time I came over. The man asked me to raise my hand and take an oath, and then to confirm that I was acting on my own free will. All of a sudden I found myself suppressing a giggle—the military command center atmosphere of the FBI apartment and the euphoric feeling of escape that I was beginning to feel were in such contrast to this bureaucratic request for signing forms that I almost missed the significance of the moment. It was not until the man shook my hand solemnly and said, "Congratulations, you are now a permanent resident of the United States," that it finally dawned on me that this was The Moment I had been waiting for during all those months of nerve-racking danger. I did not know at that time that the INS representative had taken an extraordinary step by coming to see us in the motel. Ordinarily I'd have had to be taken to the INS office downtown, but there hadn't been enough time before my meeting with Lev. Even though the probability that Lev would somehow contact the embassy and get reinforcements was practically nil, the FBI wanted me to be protected by law.

The INS man left. I gave instructions to the babysitter about feeding the children and left them with the agent who'd been in the room when we arrived. The cab was gone. Larry, John, Jim, and I got in the car parked outside and drove back to the apartment building.

There were two more cars waiting for us in the parking lot in the back of the building when we arrived. I shook hands with other people; everybody smiled and congratulated me. One of them looked familiar, but I could not figure out where I knew him from. Suddenly I remembered—the "cabdriver."

"You change cars fast," I said.

"Thank goodness." He laughed. "That one was really a wreck. I wasn't sure we'd make it to the motel."

I did not really believe it, but it was good to see everybody in a cheerful mood. In a few minutes, one car drove away. Larry parked ours so it could not be seen from the patio of my apartment where, we knew, Lev would drive up and park. It was only a few minutes after noon. We walked over to the apartment. Through the patio door I could see the table with my letters on it. I could just go back in, throw away the letters, and pretend that nothing happened, I thought. Nobody in the world except me and the FBI knew how I had spent that morning. I knew that I could ask them to bring the children back and call the whole thing off. Lev was probably still in the office, and I could call him and delay his arrival until the children came back.

As if he had read my thoughts, John took my hand. "Everything will be fine," he said. "Don't worry, we are with you." He paused and then said, "What do you think he will do?"

"Fifty-fifty," I said. This was not the first time we had tried to figure out what Lev would do when I told him of my decision. Although John assured me that my safety was their only concern, I knew that it would be a major political coup for the FBI if he defected. I did not have the answer. I had been married to Lev for seven years. He was a complex man, brilliant and unpredictable. There was a chance he would stay with me, but I also knew that his soul was deeply rooted in Russia. With all the polish he had acquired in the past fifteen years of high position in Moscow and foreign travels, he often bragged about his family roots going back to generations of Central Russian peasantry, of being of the true Russian stock. Other circumstances that would influence his decision also had a pull—although I was taking our children, his beloved mother and sister and his daughter from his first marriage were in Moscow.

Did I want him to stay? I did not have an answer for that, either. Our marriage was faltering but not dead yet. I knew, however, that if he stayed because of the children and then later regretted it, he would start drinking again, and then I would divorce him, thus leaving him alone in a country in which he was far less comfortable than I was by now. I was not prepared to take that responsibility. I pushed the thought out of my mind. Whatever happened, it would be his decision. I was not going to do anything that would let him say later that I had pushed him into something he did not want.

One of the agents in another car motioned to us to come back. They had received a message that Lev had left the office and was on his way home. I began to feel my heart flutter again. The other car was apparently equipped as a communications center. Messages began coming rapidly—crossed the bridge, five blocks away, two blocks away, pulling into the parking lot, went into apartment . . . found the letters . . . reading . . . coming out!

I gripped John's hand and went to face my husband.

CHAPTER 2

OUR assignment to the United States had been through an unusual route—Lev was not a professional diplomat. The opportunity had presented itself when, in 1973, after many years of pirating foreign books and films, the Soviet Union had finally signed the Universal Copyright Convention. The convention, which had existed for many years by then, provided for protection of copyright and proper compensation for authors in all countries that signed it, and most countries had. Except the Soviet Union. There, books of foreign authors were translated and printed in hundreds of thousands of copies, songs of foreign composers were played on the radio and in concerts, and neither the authors nor performers got a penny for it—until the government finally decided it was politically expedient to go along with the rest of the world.

One of the reasons for the Soviets' signing was that the same piracy applied to works of Soviet authors published abroad. My own father had fallen victim to that system. Many times champion of the Soviet Union in marksmanship and a holder of many world records, he'd retired from active sport in 1952, at the peak of his sports career. It had been a forced choice. In 1952 the Soviet Union was set to participate in the Olympic Games for the first time. Marksmanship being an Olympic sport, my father was an obvious candidate to head the Soviet Olympic team. The problem was that he was also a ranking officer in the Air Force Academy, which contained extensive research facilities, and he held a high-level security clearance. Traveling abroad and keeping his job at the same time was out of the question. He was told that he must resign his job—he was too valuable a sports figure to be permitted to resign from the team. The prospect did not please him. He was thirty-six and had maybe a few more years to stay in top shape, after which the only avenue open to him in sports would be coaching. On the other hand, he had at least twenty years of Air Force career ahead of him if he stayed with the academy.

The Olympic Committee ignored his plea—in the Soviet Union, sports is a State matter. Sports showmanship and frequent victories in international competitions are too important as propaganda tools and morale builders for an individual's career to count much. Finally he obtained a fake certificate that said his vision was failing and only then was let off the hook. He maintained his interest in the sport, however, and after extensive studies wrote a comprehensive book on marksmanship. It was a new approach that had never been attempted before. Besides covering such standard topics as ballistics and training procedures, he approached the subject from the point of view of physiology, human anatomy, and neurobiology, and the book instantly became the Bible of the sport. It was translated into most foreign languages in both Eastern Bloc and Western countries, but, because of existing copyright—or, rather, noncopyright—practices, he never received a penny from foreign publishers. Some publishers did not even bother to send a complimentary copy to him, and we found out about some translations only from members of Soviet teams who brought copies as gifts to my father.

Foreign piracy of Soviet works was not the main reason the Soviet Union finally decided to join the convention, however. Since many more foreign books were translated in the Soviet Union than Soviet books published abroad, it was an economic disadvantage—more money would have to be paid out than brought in. Basically, it was part of the fallout of détente, a gesture to the Western world to show that the Soviet Union was a civilized country that complied with international standards. Shortly thereafter, a new governmental entity was formed—the All-Union Copyright Agency, known by its Russian abbreviation, VAAP. The agency was granted the power to open foreign offices to handle all exchange of copyrighted material between foreign countries and the Soviet Union, to promote Soviet books and published music abroad, and to make recommendations on the choice of foreign works to be published in the Soviet Union.

The chairman of VAAP was Boris Pankin, a former secretary of the Central Committee of Komsomol—the Soviet Young Communist League—and later an editor in chief of its national newspaper, *Komsomolskaya Pravda*. He had his own vision about who would represent his agency in key foreign countries. He did not want any bureaucrats. He wanted to have people who were thoroughly familiar with the culture of each country, who knew the language, and had either been stationed there or traveled to that country before and so had a certain status and name recognition. He appointed a prominent journalist to head his West German office, and approached my husband, Lev, who had been his classmate at the university and later his deputy secretary of propaganda in the Komsomol Central Committee, to be the VAAP representative in the United States.

Lev had impressive credentials. After completing his graduate study in philosophy, he had chosen a party career and quickly risen through the ranks to a high position in the Central Committee of Komsomol. At the age of thirty-four he had been offered a position as deputy editor of the official Communist Party newspaper, *Pravda*. At that time he changed direction. He was contemplating a divorce from his first wife, which would immediately become an impediment to his career in the party, so he decided to go back to the academic world, which was more permissive in terms of people's personal lives. By thirty-six he was the youngest doctor of philosophy in the social sciences and, with his past achievements in the party, was on the fast track again.

For the last ten years he had specialized in modern American philosophy and the history of political movements, published several books, including one on the Black Panthers, visited the United States and England many times as part of academic exchanges, and had become fairly well known in his field in the American academic community. His academic status also suggested no connection to intelligence matters—an appearance that Pankin was firmly resolved to avoid at all costs.

Lev was pleased with the offer but declined at first. At the time he was a deputy director of the Institute of Philosophy of the Soviet Academy of Sciences, the most prestigious body of social research in the Soviet Union, and just then the social-research community was embroiled in a bitter factional fight between the old generation of dogmatic Marxists and the younger generation of more liberal social scientists. The Young Turks had joined their forces with members of the emerging new science of sociology, which only a few years before had been denounced as nonscience and a capitalistic tool, but was now the hottest new field in the social sciences. Lev felt that leaving Moscow at that time would give the opposition an opportunity to place their man in his critical position in the institute, and thus weaken the liberal forces to which most of his friends belonged. He also had personal reasons—his beloved eleven-year-old daughter from his first marriage. He felt that his weekend visits contributed substantially to forming her outlook on life— something he did not want to leave entirely to his ex-wife.

My own view of the situation was exactly the opposite. We'd been married for three years by then. I knew the situation in his institute, and many of his colleagues, very well, having been a member of the Leningrad branch of the same institute for several years before I had met Lev. I felt that the tide of euphoria over liberalization of the social sciences was ebbing. The Institute of Sociology, where I had done my graduate study a couple of years before, was undergoing rapid transformation from a hotbed of Western ideas, toward "ideological purity." There had been a severe personnel shake-out, with some people forced to leave, others resigning voluntarily. I feared that the hatchet job that was being performed on the Institute of Sociology would spill over to the Institute of Philosophy, and Lev, being in such a visible position, would be one of the first people to get the ax. It was safer, I argued, to sit it out in the cozy comfort of a foreign assignment until the dust settled in the social sciences field.

On the personal front, I had my own reasons for wanting to leave Moscow. Sonya, Lev's ex-wife, was making my life miserable. We'd never met, and Lev had already been separated from her by the time I had met him, but I knew that she had never wanted a divorce and that she believed that she had had a fair chance of getting Lev back until I'd come along. She maintained a good relationship with many of Lev's friends, and the sympathy of some of their wives was on her side, not always because they liked her but because they considered me an outsider in Moscow life. The fact that I was fourteen years younger than Lev didn't help, either—in the eyes of those women, I was setting a dangerous precedent, and they were afraid that Lev's apparent happiness in his new family life would set their own husbands' thoughts in the wrong direction.

In addition there were continuous demands for more money. The Soviet law regarding child support is very clear: 25 percent of the ex-husband's salary to support one child, 33 percent for two, 50 percent for three or more. A quarter of Lev's gross income, coupled with Sonya's own salary, came close to what my father, an Air Force colonel, was making to support our entire family, and about as much as Lev and I had left after deducting the money he gave monthly to his mother and paying the exorbitant rent on our apartment—he had left the apartment he had had before to Sonya as well. It wasn't enough for her, though. Sometimes she used his daughter, Xenia, as a weapon. Lev would pay his weekend visit to her home and have to run out to the grocery store because he found an empty refrigerator and Xenia had told him that she was hungry and had had nothing to eat since the previous night.

Those Sunday visits took a heavy emotional toll on Lev. He would get moody and irritable and start drinking on Saturday in anticipation of the scenes he would have to endure the next day. Sunday night he could come back depressed and drink heavily. Monday was "recovery day." We were expecting our first child, and I resented the fact that I had a normal family life only from

Tuesday to Friday, and even on those days, midnight telephone calls from Sonya and two-hour conversations, ostensibly on the subject of Xenia's upbringing, were not all that unusual. Most important, I felt that the situation with his former family aggravated his drinking problem, and hoped that removing him from that environment would help him. I was not unaware of the fact that drinking was not encouraged in Soviet missions abroad, and that he would be under some pressure there to give it up, or at least to scale it down.

In addition to my concern about Lev's job and the strain on our family life, I was worried about the future of my own job. Until then, my life had been progressing smoothly. I'd grown up in a comfortably well-to-do family in Leningrad. Although my father was in the Air Force, he was never a field officer. From the beginning, he was attached to the Air Force Academy based in Leningrad, and we lived on the same street the whole time I was growing up, moving a couple of times only to better apartments. After graduating with honors from high school in 1960, I had been accepted by the University of Leningrad, where I majored in Scandinavian languages. For a year after graduation I worked as a translator at the patent bureau—a tedious but nontaxing job, then I went to work at the Leningrad branch of the Institute of Philosophy, whose then-director, Anatoly Kharchev, was a prominent researcher in family sociology. He was interested in doing a comparative study of family sociology in Sweden, and hired me as a research assistant for an elderly Member of the Academy of Sciences attached to the branch, with the promise that I would have enough free time to do some translations for him and to pursue my own degree if I wished to do so. His word was good, and within a year I took my qualifying graduate exams and started to work on my dissertation comparing the effects on women's professional work on their family life in the USA, Sweden, and the USSR. In 1970 I transferred my graduate study to the Moscow Institute of Sociology because I wanted to be closer to Lev, and there completed my degree.

For the past two years I had been teaching Marxism in a special institute for foreign students, where all subjects were taught in native languages. My degrees in Scandinavian languages and sociology, considerably reinforced by Lev's connections, had gotten me the job in this very privileged institution, which had its own foreign goods store and commissary—the perks that even my husband did not have. Another, hidden, benefit of my work was the unusual degree of freedom provided the instructors for teaching even such dogmatic subjects as Marxism. Marxism is taught in every single college in the Soviet Union—it is a mandatory subject, and even the most brilliant student in a technical field may have trouble graduating if he or she does not pass an exam in it. The teaching is extremely rigid and consists mainly of standard interpretations of works by Marx, Engels, and Lenin. The students essentially memorize proper answers and a few quotations, and that is enough to get them through the exam.

That kind of teaching was not possible in our institute, nicknamed "the School." Our students mostly came from Western countries and were very well informed on world events—and not necessarily from the Soviet perspective. Although they were all members of foreign Communist parties, that did not preclude critical thinking on their part. In order to be believable, all instructors had to do some thinking as well. We had an excellent library, filled with the most recent Western books and periodicals, and special information bulletins issued daily for the Central Committee of the Communist Party which contained translations of the most significant articles in the leading Western magazines. Although we taught the basics of Marxism and could not deviate from the party line, we tried to stay away from the most obnoxious dogmas and were expected to be able to defend our statements with facts or good logical reasoning in the open classroom discussions. As a result, we had some very controversial instructors—people who were considered "revisionists" by the formal establishment, and who were often in danger of losing their full-time jobs in other Soviet institutions. These people were often some of our best part-time instructors, and were highly regarded both by the students and their own colleagues.

We were encouraged to socialize with our students and spend some of our free time with them in the school cafeteria or during

informal gatherings at their dormitories. And that eventually became my undoing. I became very friendly with a group of Brazilian
students and began spending a lot of time with them, although I
was not their immediate instructor. One day my friend Marina,
who had worked at the School longer than I had, took me aside.

"Your Danes are complaining that you are neglecting them by
spending too much time with the Brazilians. They'll get you in
trouble. You know, in this place the student is always right."

"My Danes are nothing but a bunch of snooty kids," I said. "I
have no problems with my Finnish or Australian groups. They like
me and will support me. Besides, we are told to be friendly with
students."

"Not *all* students," Marina said. "Sure, Brazilians are fun to be
with, but there are some rumors already that your relationship
with some of them is more than friendly."

I was stunned. Nothing could have been further from the truth.
I was solidly and happily married, and although I suspected that
one of my Brazilian friends had a mild crush on me, I treated them
all equally.

"That's ridiculous," I said. "Who is going to believe it?"

"The KGB."

I disregarded the conversation, but Marina was right. The Danes
did complain at the end of their school year. The head of my
department, one of Lev's closest friends, warned me that the clouds
were gathering over my head and recommended an extended leave.
I was protected from being fired—I was expecting a baby, and it
is against the law to fire a pregnant woman, no matter what the
reason. In addition, I could take a year of unpaid leave after the
baby was born. By then things would have quieted down. However,
a foreign assignment was an even better solution. If I went abroad,
I was not quitting my job; I was taking a leave of absence and
could claim my job back after my return from foreign duty.

On top of all those reasons, I knew that since we were not
professional diplomats, this might be our once-in-a-lifetime chance
to spend several years in the United States—a country in which I
had considerable interest. And to pass up the opportunity would
be plain stupidity.

Finally, with help and cajoling from both families and friends, we reached a compromise—Lev would accept the post, and we would take Xenia with us to the States. He would be attached to the Soviet Embassy in Washington in the rank of counselor, but essentially we would be independent from the embassy. Later, as soon as the Soviet consulate opened in New York, we would move there to be closer to the publishing community.

Although the Ministry of Foreign Affairs later changed Lev's rank from counselor to first secretary because of quota changes in counselors' positions, he still retained the pay and allowances consistent with that of counselor's status. We started preparations for our trip.

The first thing to do was to get as many tips as possible about life in the United States from our friends. In a sense we fell into a crack between different jurisdictions of Soviet bureaucracy and so received no formal briefing on embassy procedures and the do's and don'ts of life abroad.

Because we were not professional diplomats, we received no formal training in diplomatic protocol in the Ministry of Foreign Affairs. The security briefing was to be conducted upon our arrival in Washington. But meanwhile we needed to know a myriad of practical everyday things—what to take with us? How to behave in a strange country? What to watch out for? What could we anticipate and take care of before leaving our home, rather than after?

Our friend Gennady had been assigned to Washington a few months before, and we knew we could count on his help there, but he was not planning to visit Moscow before our departure. Therefore we turned for advice to our neighbors, Eugene and Lilian, who had spent six years with the Soviet mission in New York. Although they had returned to Moscow in 1968, things could not have changed that much in a few years. Lilian undertook the task of coaching me in practical household matters, and Eugene gave us tips on how to cope with the "hostile environment."

"Do not take too many clothes," Lilian said. "Take only enough to last for a few months, because you will have to buy a whole new wardrobe there."

I was surprised. I had always been well dressed by Moscow standards. The special store in our school had a good selection of foreign goods. I did not have a single Soviet-made piece of clothing. I remembered the groups of American tourists I'd often seen on the streets of Moscow; they consisted mostly of elderly ladies who almost invariably wore polyester pantsuits in four basic colors— pink, lettuce, yellow, and baby blue—and straw hats. Was that the way I was supposed to dress in the States?

"Don't misunderstand me, I am not saying that you look shabby." Lilian laughed. "It's just that you look, well, different—maybe too European. Americans dress—well, you'll see it when you get there. Besides, clothes are cheap there, and if you sell most of what you have here for even half of what you paid for it in rubles, you will net a tidy amount of cash. I know you could use that money right now to help make the downpayment on your co-op apartment. Also, sell your stereo system. You can't take it there because the United States is on different voltage and current frequency."

At least I did not have to worry about the furniture. We did not have any. Lev had left his apartment, with everything in it, to his former wife, and we were renting a furnished apartment from diplomats who were abroad. The rent cost us the equivalent of a schoolteacher's monthly salary, but we were lucky to have it at all. You cannot rent apartments temporarily in Moscow. Either you get an apartment from the State, or you don't get one. Generosity in leaving your apartment to your ex-wife does not qualify you for a replacement. Therefore, there is a booming business in private rentals, mostly apartments of people who are away from the city for a couple of years. Since it is illegal to charge rent in excess of the government rate, and what we were paying was about twenty-five times more than the State apartment would have cost us, the prospective tenants are chosen by references from trusted friends and checked for their trustworthiness by prospective landlords. All agreements are oral, and the apartment owners always face the risk that the tenant will renege on the agreement and refuse to pay, in which case the owners have no legal recourse. Apparently our references had been good. We were renting an apartment in one of the most fashionable co-ops in the city, and all the furnishings had been left there in our care.

"Take all the dishes, pots, and pans and everything that is non-electric that you need for the kitchen," Lilian continued. "Those things are relatively expensive there, and have no resale value here. For the cost of a skillet, you can buy a pair of shoes that cost an equivalent of twenty skillets here."

As we went through the list, the basic philosophy became clear: anything that was inexpensive in the States but had high market value in Moscow had to be disposed of; things that were relatively expensive in the States had to be brought from home to conserve valuable currency. We could take an almost unlimited amount of luggage—anything that we did not need right away would be shipped by sea, and the agency would pay the freight charges.

"You will only have three years there, and the cost of living is pretty high," Lilian continued. "In terms of making money, African countries are better. Same salaries, but the cost of living is next to nothing. You can even afford domestic help. Nobody comes from a tour in Africa these days without at least a car and a co-op. In the States you have to spend more, but you can at least try to save enough for a car."

Then she went through the list of favorite shopping places where the prices were best. Orchard Street in New York was the best source for buying gifts for relatives and goods for resale—they would not know the difference—but things there were too cheap and outdated to buy anything to wear in the embassy in Washington. G. C. Murphy and K-Mart were OK. For better things, go to Hecht's. Always keep an eye on sales in good stores, sometimes you can get real bargains, and remember that the Soviet community is a hornet's nest and everything you buy and wear will be instantly appraised for its exact value, give or take a penny. We spent days going through minute details until, armed with the long list, I set upon rearranging my personal possessions and packing.

Eugene gave us a different kind of briefing.

"First of all, try not to follow any patterns," he said. "Your apartment and your car will be bugged—there is nothing you can do about it. If the bugs are removed, the Americans will get suspicious and you will only get more surveillance. Do not do anything to irritate them—they are just doing their jobs." He told us how Lilian had once returned to their apartment shortly after leaving because she had forgotten something, and encountered two men there who had quickly departed without doing her any harm. "Thieves?" I asked. "No," he said, "just the CIA checking on their equipment, thinking she was gone for the day. Don't do things like that on purpose, it won't do you any good and only make them mad."

"Obviously you know better than to discuss any embassy business in the apartment," he continued, "but what some people don't realize is that 'they' can use your personal relationship and whatever family disagreements you may have either to blackmail you or to try to recruit you. So if you want to quarrel, go for a walk, but even there, take different routes and don't start talking until you are a couple of blocks away from your apartment building. A couple of times we found bugs in the trees in Glen Cove over our favorite picnic spots, and you can be sure that every tree around the embassy is bugged, because people often take a walk around the block at lunchtime but rarely have time to go too far."

I was beginning to feel nauseated. "But how can you live in an apartment where you know that everything you do, everything you say, is heard by somebody else?"

"You get used to it," he said. "And if they want to know how often I f— Lilly, they are welcome. Besides, there are even some advantages to it." He recounted an anecdote popular in the diplomatic community about a wife who was constantly nagging her husband about buying her a fur coat. One day he came home and found a thousand dollars on his desk, with the note, "For Pete's sake, buy her that damn coat!" We laughed politely, but an uneasy feeling persisted. Was it really such a great idea to live in the States? Here we were seeing the other side of the coin—loss of privacy, suppression of all emotion, constant awareness of every word you said.

Eugene went on, telling us stories about tricky ways he used to shake off a tail. Some of his stories suggested that his duties somewhat exceeded those of a mere administrator attached to the Soviet mission. Why else would he even care about the tail? I doubted that I would have much use for such techniques, but the general idea was, nevertheless, disturbing—being watched, being followed.

"What about provocations?" I asked. "I've heard stories about people being lured into compromising situations and then photographed."

"Not too much of that anymore," he said, "although they won't miss an opportunity to take a snapshot if you get yourself in a mess. The press, too—they'll be only too happy to blow everything over the front page."

He told us several stories of diplomats who had been photographed drunk in public or even in bed with prostitutes. "In most cases, however," he said, "those people got themselves in such situations by their own stupidity and then later tried to blame it on CIA setup. But sometimes 'they' can still play a trick on you if they want to create an incident. So if you have a habit of stopping in a bar for a beer after work, change bars all the time. If you start going to the same place, 'they' may recruit the bartender to slip something in your drink and then create a public disturbance, and you won't even remember afterwards what happened."

The more I listened, the more depressed I was getting. What kind of a place were we going to?

————

We arrived at Washington's Dulles Airport on August 24, 1975. Our friend Gennady met us at the airport. My very first impression of America was a feeling that I had stepped into a sauna—I was unaccustomed to the heat and humidity that is typical of Washington's summers. Although summer temperatures in Moscow occasionally reach 90 to 95 degrees, the climate there is much dryer and the heat is more tolerable. It was a relief to get into an air-conditioned car (another alien thing, since Soviet-made cars do not have air conditioning). The size of the car was impressive, and I thought briefly that it must require quite an effort to handle it. Watching Gennady handle the steering wheel with what appeared to be just one finger, I could not help but ask him how he managed to do it.

"It's not me." He laughed. "On cars of this size, the steering and brakes are electrically enhanced. It only gets heavy when the electrical system is out of order, which is not often."

The car slid smoothly out of the airport onto the Dulles Access Road and then took a turn to the Capital Beltway. Things got more and more confusing. I expected to see an "industrially developed" country, as it is traditionally described in the Soviet press: buildings crowding each other, heavy smog. Instead, I saw mostly open space, clusters of trees, occasional high-rise buildings and small houses, and very blue sky. I asked Gennady how far away from the city we were.

"We *are* in the city," he replied. "Just about in the middle between the center and the outer bounds." He caught my puzzled look and added, "It'll take some getting used to, but we'll guide you through the first days. It happens to everybody who comes here for the first time. We all help newcomers to adjust."

The embassy had arranged for us to stay in the apartment of an embassy family on vacation in Moscow at the time. That way we had a couple of weeks to find an apartment and arrange for other necessities and still be comfortable, rather than having to live out of suitcases in a hotel. There were other Soviet families in the apartment complex in Riverdale, the Washington suburb where we were to stay, and one of them volunteered to assist us in the transition. The apartment was ready for our arrival. Gennady and his wife had even done some grocery shopping for us, and we found that the basic necessities such as milk, eggs, and baby formula were already in the refrigerator; on a coffee table was a box of disposable diapers for our baby daughter—another new thing! Gennady only waved back when we offered to pay for the groceries. "Forget it," he said. "What are friends for?"

Within minutes of our arrival, the apartment was filled with people from the embassy, each bringing something for the table, and we had a welcoming party. We were prepared, too. Before we'd left Moscow, we'd been told that certain simple things from home, such as black bread, salted herring, and smoked salami were always in demand in the Soviet colony abroad, and we'd brought a generous supply with us. We put it all on the table as our contribution, and I saw the nods of approval from the people around us. We had done our homework and made the first step toward being accepted in the community. The party lasted several hours, with people coming and going. Although we were completely exhausted from the long flight, our friends explained that they were keeping us up intentionally in order to break the jet lag. Otherwise the eight hours' time difference would be felt for days. The trick worked—we were so tired that the next morning we slept late and got up at the normal Washington morning hour.

Gennady arrived soon after breakfast to take Lev to the embassy for introductions and a discussion of future arrangements. Before they left, he said, "First thing you have to do is buy a car. Without it, you are helpless here. I will make arrangements with our senior mechanic to take you to the dealership tomorrow."

The men left. I cleaned up the apartment and tried to get familiar with the things in it. I figured out fairly quickly what a few containers on the kitchen counter were for. Most appliances were familiar. The stove did not look all that different from the one we had had in Moscow, although I would have to get used to the fact that I did not need matches to light it—Soviet stoves do not have pilot lights. The toaster on the counter was similar to the one I used in Moscow. Earlier, Gennady had shown me how to use a coffeemaker.

As I started to do the dishes, I remembered that nothing on the counter seemed to be a dishwashing liquid. Perhaps the apartment owners had run out of it before they left. I took the soap from the bathroom and used it for the dishes. It also seemed strange that there was no rack or some other place to put clean dishes to dry. I started looking in the cabinets, and discovered that one of them had several rows of drying racks. Some still had glasses and plates on them. I put the dishes in and called my new acquaintance next door, a woman named Valentina, to tell her I was ready to go shopping. She came over and we started making a shopping list. I mentioned dishwashing liquid. "But you have a whole box of detergent, right here," she said, and pointed to one of the boxes that I thought to be a clothes detergent. "You should not use liquid in the dishwasher." Seeing incomprehension in my eyes, she laughed. "Of course, I forgot," she said. "You know, after you spend several years here, you begin to forget all the things that do not exist back home." She opened what I thought was a cabinet with the racks. "This is a dishwasher. Here you don't have to do dishes by hand." And she showed me how to use the machine.

My first reaction was embarrassment. The rest of my feelings were more difficult to sort out. What else was in store for me on my first day in this strange country? Here I was, a wordly woman by Moscow standards. Lev and I were very well off back home. Our apartment was well equipped, or so I had thought up till now; we had access to special stores and many things that were out of reach for most of my countrymen. I had traveled to several foreign countries as a tourist, and Lev had visited many countries, including the United States, as a member of scientific delegations. He had often told me of his travels and of the different things he had seen. And yet I could not figure out some of the obviously everyday things in this rather modest apartment. What next?

"Next" turned out to be the supermarket where Valentina took me after we had finished the list. The shopping trip turned into a guided tour. At least half of the items simply did not exist in the Soviet Union. The produce and household goods isles were most confusing. I did not even know that so many varieties of fruits and vegetables existed on earth, let alone on supermarket shelves. The household goods took at least half an hour to go through while Valentina patiently explained the merits of such things as plastic wrap, various detergents, "quickie" floor mops, and the myriad of other items. I had already been introduced to the wonder of disposable diapers the night before, but the selection of baby food and instant baby cereals stopped me dead. In Moscow, having a baby meant hours of labor every day: washing diapers, cooking cereals, grating and mashing fruits and vegetables by hand. All of a sudden it occurred to me that having a baby here did not mean being tied up in the kitchen for half a day. What a wonderful surprise! I remembered my American friends who had visited us in Moscow. When they had mentioned that they had six children, it had sounded unbelievable to me that a charming woman such as my American acquaintance would want to spend her life between the kitchen counter and the clothesline. Now I realized that in this country you could have more than one child and still have time and energy for other things in life.

Another incredible thing was that I could buy everything in one place, have it packed in bags, loaded into the car, and be home in an hour! In Moscow I often had to go to several different stores to do my grocery shopping: the bakery, produce store, general grocery store, and on and on. Without a car I had to make several trips to complete my shopping because I could only carry so much in two bags. Even in larger stores that had produce and bakery departments, each department had its own counter and, naturally, its own line. I decided that someday I would calculate how many years of my life I had spent standing in lines and doing household chores. Even without exact calculations, I knew that this country was already giving me the greatest gift I could dream of—my time.

But the most amazing thing was the profusion of color. Color, color everywhere. Things *looked* pretty. Soviet life is essentially colorless. The consumer products are generic and often scarce. An item may be produced by hundreds of factories throughout the Soviet Union, and will look the same everywhere. A bar of low-grade household soap is invariably brown; a better hand-soap is always pink. A typical grocery shelf in the Soviet Union looks like a generic brand section in the supermarket—plain paper with dark lettering on everything. There is no need to make things attractive. First, if you need something, you buy it no matter how it looks; second, the factories are compensated by the quantities they produce. Whether an item is sold later or not, and whether things produced by one factory sell better than from another, is not the concern of the factory directors. Many things such as butter, sausage, and sour cream are not packaged at all but sold by weight. If the item is solid, it is cut, weighed, and wrapped in plain paper at the counter. For things that cannot be wrapped—such as sour cream—it is necessary to bring a container from home. All this weighing and wrapping at the counter is time-consuming and creates those infamous lines so often described in the Western press. In many instances, however, the lines are not the result of scarcity but simply inefficient organization.

The scarcity of man-made color does have at least one positive effect. The Russians are very appreciative of the beauty nature provides and try to make it a part of their lives as much as possible. The first fragile flowers appear on the streets of Moscow early in the spring, sold on the street corners by private entrepreneurs from the southern republics. From then on, there are tiny flower markets everywhere until the end of fall. The flowers are not inexpensive, since most of them come from private sources, but people buy them anyway. In Moscow it's not the migrating birds that signal the spring; it's when you see people in the crowd carrying the first bunches of yellow mimosas.

The lack of color partially explains the fascination Russians have with foreign goods. Not only is the product better, it also looks pretty and brightens up your apartment. It is not unusual to keep empty containers from foreign-made hairspray in the bathroom, or a dishwashing liquid in the kitchen, long after the contents are used up, just for decoration. When I was a student of foreign languages, I often worked as an interpreter with foreigners and received a lot of small gifts, especially cosmetics, and my friends always asked me to give them the empty containers.

By the time we got home from the supermarket, my head was spinning from all the new information I was trying to absorb. And, as though everybody conspired to finish me off, Gennady had already made arrangements for us to go to buy a car the same afternoon.

Buying a car in the Soviet Union was an experience that could rival anything Kafka ever put on paper. You have to live through it to believe it. It has to be planned long in advance, much as young families here plan for their dream house. My particular encounter started in 1967, when the Soviet Union put in operation an Italian-built plant in Togliatti which was to produce a Soviet version of the Fiat-124 called the "Zhiguli." The local newspapers announced that on January 20 the automotive store in Leningrad, where I lived with my parents, would be "signing up those citizens who desire to purchase a car." It also announced that any previous signups through the automotive club and other semiofficial groups would not be honored—strictly first come, first served.

There was only one automotive store in Leningrad, a city with a population of four million. There is no need for another—the cars are allocated by quota through the country. This store's annual quota was six hundred cars.

The line started to form on the eighteenth. In order to prevent blocking the street, the sign in the store window directed people to the back door, where it had a large empty lot capable of holding crowds.

By the time we arrived in the evening of the nineteenth, our number in line was somewhere over twenty-five hundred. Volunteers from the line were keeping track of arrivals and conducting roll calls every hour. Anybody who missed the roll call was struck out from the list. It was about twenty below, and almost impossible to stay in place. People were bundled in several layers of clothing and used their ingenuity to keep themselves warm—some with coffee mixed with brandy, some with vodka straight from the bottle. Most came in families, with family members taking turns out in the cold while the others were warmed up in shelters—heated staircases of nearby buildings, or for the lucky ones with older cars, inside their cars parked on the street with motors running. There were only two of us—my mother and I, but we struck a deal with a couple next to us to take turns on the roll call for each other so we could spend less time exposed to the cold.

By seven in the morning the crowd had grown to over four thousand people, and the police closed the entrance to the street to everyone except the residents and store employees. The store opened at eight. Signup cards were distributed quickly. All we needed to do was to fill in our names and addresses, hand the card over, have the number assigned to it, and go home. Within three hours, our turn came. Our number was 1856—apparently some people had left the line during the night or missed the roll call. I was jubilant—in three years I would be able to buy a car. It did not matter that I did not have 9000 rubles—I doubted that many people in the line did either.

For three years, once a year I received a postcard from the store requiring me to appear in person to confirm my registration. Finally, in 1970 a notification arrived that I could purchase my car. By then I was living in Moscow. Luckily, as a graduate student, I had only a temporary registration for Moscow residence. My permanent residence was still in Leningrad and I was eligible for car purchase.

I still did not have 9000 rubles, however. My father could cover about half the sum, but he was happy with his old car and did not want to spend money on a new one. Finally, after lengthy negotiations he agreed to lend me the money. I was planning to marry Lev, and it was obvious that he had the means to repay the debt. Under the worst circumstances, I could always resell the car. It just did not make sense to go through what we had for registration and not take advantage of it now.

The Soviet Union has no financial system from which people can borrow money—banks, credit unions, or anything like that. There is a State equivalent of a savings bank where people can keep their money and earn 2 percent interest, but you cannot withdraw more than you put in. The only source of financing is friends, and money is constantly borrowed and repaid between friends—sometimes "till the paycheck," sometimes "until needed." It is always a gentleman's agreement, and no interest is charged, although I've heard of loan sharks who do it for profit. Primarily, the habit developed from the fact that most major purchases cannot be planned in a timely manner, but depend on supply and luck. It was not uncommon to get a phone call from a friend who found herself in a store at a time when an imported refrigerator or piece of furniture was announced to be available for sale, and was strapped for money. Since most of those rare commodities sold out in a matter of hours, the only way to cope with it was to get a cashier's reservation, usually good for an hour or so, and start calling friends to see who had money on hand. A couple of times I had to catch a cab and deliver money to a friend in need at the other end of the town. It goes without saying that my friends did the same for me more than once.

Therefore it did not take long to collect the necessary amount—we had only one week from notification date to claim the car—and soon I was the owner of a shining new Zhiguli. For two weeks I happily drove it around Moscow. Then Lev and I broke up. Angry and frustrated, I contacted a friend of mine who was not an unfamiliar figure in the Moscow black market and asked him to help me to sell the car, splitting the profit fifty-fifty with him for his services as a mediator.

Selling a car in the Soviet Union is an easy way to make a profit, since there are always people who want to buy them but cannot do so legally, either because they live in remote places where the allocation of cars is next to nothing, or because they have illegal income, which quite a few Soviet people do—from moonlighting or taking bribes. Of special value are cars won in the State lottery. The ticket is often purchased for twice the value of the car since then the owner can claim that he won the car in a lottery rather than having to explain to the authorities where in the world he had gotten that much money on a grocery clerk's salary. Another way of reducing the offical value of the car is to sell it through the State-owned consignment store. Since the seller names the price at which the car is consigned, the purchase price can be officially low. The store takes 7-percent commission and does not ask any questions. The rest of the money for the actual price agreed upon is paid on delivery, in cash. It took my friend only two days to find a buyer who was willing to pay 19,000 rubles for my Zhiguli. A week later I paid off my debts to my friends and spent my share of the profit on a nice Phillips stereo system in a consignment store for foreign goods. Soon Lev and I reconciled and decided to get married. I had my fiancé back, but the car was gone.

Obviously I did not expect to find anything close to that car-buying nightmare here, but I did not expect what I saw, either.

Oleg, the embassy senior mechanic, took us to an Oldsmobile dealership where the embassy bought most of its official cars. It did not occur to me to question the choice. At the time I could not tell the difference between one car and another. I had seen American cars parked in front of the American Embassy in Moscow, and they all looked the same to me—long, sleek, and elegant. Gennady drove a Delta Royale, and it certainly looked good enough for me.

The salesman, introduced as Derek, greeted Oleg as an old friend—which he almost was, since he was in charge of car purchases at the embassy. We walked to the new car lot, and there I got my second shock of the day. There they were, rows of long, sleek, shining cars—just walk in and pick one.

"I want a silver one," I managed to say. The salesman started to explain the standard features, most of which did not make any sense to me. Finally he said, "What options do you want on your car?"

Options?

I was saved from total humiliation by Oleg who said, "We'll take it out of stock, and there is only one silver car." He then launched into the price negotiations, which made me feel even more confused. Finally the salesman started to write a long bill of purchase. Out of the long list I made out the word "discount." Was it because the embassy was getting a special consideration?

"You can pick up the car tomorrow morning," the salesman said.

"We'll pick it up in three hours," Oleg replied, and, without listening to Derek's protests that it was not enough time to prepare the car properly, shook hands with him, took me to his car, and drove away.

"Actually," Oleg explained on the way to the embassy where we went to get the voucher since we did not have a separate office account yet, "we could get a better deal someplace else. The old fox is charging us an arm and a leg, and we are just too lazy to switch to another dealership. This one is the closest to the embassy, and old habits die hard, but one of these days I'll go someplace else and get a better price." He proceeded to explain that the discount had nothing to do with us being diplomats, and that each dealer charges what the market will bear.

"Why do we need the car today?" I asked. "I don't have a driver's license yet."

"You'll have it by the end of the day," he said. "We are going to the traffic department now, and they will simply issue you a license on the basis of your Soviet license. They know that our traffic laws are stricter than theirs, and if you still have a valid license, it's good enough for them. Of course, I will drive your car to Riverdale, and you'll need to practice a little before you get it on the streets, but I want to pick it up today so they won't have too much time to tinker with it."

He explained then that since the embassy bought most of its cars in the same place, a routine assumption was that the FBI would be notified as soon as we left, and given the opportunity to go over the car and to plant bugs. The less time they had to do it, the less likelihood that they would plant anything too sophisticated. So everything Eugene told me in Moscow had been right— we could expect surveillance and intrusion in our private life everywhere.

Oleg was right about the license procedures. It took less than fifteen minutes. I was not even given a driver's test, which I knew I would have failed in an unfamiliar car.

My real test came the next morning. I decided to drive to the supermarket by myself.

It took me about twenty minutes to maneuver the car out of the parking space. It was twice as long as any car I had ever driven, and the responsiveness of the power steering was scary.

Automatic transmission was another problem. Soviet cars don't have them, and it was confusing not to have to use my left foot on the clutch. It must have been a hilarious sight for any observer who happened to be on the lot. The car was swerving, moving in fits, and every time I hit the brakes it came to an abrupt stop, shaking me inside out until I got used to the sensitive brakes. It took another twenty minutes to cross the street to the mall parking lot. I waited and waited until the street was completely empty, gripped by fear that somehow I would do something wrong and stall the car in the middle of the street, ending up with a mangled mess instead of this beautiful machine. That I could be mangled in the process did not occur to me. By the time I found the place on a mall that had at least three unoccupied parking spaces on both sides, I was drenched in perspiration and my hands were shaking.

Amazingly, I was not as scared when I started on my way back. I even took a drive around the block and finally—the ultimate challenge—made a left turn at a traffic light. I arrived home, proud and convinced that I was ready to face the American way of life.

My confidence was crushed the very next day. Kitty, my seven-months-old baby daughter, had developed a mild fever, probably from travel and the change of food and water. I called the embassy and got the name of an embassy-approved pediatrician. The embassy had its own pediatrician, but she handled children only from the age of two. Since Kitty was only seven months old, I was to go to an American doctor.

The doctor's office was on Connecticut Avenue, some ten miles from Riverdale. I looked at the map that I had bought in the supermarket the day before, and decided to stick to major highways rather than try to find my way through the maze of streets. My plan was to take the Beltway to Connecticut Avenue, and then a few easy blocks to the doctor's office. The route seemed to be easy and straightforward—how can you miss a major highway like the Capital Beltway?

Very easily, if you are not familiar with route numbering conventions in the US. In the Soviet Union streets and highways have names. In the US they have numbers—a little detail I had completely overlooked.

I knew that we were only a few blocks from the Beltway, and in which direction I should drive. As I approached what I thought was the Beltway exit, and did not see any sign saying "Beltway," I stopped at the gas station and asked for directions. I was instructed to take the next right turn and follow the signs to I-95. I did as instructed, saw a large green sign sitting high above what seemed to be a major highway, and happily set on my way. I remembered from the day before that the Beltway had similar signs on it, and that the streets didn't.

I drove for almost half an hour before an uneasiness began to creep in. In my estimate, I should have passed the Connecticut Avenue exit by then. The green signs were now few and far between, and the highway seemed almost deserted. Kitty was whimpering; I had not anticipated a long trip and had not brought her bottle.

Finally, I saw a car on a road shoulder, pulled over, walked to the man checking under the hood, and asked him to show me where I was on the map. He looked at the map and said that it was a wrong map. I thought he did not understand what I wanted, and tried again. Finally, he looked at the tag number of my car, and between that and my broken English probably figured out what had happened.

"Lady," he said slowly, "you are outside of this map. You are two miles away from Baltimore. If you need to go to Washington, you have to turn around and go about thirty miles back."

My first reaction was panic. I was outside of the twenty-five-mile zone. One of the first things we'd been told was to observe the twenty-five-mile limit on travel from the center of the city that was imposed on all Soviet diplomats. Had I been followed? Had anybody seen me? I'd heard a lot about American agents following Soviet diplomats around. If they'd seen me, would I get in trouble, or would they believe that I'd simply gotten lost?

I thanked the man, made a U-turn, and started driving back. Kitty was crying in full voice now and started trying to crawl out of the portable crib that was strapped to the front seat next to me. For a while I tried to keep her down with one hand while steering the car with another. Finally, desperation overcame me. I stopped the car and burst into tears. For a few minutes we cried together. Then, by some miracle she quieted down. I put her back in the crib, started the car, and, after ten more minutes saw the Riverdale exit. I decided not to tempt the hand of fate, and to go home while I knew where I was. We never made it to the doctor that day. And I realized that it would take many more days and more mishaps like that one to get used to the American way of life.

CHAPTER 3

WHETHER it was due to the fact that seven years had passed since Eugene and Lilian had returned to Moscow, or because of the differences between the Soviet communities in Washington and New York, a lot of their advice would turn out to be useless or outdated. Occasionally, though, I had sharp reminders of the reality Eugene had talked about before our departure. Those reminders came in unexpected ways, but they were there.

We stayed in Riverdale for almost two weeks while waiting for the transfer of VAAP money from Moscow. We had been issued a start-up advance in Moscow, but the bulk of the money was scheduled to be transferred to the embassy account through an international bank transfer. Meanwhile, I tried to learn as much as I could from Valentina, and to use my relatively free time getting used to my new family member, Lev's daughter, Xenia. I had met Xenia several times when she had been about eight. Now she was twelve. At that time my status with Lev had not been official. Lev's mother usually rented a small country cottage outside of Moscow in the summer, and Xenia often stayed with her. Whenever Lev and I had visited, I had been introduced to Xenia as a friend of Lev's sister, Tatiana. Since Lev's divorce, however, one of the conditions Sonya had set for his visitation with Xenia was that he would never take her to our home or introduce her to me, so the meetings always took place in her home. Whatever I knew about Xenia, I knew from Lev—that she was exceptionally bright, was attending a special workshop for talented childen, was very good at modeling, and was trying her hand in writing short stories. I suspected that Sonya had not given me rave notices before Xenia's departure from Moscow, but I was hoping that the girl's natural intelligence would lead her to make her own judgments.

Things seemed to be going well—she was polite, though sloppy, and I tried to excuse that by keeping in mind some of the details of her childhood. One of the reasons for Lev's divorce had been his resentment of Sonya's very active social life away from home. Sonya was an attractive and bright woman and worked as an editor in a prestigious publishing house in Moscow where she came into contact with a great many people. She liked to go out as much as possible, and from the age of three Xenia had been boarded out, spending the entire week there and coming home only on week-ends. When she started school at the age of seven, she spent the rest of the day in an after-school day-care center and was often alone in the evenings. As a result, she did not have much of a sense of family. I did not want to push her too hard, but I felt that, being a member of a family now, she should participate in the chores and other family activities. She tried, but wasn't much good at it.

Other than that, she seemed to be agreeable and intent on making the relationship work. Knowing how much Lev wanted her to be with him, I was happy that he no longer had to be torn between his past and present families.

My illusions were shattered very soon. It was exactly two weeks after our arrival. Aeroflot had one flight a week from Washington, and that morning I had given Lev letters to our relatives to drop into the embassy mailbox. I was surprised that Xenia did not have a letter ready for her mother, but that was up to her. After Lev left for the office, Valentina came to see me.

"Let's have coffee in my apartment," she said.

The request was not unusual—we shuttled back and forth most

of the time. I took Kitty and we went to Valentina's apartment on the same floor. When we sat down at the kitchen table, I noticed that she had an unusually serious expression.

"Xenia gave me a letter to send to Moscow," she said. "The envelope was open and a few words caught my attention. I think you should read it before it goes any further."

I wondered if she had read the whole letter. If she had, she did not show it. Anyway, after I read it, I silently handed it over to Valentina to read.

The letter was a complete shock. It was four pages long, and had obviously been written at night, since I had not seen her writing it. Hatred poured from every word. She described every little happening in detail, and tried to find the bad side or hidden intent in everything I did. Her main complaint, however, and a revelation to me, was that her father was completely under my thumb and unable to say a word for himself, thus leaving her unprotected against a mean stepmother.

From what I read I deduced that Sonya had sent Xenia with clear instructions: ignore "that woman," listen only to your father, and anyway, it is all a temporary inconvenience—as soon as they buy you the things you need, I'll have you back before the New Year.

That last part was another surprise. Lev had told me he'd reached a clear understanding with Sonya that Xenia would stay with us all three years in order to become fluent in English.

"What do I do?" I asked.

"What you do," Valentina answered, "is keep it and show it to Lev. First of all, he'll need to explain to her the simple fact that letters sent through the embassy mail are read by you know who, and that she can cause trouble for him writing things like that. More, she will start school soon, and if she keeps talking like that, it will be all over the embassy. That's the formal part of it. Informally, I do not envy you, and if I were you I'd send the girl home at the first opportunity."

"I can't do that," I said. "Lev is so happy to have her here." I briefly explained the problems we had back home because of his separation from Xenia.

"It will be different here. When he is three thousand miles away from her, he'll miss her but he'll get over it. If she stays, she'll destroy your marriage."

Valentina was ten years older than I, and what she said made sense except that, in practice, I did not have any choice. What bothered me most was the possibility that Lev had made a deal with Sonya behind my back about the line of authority in the family.

To my surprise, he admitted doing exactly that.

"You mean," I said, "that if I want her to wash her hands, I have to tell you first, and then you tell her to go and wash her hands?"

"Well, not exactly," he said. "But she does need to change a lot of her habits, and it would be better if it comes through me."

"Need I remind you that you are often not home during the day and I am alone with her? What am I supposed to do—wait till you get home?"

"Why not?" He shrugged. "Anyway, as soon as we move, the office will be in our home, and I'll be there. Meanwhile I'll find some pretext to talk to her about things that can be said or written without letting her know that we detained this letter."

I did not like his attitude, but I decided to let it go for now. It was too early in the game; the girl was homesick and missed her mother; maybe she'd come around in time.

———

Contrary to Eugene's predictions, we found the members of the Soviet Embassy in Washington to be sharp and dedicated professionals, well versed in the affairs of the world and culture, and congenial as friends, at least in our immediate circle. The Soviet Embassy is very stratified according to rank. This stratification has little to do with snobbism but is mostly a result of difference in pay and allowances. The differences start with the ceiling on rent reimbursement which determines who lives where. Most embassy officials in the rank of second and third secretary live in apartment buildings in Arlington and Alexandria or Riverdale where rents are low. People are encouraged to find apartments in buildings where other Soviet families already live. There are several reasons for that: for one, neighborly support and help are often important; for another, embassy employees of that rank have to buy their own cars, usually used ones bought from their departing predecessors, and pay for their own gas, so car pooling is widely used to save money. Another unspoken but clear reason is that, living in clusters, they can keep an eye on each other and, presumably, report any deviations from expected behavior to embassy security.

High-ranking officials—counselors and some first secretaries—live in a Chevy Chase cluster of high-rises at Friendship Heights, and that was where we were steered upon our arrival. We rented a three-bedroom apartment on the twentieth floor in the Willoughby. Kitty was only seven months old and could share our bedroom; Xenia had her own room; and the third bedroom was to be used as an office. The size of the apartment was awesome by Moscow standards. In fact, we got immediately embroiled in a bitter bureaucratic argument with our Moscow office. The guidelines for "living-space allocation" that VAAP had issued for its foreign representatives had been fashioned according to Soviet standards of housing allocation, with no knowledge or regard for the realities of living in a foreign country. Those guidelines dictated that the total living area of our apartment—everything but the hallway, bathrooms, kitchen, and closet space—could not exceed 9 square meters, approximately 90 square feet, per family member, plus an additional 9 square meters for common areas—in our situation, approximately 450 square feet altogether. We were required to submit a floor plan with exact measurements and have our choice of apartment approved by the Moscow office. Although our rent allowance was more than enough, the total area of our apartment was double the permitted maximum.

After an exasperating exchange of letters, with Moscow demanding that we move to a smaller apartment, Lev called on the embassy for help.

"Oh, no, not again," sighed Peter, a high-ranking embassy official who'd become a new friend of ours. "When will those idiots in Moscow get in touch with reality?"

Peter lived in a building across the street from us. We liked him very much and quickly became close. His advice was invaluable—he had been assigned to the embassy for more than ten years by then, his term continually extended because, with his experience and knowledge of the United States, he was almost irreplaceable. "Don't worry," he said, "we've dealt with things like this before."

Within days an official letter was sent from the embassy to the VAAP office in Moscow stating that because of American housing regulations and because of the embassy practice of assigning high-ranking officials to areas that were appropriate to their status in American eyes, we could not be moved to a smaller apartment. In not so many words, the letter told VAAP to lay off and let the embassy decide what was appropriate for its members.

That solved our immediate problem and turned out to be of help for years thereafter. Whenever our official delegations visited us and gasped at what was in their eyes an extravagant car, we simply pointed out that Oldsmobiles were a standard choice of the embassy and that we had to comply with embassy practices. End of argument.

Other things were also different from what Eugene and Lilian had told us. Gennady's wife, Alia, became my mentor in practical matters. Within days I replaced the bulky four-wheel baby carriage I had brought from Moscow with a folding stroller, got a baby car-seat and became completely mobile—a luxury not attainable in Moscow when you have a young baby. I remembered how stranded I had been when Lev had taken a ten-day vacation with Xenia, leaving me alone with one-month-old Kitty. It had been February and minus twenty outside. Soviet teenagers do not babysit; the only source of help, unless you have a housekeeper, which is extremely rare, is relatives and neighbors. Therefore I had had to take Kitty with me wherever I went. There was a grocery store within two blocks, but Soviet stores do not have shopping carts—everything you buy you have to carry in your hands. Neither could I take Kitty's carriage into the store—it was too large to pass the checkout line. With a baby in my arms, there was little I could put in a bag hanging from my arm, and within a few days I had been completely dependent on my neighbors to bring me groceries. All other shopping had had to wait until Lev came back. I'd been angry at him for leaving me stranded like that—it had already been decided that Xenia was going with us to the States, and he would have plenty of time to spend with her, but he had been reluctant to give up his semiannual vacation alone with her, and I had been reluctant to argue when it came to his daughter.

Other things had to go, too. The bed linens I had brought from Moscow were too small for our queen-size bed and required ironing. It had been no problem in Moscow, since all I had had to do was drop the linens at the laundry and pick them up three days later, clean, starched and pressed for a nominal charge. In a way, there was no other way to do it, since there is no such thing as a clothes dryer in a Soviet apartment. When I was a child, my mother had had a washing machine—a rarity in those times. Afterward we had had to take the laundry to the building's attic and hang it on clotheslines to dry. Twenty years later my washing machine was still not much more sophisticated than the one my mother had owned, but our modern building did not have an attic. I could dry small items on the clotheslines stretched between kitchen walls, but large items always went to the commercial laundry. The real problem started when Kitty was born. Since there was no such thing as disposable diapers in Russia, our small kitchen became almost impassable most of the time because of all the diapers drying on the clothesline and hanging down to shoulder level.

Alia guided me through a big shopping trip to Hecht's where we bought all the time-saving miracles of modern technology unknown in the Soviet Union—no-iron sheets, Teflon-coated pans (what was I going to do now with the dozen skillets that were on their way from Moscow?), and small kitchen appliances. "And now," said Alia, "we'll take care of your wardrobe."

Our initial start-up advance was rather limited, so there wasn't much we could do in that department. Alia, however, set firm guidelines that I followed for the next several months. The instructions were brief—no polyester, no K-Mart. Go shopping with other embassy wives—they knew all the nice outlets in town where you could find decent clothing at reasonable prices. Don't hesitate to ask for advice—better to ask now than be embarrassed in front of Americans.

Clothes were not on my priority list anyway. I knew I had at least a couple of months until we settled down, established business contacts, and started to make business calls and entertain. I had not exactly followed Lilian's advice, and had brought some of my better things with me. European look or not, they were well made and would suffice for a while. My immediate concern was Xenia. Her mother had packed her with one small suitcase, half of the space occupied with books, and a simple instruction: "They'll buy you everything you need in the States, and don't hesitate to ask." In addition, she'd given Lev a long list of nonclothing items that she felt the child was entitled to. The list was several pages long and included such items as a tape recorder and Barbie dolls.

Barbie dolls or not, Xenia had nothing to wear but a pair of shorts and a change of shirts, and I knew it would take whatever was left of our first month's salary to get her even the basic necessities.

Alia sensed my mood. "I know what you must be thinking," she said. "I was in the same situation a year ago. Most people around you in Chevy Chase have been here for years. They have already provided for the rest of their life in Moscow, and can afford to spend a little more freely now. We only have a limited time here, and naturally you want to put something away or to buy major things you can take to Moscow. But we don't have any choice. We are paid a fraction of what American diplomats are paid in Moscow, and yet we must appear prosperous and entertain in order for our husbands to be treated as equals by their American counterparts. Appearances are important in this county, and you would do your husband a disservice if you don't dress him well. You know, sometimes I envy the wives of our security guards who live in an embassy compound, can get by with a simple change of clothes, and don't have to spend money on anything except food. They are the ones who will go home with a car certificate fully paid for, not us."

Despite initial difficulties, I was beginning to like life in Washington. Quite often, though, I had a feeling that I had been thrown into some kind of parallel universe where all meanings and values were reversed. The discrepancy in the cost of material items was just one small part of it. Even more bewildering was the difference in attitudes between people in the embassy and our friends in Moscow. We were used to long evenings with friends where conversations were often confined to political gossip, exchange of the latest rumors, and discussions of bickering in the institute. Newspapers were largely ignored, and television was boring. The rest of the world was incidental. In the embassy, nobody would start the day without reading the *Washington Post,* and Walter Cronkite's news program was sacred—in the middle of the party the conversation would cease and everybody watched the news. Our embassy friends engaged in long discussions of upcoming Presidential elections and how the outcome would affect relations between our countries. Like most people in the Soviet Union, I had almost no knowledge of the American political system, and the conversations initially bored me. Their wives were more interesting company; most of them were very much on top of the latest in books and movies—the subjects in which I was always well versed.

One thing that puzzled me for a while was that all those lively political discussions and frank exchanges of opinions were taking place in our apartments. I remembered what Eugene had said in Moscow about bugging, and finally decided to ask Peter about it.

"Oh, don't worry about it," he said. "They simply don't have the manpower to keep all of us under surveillance all the time. They do it on a rotating basis, and if something interesting comes up, they may put more resources into watching a particular individual. Political jokes are so common that it is not a sufficient cause for interest. But"—he suddenly became serious—"there are people you should be careful with, and it's not Americans. You already know some of them in the embassy, but some are not as visible. Right now you are in good company—we've known the people who come to your parties for years, and they're OK—but in the embassy, be careful, or you will have all the surveillance in the world, and it will be Soviet-made. Be especially careful with your women friends. They don't have much to do and notice a lot of things, and the embassy is a gossipy place."

I was also learning a lot. One immediate concern was the language. I was rather fluent in English, having taught philosophy in

English back home, and I could read anything without a dictionary. However, understanding spoken American was a different matter. The idioms were unfamiliar, and I had to get used to saying "apartment" instead of "flat"; "call" or "phone" instead of "ring." I was amazed how many everyday words were different here from the British English which is taught in Soviet colleges. My Russian accent did not make things any easier. I decided that my two best sources were newspapers and television. I discovered soon, though, that the *Washington Post* had a language of its own which wasn't of much help in a supermarket line. That left the TV.

I became an avid viewer, watching anything from *Electric Company* to *Kojak*. Besides being a feast for the eyes—color TV was a rarity in the Soviet Union, the sets being very expensive and most programs still being broadcast in black and white—everything was so different: the programs, the totally new phenomenon of commercials, and, mostly, the news. Especially unusual was the way the news broadcasters behaved on TV—they actually talked to each other, made jokes, and when they talked they appeared to be doing just that—*talking*. Of course I did not know about the use of TelePrompTers then. On Soviet news programs the news is usually read from paper by two somber-faced announcers, and there is much less visual material in the program. Of them all, action shows became my favorites; there was nothing like that in the Soviet Union—pure entertainment, no propaganda. I never got into soap operas, mostly because I did not have time for TV during the day, and I intensely disliked sitcoms—the laugh-tracks were such an obvious insult to anybody's intelligence that I wondered how the people here could let the TV companies get away with it. I did not mind the commercials, though—I was still learning about a lot of things I saw in the stores, and commercials were helpful. It wasn't until much later that I learned that "new and improved" is nothing new, and that celebrity endorsements did not necessarily mean that those people actually used the products.

Gradually, after the initial fascination wore off, I became more selective in what I watched, and learned to estimate whether a movie was worth the time from the first ten minutes of the show. Some Hollywood clichés were irritating, such as their portrayal of

Russians—always dumb and uneducated. The producers did not take the trouble to make actors reproduce anything that sounded even close to the Russian language, and whenever Russian life was shown, it was ridiculously wrong in many details. With all the emigration coming from the Soviet Union, I wondered why nobody bothered to hire a consultant, and finally decided that the producers probably did not care about the Russians watching their movies, and figured the American audience would not know the difference anyway.

The only show that was markedly different at that time was *The Six Million Dollar Man,* which we always watched. I liked the spirit of the show, and several episodes where Steve Austin, the main character, dealt with his Russian counterparts were a pleasant surprise; for the first time I saw Russians portrayed as intelligent human beings, with human emotions, able to overcome their distrust of Americans and join forces at a critical time to save humanity. Maybe it was the still-lingering spirit of détente and the joint Soyuz-Apollo flight, but it was pleasant to see Russians being treated as equals for a change.

We did not know then that many series were repeated in summer reruns, and that successful ones went into syndication. The assumption was that although theatrical movies were shown on TV several times, a series episode was shown only once, and we tried not to miss any. A few times I broke speeding records trying to get home from the embassy retreat on the Eastern Shore, where we spent most of our weekends, in time for *The Six Million Dollar Man* at seven o'clock on Sunday evenings.

Another delightful treat was the discovery of *Star Trek.* I'd always liked science fiction and had a very good collection of science fiction books in English back in Moscow—Clarke, Heinlein, Bradbury. I'd read one of the *Star Trek* books by James Blish, but had not known it was based on a hit television series. Although the stories had been interesting enough and the idea of the importance of universal understanding between different cultures appealing, it had been nowhere close to the quality of social thought I'd found in Ray Bradbury's books. On screen, however, the characters took shape, and the show made a much more powerful impression on me. It is still one of my favorite shows. I firmly believe that what made *Star Trek* a success was not the material itself but the perfect casting. The actors were totally identifiable with the characters they played, and therefore as real and familiar as one's friends are in real life.

I also started catching up on all the movies that I'd known about but had never had a chance to see. I had been a movie buff all my life, but my knowledge of them reflected the strange system by which movies are chosen for showing in the Soviet Union. There are two criteria: cost and ideological suitability. The cost factor means that movies are purchased when they are already old, have been shown all over the world, and the licensing rights can be obtained for next to nothing. A five-to-ten-year lag between the first release of the movie in the West and its showing in the Soviet Union is not unusual. The ideological factor dictates that the "socially significant" movies—those that show the deterioration of Western society—are given priority. Another category is mindless trash that is "ideologically safe" but provides some entertainment for the populace. Sex beyond kissing is censored out, although quite a lot of violence stays in.

The combination of those factors gives the Soviet moviegoer a strange knowledge of the international movie scene. Among the names unknown in the Soviet Union: Clarke Gable, Cary Grant, Charlton Heston, Rock Hudson, Clint Eastwood. The only movie I'd seen with Elizabeth Taylor was a totally forgettable one called *Rhapsody* that broke records in Soviet movie theaters. Jane Fonda is well known, but the only movie shown with Henry Fonda was *War and Peace*.

I would have not known about the great movie stars of the past myself if it hadn't been for a small movie theater in Leningrad that showed undubbed and very old foreign movies for educational purposes. The theater sold tickets to a series of ten movies each season, and quite a few of those tickets were distributed at the foreign language school in the University of Leningrad where I studied. That was where I saw Cary Grant for the first time in *Arsenic and Old Lace* and Clark Gable in *It Happened One Night*. I still did not know who Rock Hudson was until I saw *McMillan & Wife* on American TV.

As to the more recent movies, I'd seen a limited and totally arbitrary sample of them through several channels. The Soviet government has copies of practically all the newest Western films. However, they are not shown to the public but are restricted to so-called closed showings. The reason is simple: the copies are often illegal. When a movie is sent to the Soviet government for review, or offered for sale after a film festival—in fact, some film festivals require the participant countries to purchase the films that win the festival's major awards—a copy is made, and the original film returned without being purchased. This copy, usually black and white, is then shown to exclusive audiences: the higher party apparatus, professional clubs of writers, actors, filmmakers and journalists, or places like the school where I taught, to keep our students entertained. That was where I saw *The Godfather, A Clockwork Orange,* and other films that never saw general release in the Soviet Union.

Catching up on movies and discovering television was fun and a necessary language exercise. The other part of my discovery of everyday life in the United States consisted of getting to know things that simply do not exist in the Soviet Union: bank accounts, credit cards, car insurance.

Fortunately we were spared the necessity of hunting for an apartment and the car—both were found quickly under the direction of the embassy. We did have to open a bank account, however, since the money for our operations had to be kept separate from embassy funds. The account was opened in Lev's name, but my signature was also at the bank so I could sign checks. As time went by, however, it turned out to be insufficient for my own purposes. First of all, although I was doing all the bookkeeping and shopping for the office, VAAP objected to having my signature on the checks. I was reluctant to carry a checkbook with blank checks signed by Lev, in case I lost it, so with his blessing and a little practice I learned to forge his signature perfectly.

However, it did not solve the problem of my personal shopping—I could not use the VAAP checkbook to pay for our household purchases. The embassy does not permit its members to have bank accounts or credit cards, except oil company cards. The ostensible reason is that all embassy members live in a precarious situation where they can be expelled for no good reason and have to leave for home almost on a moment's notice, thus possibly leaving the embassy with unpaid bills. A more practical reason, I suspected, was that the high officials were afraid that plain human greed would take over and people would run up bills they could not pay.

Money brings out the best and the worst in people. It is an excellent litmus test of human nature to see how Soviet people handle their money when they are abroad. Back home, the distinction is blurred: Russians are normally very generous and hospitable people, ready to share the last they have with friends and often strangers. That ingrained generosity is aided by the fact that Soviet money is looked upon as almost worthless—what's the use of saving money if there is nothing to buy anyway? It's better to spend it on pleasure and good times with friends. Going abroad, the Russians are suddenly confronted with the phenomenon of a limited supply of money with tremendous buying power, and their mentality often changes to reflect this new reality. Whereas Americans think of a bottle of Coke as something that costs fifty cents, in the Russian mind the same bottle of Coke is only one-tenth of the cost of a sweater. Everything is instantly translated into the equivalent of Soviet black market selling prices, and in those terms the same bottle of Coke becomes very expensive indeed.

Even without dabbling in the black market, the incentives to save money are powerful. The Soviet government always tries to limit the outflow of foreign hard currency. In order to make people bring home the money they earn abroad, special diplomatic stores exist in every major Soviet city. Soviet citizens are not permitted to keep foreign currency once they return. Instead, the money is exchanged for special certificates that have the same buying power in diplomatic stores. Through such stores, Soviet diplomats can not only buy Western goods, but also make a payment on a Soviet-made car, with immediate delivery instead of a normal five-year wait, and at a price of about one-fifth of what a car costs in rubles. The same applies to cooperative apartments.

Stories about extremes in saving money abound in the Soviet missions. I was told that Russian mothers could always be spotted on the beach because they bring plain water from home to give their children on a hot day. In England, the Soviet Embassy once formed a special commission charged with paying regular visits to employees' apartments to check their refrigerators and make sure that there was a minimal amount of food there. The action was prompted by the fact that several people had fainted at the embassy and the cause was diagnosed as malnutrition. Another startling phenomenon is shoplifting. Although not widespread, there are a few incidents every year in which Soviet women are caught in the act. They usually blame foreign intelligence services for putting things in their shopping bags or purses in order to embarrass them, and most of the time the matter is resolved quietly by reimbursing the store or returning the goods. The embassy usually takes the side of its employee or his or her family, and no action is taken, but in some outrageous cases the culprits are sent home. One of those incidents involved the wife of a military attaché who was stopped in the supermarket with a couple of pounds of meat stashed inside her dress—nobody, including the embassy, would buy the story that it had been put there by somebody else without her noticing it!

Not used to such behavior, we were pleasantly surprised and relieved to find that it did not affect the people with whom we socialized in the embassy. When we'd offered to pay Gennady for the groceries he and his wife had bought for us on the eve of our arrival in Washington, he'd given us a look as if we were out of our minds. Whenever we went out, the charges were usually split evenly, and nobody ever counted who ordered what. More often, somebody simply paid the bill, knowing that in our regular little circle somebody else would pick up the tab the next time. It was the normal civilized behavior we were accustomed to back in Moscow, and it was good to see that our friends at least were not affected by the money mania that so often afflicted Soviets traveling abroad.

With all the restrictions on credit cards and checking accounts, however, we were all warned not to carry too much cash, either, because of the possibility of being mugged, especially in some areas of Washington, DC. At the same time we were advised to carry at least some cash so the muggers would not get angry if they found nothing. We were also told to surrender money without argument if stopped on the street in order to avoid getting seriously hurt. Several Soviet diplomats were robbed in New York City, but got off with the loss of a few dollars and other valuables. The tactic did not always work, however. A most tragic accident took place in Washington while we were at the embassy. One of the maintenance people was stopped at gunpoint after leaving the Safeway supermarket on 18th Street. Remembering instructions, he quickly reached for the money in his pocket to give it to the robbers. He spoke very little English and could not explain to the robbers what he was doing. Unlike American men, who usually keep their wallets in their hip pockets, Russians carry their wallets in the breast pockets of their coats. What happened was unclear, but it appeared that the robbers thought he was reaching for a gun and shot him in the head. One of the bullets could not be removed, and two weeks later he died in a hospital.

The fear of being robbed partially explains why most Soviet diplomats' wives go shopping in groups. I was certainly just as scared of being mugged as everybody else, but group excursions did not fit my schedule either. For some reason Lev left all the driving to me. Although he often bragged of how he had driven his father's car when he was sixteen, and said it would be no problem for him to get a driver's license, he consistently refused to do it. I could not figure out why; the only possible explanation was that he wanted the freedom to drink whenever he felt like it. Gradually, however, I started to suspect that my husband was far less comfortable with our life in the States than I was. It was difficult to believe, since he had visited the States six or seven times before, and in the beginning had known more about certain things than I had. I finally came to the conclusion that during those trips he had been part of the official delegation and had not had to deal with things on an individual basis. My suspicions were confirmed when I received a canceled check from the bank for Lev's recent trip to New York. The check was for the hotel and had Lev's signature on it, but had been completely filled out in strange handwriting.

"What happened with this check?" I asked.

"Oh, nothing," he said. "I asked the hotel clerk to fill it out."

I did not say anything, but at the earliest opportunity asked Peter if we could get the embassy to permit Lev to have a credit card. I explained that VAAP did not accept any expenses without a receipt, and sometimes it was difficult or embarrassing for Lev to ask for a receipt in bars or restaurants. Permission was granted, and soon I handed him a brand new American Express card.

"Here," I said. "All you have to do is to sign the slip."

His card still did not solve my own problem. The rule about cash and carry continued to irk me. I never liked rules that did not make sense. For many Russians, getting around the law is a national game. The Soviet bureaucracy is so vast that often the only way to get anything done is to find a way around it. This goes from paying the construction crew to bring you hard-to-get materials after hours while they maintain with a straight face during working hours that the materials are simply not available, to paying extra to your gynecologist to have anesthesia during an abortion. Back home, it's the name of the game. Here, however, the risk of being discovered carried a potential penalty of being sent home if the offense was serious enough. We were watched much more closely here than at home. Still, I decided to take a chance. Soon I was in possession of a separate checking account and a Central Charge from Riggs Bank. I was careful to use only the checkbook in the presence of other embassy people, though. It was known that we had an official checking account, and nobody noticed that I was using a checkbook with my own name on it.

By the end of the first month we had our apartment furnished, had bought a typewriter, had our stationery and business cards printed, and had gotten down to business. We sent an announcement to all the major publishers about opening our office, invited them to refer all copyright matters to us, and started regular mailings of VAAP catalogs and informational materials. Lev made several get-acquainted visits to New York where he met major publishers, and we established a good working contact in Washington with the Copyright Office of the Library of Congress and with the Association of American Publishers.

We also brought with us several ongoing investigations of copyright infringement that VAAP had been trying to resolve for some time. One case involved plagiarism, and that was when we discovered what a convenient cover a post office box is: we could not reach the guilty party—there was no way to find a real address, the author was not listed in the telephone book, and all our letters went unanswered. Another elusive entity was a publisher called Joint Publications Research Service, which had apparently translated several very recent scientific works by Soviet authors. That one did not even have an address printed on its publications, and all our efforts to locate the publisher were in vain. It was not until several years later, after I had departed from the embassy, that I discovered we had been wasting our time—JPRC happens to be an arm of the CIA that translates and prints scientific research articles from foreign countries in limited quantities. Since the distribution of those translations was intended for the government only, they apparently had not counted on some of the copies winding up in VAAP's hands.

I was enjoying my new job. It was essentially an executive secretary's job, but most of our contacts knew that I was Lev's wife and did not hesitate to discuss business with me if he was not around. Lev was undoubtedly in charge of the business, and I was quite content doing what I was doing. I always liked doing things of an organizational nature; my former boss in Leningrad had discovered that quickly, and although technically I had been a researcher, most of the time I had acted as his executive assistant— organizing conferences, coordinating the itineraries for the visits of our foreign colleagues, and so forth. Having an office at home also helped—I officially worked part-time and could easily manage both business and household duties.

My tenure, however, was short. Rumors started to circulate that we weren't doing much work. Then all of a sudden we received a notice from Moscow that it was against the rules for a husband and wife to work together if one was subordinate to the other, which clearly was the situation in our case.

"What in the world . . ." Lev said when we got the notice. "We've been assigned to work together from the very beginning. Surely they knew the rules then. There's got to be something else to it."

There was. Unknowingly, we had broken an unwritten rule of embassy life by which a certain seniority is observed for embassy wives' employment. Women who come to the embassy with their husbands cannot have full-time jobs—people for those jobs are assigned from Moscow. That leaves only a limited number of part-time jobs to go around, plus a lot of highly educated professional women who loathe sitting at home and being housewives. Most of those jobs were with the Novosty Press Agency—doing the mailings, clippings, mild editorial stuff—but even that was a welcome relief from the boredom of home. The fact that they were paying jobs and added even minimally to the family budget was an additional allure. Because of the scarcity of positions there was a waiting list of applicants, and nobody got a job right away—you had to pay your dues by staying at home until your turn came. My coming with a ready job in my pocket had apparently caused the complaints that had resulted in VAAP's action. Lev had no choice but to dismiss me and hire the wife of our trade attaché and neighbor, a woman named Natalie.

CHAPTER 4

IN a way I did not mind a break from work. The first thing I did was to take Kitty and fly to Moscow for three weeks in the middle of January. The co-op apartment that we had paid for before leaving Moscow was finally finished; Lev's sister had the power of attorney, but she was working full-time and could not deal with all the practical issues on hand, and my mother was not feeling well enough to make frequent trips to Moscow. The apartment needed to be fixed, minimally furnished, and rented out. All of that required my presence. Besides, I was only too happy to leave Lev to deal with Xenia.

Since that fateful letter, we had kept an eye on her mail. She'd toned down her complaints after Lev had talked to her about possible repercussions, but still asked her mother regularly to keep her promise and bring her back to Moscow by the New Year, saying that she had never agreed to stay for three years as Lev was now telling her. We'd bought her most of the things on Sonya's list, and she felt that she had kept her part of the bargain by tolerating me long enough to fulfill her mother's wishes. Ignoring me had not worked—Lev was too reluctant to interfere in any disagreements and had finally left all household-related decisions to me. Xenia had finally accepted the fact that she had to deal with me; she was always polite but spent most of the time locked in her room.

In a way, I sympathized with her—I would not have wanted to be in her situation, forced to live with and to take orders from somebody I hated, and I did not blame her. I could only blame Sonya, and Lev for his refusal to see the truth. Most of the things that he dreamed about for Xenia did not materalize. His idea was that she would learn to speak English fluently; however, he ignored the fact that in Moscow she had attended a special school with early foreign language education, and the language had been French. At first Xenia had refused to study English at all, claiming it would spoil her French accent. She had little choice, however, when school started, and she entered fifth grade. She did well, but still hated English and spent time at home going through her French textbooks. I suspected that the issue of language had a symbolic meaning for her, as well—Sonya was fluent in French, while English repesented me and our life in the States.

Lev did not seem to notice the tension. He did not spend much time with her—I drove her to school and took her shopping; he was merely content to have her around.

Finally, by the end of November, I brought the subject up with him.

"I think we should send her home during the winter school break," I said. "Sonya promised to take her back by the end of the year, and she is looking forward to it. The idea of learning English is not working, she is miserable, she hates me, and it is beginning to get to me, too."

"I want her to stay. She'll get used to English and it'll be invaluable for her future. And she'll get used to you once she realizes that she is not going home soon."

"Yes," I said, "she can get used to anything, but at what price? She's been torn away from everything she loved—her mother, her school, her friends. She is twelve and a half, practically a teenager, which is a difficult time by itself. At this age children are difficult even for their own parents. I cannot handle my job, the baby, and her for much longer."

"OK," he finally said. "I'll talk to her."

"Talk about what?"

"I will ask her if she wants to leave. If she says yes, I will send her home."

"She will never say yes, not to you. She wants to please you, and she knows that you want her to stay. And how can you leave a decision like this to a twelve-year-old child? This is something that only you and I can decide."

"I'll talk to her," he repeated.

I gave up. "OK—as long as you do it before the school break in January."

December came and went. I reminded Lev several times about his promise, but he kept stalling, saying that he could not find the right moment to bring it up. Finally school started again in the middle of January, and I finally realized that he would never have that conversation. He was too comfortable with the status quo. The fact that both Xenia and I were miserable did not matter. It was Lev's way of making a decision—by doing nothing and letting things take care of themselves.

Not that the pattern was unfamiliar. I still wondered sometimes how he ever managed to make the decision to marry me.

We'd met in 1969 at a conference in Leningrad. I was working at the Leningrad branch of the Institute of Philosophy then; the institute itself was located in Moscow, and Lev was the head of a department there and was attending the conference as chairman of one of the committees. We started seeing each other—I came to Moscow several times, and he visited Leningrad. He was separated from Sonya and living with his mother and sister.

I was then twenty-five years old, and already had one disastrous marriage behind me. When I'd been nineteen, I'd married a boy my own age whom I had met through my university friends. Leonid was bright, imaginative, and a little wild. Within six months we were wed, despite strong opposition from my family. My father was particularly unhappy with my choice.

"Something is not quite right," he kept telling me. "Leonid is draft age and he is not a student, so why is he exempt from the Army? I don't buy his explanation of sinusitis—people don't get exemption on that basis."

I had never listened to my father, and I was not going to start now. Our relationship had always been quite distant, and was growing more and more so. He was an older-generation dogmatic Communist whose philosophy was the front page of *Pravda;* I spent most of my time in the company of my mother's friends, the journalistic and literary elite of Leningrad, and was already four years into my university studies, where I was being exposed to more and more Western books and ideas. We never had anything in common to talk about.

For once, though, my father was right. Leonid's "wild imagination" turned out to be an incurable form of schizophrenia, and nine months later I got a divorce on medical grounds. Devastated and disappointed, I started dating older men with whom I felt more secure and comfortable, and from whom I could learn more about life and human relationships than I could from my father.

Lev was the answer to my dreams. I was fascinated with his brillance and erudition, his aura of power and secure knowledge that came from being in control of one's own life. Our first meeting was unforgettable.

The organizational side of the preparation for the conference had hit several snags in the past few days, and as a result the papers submitted to the conference had been printed in small quantities. There was no way to provide papers for all the participants, and I had had to restrict the distribution to committee chairmen and authors. After the session started, I was sitting in a hallway with the few remaining copies, exhausted from battling all the people who wanted the papers, my throat sore from endless explanations of why we had the shortage, and certainly not looking my best.

I was ready to leave when a man came out of the conference room. I had never seen him before and was not prepared for what I was about to hear.

"What idiot invented this imbecile distribution by the list?" he said. "Meanwhile, I want my copy."

"I invented it," I said angrily. "There was no other way. Is your name on the list?"

He seemed to be taken aback by the fact that I did not know who he was, and his contempt for me was visible. Finally I verified that he was entitled to a copy and gave it to him.

"And to think that people go to such trouble to get this junk."

"You seem to go through that trouble yourself," I said tartly.

"A friend of mine asked me to get it for him," he said, and left without a word. I collected the remaining copies and hurried to the hairdresser to prepare for the best part of the conference—the big banquet.

Later in the evening I caught a glimpse of him a couple of times, but I was constantly surrounded by people, talking and dancing. Close to the end, a friend from the Moscow delegation finally managed to get over to me.

"A friend of mine wants me to introduce him to you," he said. "Elena, meet Lev Mitrokhin."

After a few months I transferred my graduate study to the Moscow Institute of Sociology and moved to Moscow. We dated for almost a year; I was introduced to his mother, who had never liked Sonya and was hoping for change in Lev's life, and to his younger sister Tatiana, who was about my age. Tatiana and I became immediate friends; she hated Sonya and would have liked nothing better than to see Lev marry me. Yet, with all the support from his family, he still did not file for a divorce.

Exasperated, I finally started going out with other men, and after a while one of them, named Anatol, proposed to me. I called Tatiana for advice, and she came to see me in the apartment I was renting in the outer suburbs.

"What shall I do?" I asked. "You know I am in love with Lev, but it's been going on for almost two years, and there is no change."

"I know," she said. "My advice is—marry Anatol. You are not in love with him, but he is nice and dependable, and he is crazy about you. You'll be happy with him." Tatiana was speaking from experience. After a sizzling affair with an older, and married, man that lasted several years and left her bitter and emotionally drained, she'd married a man who had been in love with her since high school. Vadim was not the brightest man in the world, and was clearly no match for Tatiana's good looks and intelligence, but he was eager to do whatever it took to keep her happy, and she was reasonably content in her marriage.

"To tell you the truth," she continued, "I was hoping that a miracle would happen, but I don't think now that Lev would ever divorce Sonya."

"But why? I know she wants him back now, but he always says that he is not going back, and the only link between them is Xenia."

"That's true," Tatiana said. Suddenly she turned away to avoid looking into my eyes. "He will probably kill me for telling you, but the truth is that if he divorces Sonya, he will have to marry Irina, his mistress of twenty years, and he does not want to do that either. I am sorry I did not tell you earlier, but he is my brother, after all, and I did hope that things would work out."

If a bomb had dropped from the ceiling and exploded in my apartment, I would have been less surprised. "So where do I fit?" I finally managed to say.

"I honestly do not know," Tatiana said. "I don't think he knows, either. I think he is trying to keep things as they are because no matter what he does, he is going to hurt one of you."

Slowly she told me the story. When she'd been four years old and Lev eighteen, their father, a general in the Soviet militia (the equivalent of a police commissioner), had been arrested on some cooked-up charges. It was 1948, and things like that were happening. Lev was a student at Moscow University. Although he was not expelled, his future was severely limited—with his father in the Gulag and the stigma attached to the family, he could not continue his study of such a highly political discipline as modern Marxism and had had to change to the study of classical philosophy—not exactly a fast track in the social sciences. Irina, his sweetheart, was seventeen and an obedient daughter. Her parents hurriedly married her off to the son of a well-to-do and, most important, politically reliable lawyer. The affair broke off.

Lev's family fell on hard times; he continued his studies and moonlighted as a traveling lecturer to support his mother and sister. His father died in the camp in 1952, several months before he was cleared of all false charges. Lev's career went back on track; he completed his graduate study and went to work for the Central Committee of Komsomol. In 1960 he married Sonya, a provincial girl who was just finishing her studies at Moscow University. Soon afterward he met Irina again. She was not happy in her marriage;

they started an affair and Irina was ready to file for a divorce when Xenia was born and Lev decided to stay with Sonya because of the child. The affair with Irina continued, though, and when he separated from Sonya, Irina rightfully expected that she would file for a divorce at the same time he did, and they would get married.

"The problem is," Tatiana said, "that I personally think it's been going on for too long and sort of burnt itself out, but he does not know how to get out of it. Neither of them knows about you— both Sonya and Irina think it's just between the two of them."

"Sure," I said bitterly, "like two dogs fighting over the same bone only to discover that a third has come along and stolen the bone right from under their noses. Only I don't seem to have the bone either."

We talked for another hour, when suddenly Lev showed up. I did not have a phone—in the Moscow suburbs it can take several years on a waiting list to get a phone line, and it wasn't even my apartment. Lev was high, as usual, but not quite drunk. My resolve to stay calm suddenly collapsed; I started crying violently; Tatiana ran downstairs to call Anatol, who rushed over and took me away to his apartment at another end of the city.

I was resolved not to talk to Lev again, but he somehow managed to get Anatol's number from Tatiana and called me there. He was leaving for Czechoslovakia the next day and asked me not to make any drastic decisions until he returned and we had a chance to talk.

A week later I went to the airport with Tatiana to meet him. He had called Tatiana from Prague and insisted that she bring me along. I could hardly recognize the man who got off the plane. He had lost almost ten pounds and looked sick. We drove to my apartment, which was only two miles from the airport, and he brought all his bags in from the taxicab.

"I brought a full set of glasses and dishes from Czechoslovakia. They are yours . . . ours, if you want to. This will be the start of our household. But I want your decision now," he said.

I stayed. I loved him and he needed me. The next day he filed for a divorce from Sonya and a year later we were married.

Now, packing for Moscow, I was wondering whether he would

ever have made any decision if I had not forced his hand by walking out with Anatol. I'd never regretted staying—Lev was a fascinating man to be with. After several years of marriage, we still could talk late into the night; he always had interesting ideas and opinions about everything, and I had learned a lot from him. He also always seemed to be in charge of the situation back in Moscow—something that I had never challenged or questioned—until now. Whether his reliance on me in practical matters here had given me more confidence in myself, or the strain of our family situation was showing, I don't know, but I was gradually losing my unquestioning admiration for him. The god had suddenly lost his aura.

———

The trip to Moscow was a relief, although a costly one. I could not possibly afford to pay for the airplane tickets in dollars, but my friends at the embassy told me how to get around that. Pan-Am and Aeroflot flew the Moscow-Washington route jointly; any tickets purchased on this end had to be paid for in dollars; tickets purchased in Moscow could be paid for in rubles. All I had to do was to give Pan-Am a voucher from the embassy guaranteeing payment later. Then in Moscow I went to an Aeroflot supervisor who had been recommended to me by a friend at the embassy. The mention of his name and a bottle of Miss Dior did the job: the Pan-Am voucher was canceled and an Aeroflot round-trip ticket issued to me payable in rubles. The practice was illegal, and Pan-Am raised the issue more than once because the profits were divided according to the share of tickets sold by each side, and in this case the sale was rightfully Pan-Am's. Their complaints were largely ignored, however.

The reason the embassy people were so well versed in the tricks of ticket-swapping was that, although men flew home occasionally on business, their wives were entitled to only one vacation trip a year. The tickets VAAP purchased for us in Moscow, just like the tickets the Ministry of Foreign Affairs bought for other diplomats, were good for a return trip within a year; then, after vacation, VAAP would buy us another ticket good for another year. The wives of the lower-rank personnel with two-year assignments were not entitled to a vacation trip at all—two years without vacation was not considered too much of a burden. Meanwhile, the need to fly back and forth arose often; some families had teenage children living with relatives back in Moscow, there were occasional urgent family affairs; and, quite often, women flew to Moscow to have abortions.

Birth-control methods in the Soviet Union are primitive. The pill is unheard of; IUDs are smuggled in and then sold by physicians to their private clientele. Like everybody else, doctors strictly separate their State jobs, for which they are often paid less than construction workers—which explains, by the way, why over 90 percent of Soviet physicians are women—and their private practice, provided they are good enough to have private clients. Sometimes they take advantage of the fact that they work in one of the privileged health-care institutions, access to which is highly sought after and which can therefore bring money from patients eager to get into a better hospital and willing to pay extra to bribe the physician.

The rest of the population makes do the same way their grandparents did; therefore, abortion remains the most used method of birth control. Many women have more than one, and I've known a few who had over a dozen. Abortions are free and available to anybody, although in recent years the government—alarmed by the declining birth rate among ethnic Russians and the disproportionately high population growth of non-Russian minorities, particularly in the Moslem southern republics, where large families are common—has introduced some restrictions, notably, a ban on abortion during the first pregnancy. There are plenty of abortion clinics, which are usually departments within maternity wards. They are contemptuously called "meat factories," require three days' hospitalization, and issue a paper that justifies absence from work. Unlike any other sick leave, abortion leave is without pay. Therefore, the paper states clearly the reason for absence, and soon everybody at the place of work is privy to the private life of the woman. Most women who have been in one of those clinics go to extaordinary lengths to find a private practitioner for the next occasions. Those doctors use the same hospital facilities, but usually work with trusted nurses with whom they share illegal income.

Paying for an abortion means getting an anesthetic, normally not available, and better postoperational care, because nurses and orderlies are in on the take.

With respect to birth control, the women in the embassy are not in a much better position than they are back home. The embassy has a full-time physician assigned from Moscow. He is licensed to write prescriptions but is not affiliated with any hospital. Therefore his primary duty is to treat minor ailments and provide diagnostics. When a serious illness is suspected, people are referred to American specialists—the embassy has a list of physicians with whom they deal regularly. The embassy does not carry medical insurance for its members—emergencies and occasional visits are paid for by the embassy. In the case of an illness that may require prolonged hospital stay, people are sent back to Moscow. The doctor would not prescribe anything considered to be strictly a Western medication, such as birth-contol pills, and I doubt very much that anybody would dare even to discuss it with him, anyway.

The embassy also has some small medical offices in another building, equipped for pediatric, gynecological, and dental care. These specialists are not assigned from Moscow, however. If there are doctors among embassy wives, they fill the positions part-time. Since almost all Soviet doctors are female, there is always a fair chance that among the almost eight hundred members of the Soviet community in Washington, there will be one or another of the specialists. Indeed, at the time I was there, we had all three. However, they are not fully licensed to practice medicine here. Infant care is referred to an American pediatrician, as well as obstetric care—the latter for the obvious reason that a hospital stay is required eventually. For the same reason, abortions cannot be performed by the embassy gynecologist, and since it is one of the operations the embassy would not pay for, practically nobody would consider going to an American doctor, both because of the cost and for fear of a security breach. Therefore sudden flights to Moscow by the embassy wives usually cause humorous speculations unless there is another, well-known reason for the trip.

My trip to Moscow after only a few months in the United States probably caused the same speculations, but I had other things to worry about. The first vacation trip home is always a tremendous financial burden for any diplomat. Besides a natural desire to bring gifts for relatives, gifts must be brought for any friends you intend to visit. Gifts are always brought when visiting friends in Russia— usually flowers or a bottle of wine, but, coming from a foreign country, the gift is expected to be something foreign. Coupled with the fact that everybody will want to see you when you come back on vacation, this means stocking up on a substantial number of supplies unless you want to find yourself embarrassingly short close to the end of your trip. Aside from the cost of the gifts themselves, there is also the problem of excess luggage.

I made a special trip to New York, where the Orchard Street district in lower Manhattan serves as a wholesale market for the Soviet community. Many stores there are run by Russian emigrés who always know what the hottest items on the Soviet black market are and stock a variety of discontinued and low-quality merchandise at very low prices. Many stores have Russian-speaking salespeople and have Russian signs in the windows. I went with a couple of embassy women who had been there before and could steer me to the right places. It was a hard trip—I was the driver, and we had to get to New York and back in one day, but it did give me an opportunity to finish my gift-shopping quickly and inexpensively.

I bought a variety of cosmetics for my women friends and decided that a case of scotch from a duty-free shop in Moscow would take care of the rest. My main problem was to get enough supplies for Kitty to last her three weeks. She still needed diapers, and although she could eat a variety of regular food, I was also bringing a full supply of fruit juices, vitamins, and enough baby food for the first few days in the Soviet Union, to ease her gradually into Russian food. The rest of my suitcases were stuffed with gifts for our families—fake fur coats for Tatiana and my mother-in-law that would cost a fortune in Moscow, fabrics for my mother, and household items for both families.

———

My feelings upon my arrival in Moscow were mixed. I was amazed how a few short months in Washington had changed my outlook.

Even familiar things looked different. Tatiana and her husband met me at the airport. After hugs and kisses we walked out to the parking lot and got into a taxicab. I looked at the rest of the cabs waiting in line. I was used to all the taxicabs being Volgas—medium-sized sedans. All of a sudden, all the taxis were compacts.

"When did they switch taxis to Moskvitch?" I asked Tatiana.

"Where? I don't see any."

"There." I pointed to the waiting line.

"They are all Volgas." She laughed. "Don't you recognize them?"

"I guess I have lost my sense of proportion. Also, something is burning—can't you smell it?"

Tatiana looked at me strangely. "You must be tired from the long flight. You are imagining things." And then, quietly: "Is it really that different?"

"Yes." I realized by then that what I thought was a burning smell was the regular Moscow smell of car exhausts—the pollution in Moscow is much greater than in Washington.

Finally we arrived at Tatiana's apartment. We quickly walked through the foyer to her rooms—Lev's family still lived in a "communal" apartment they shared with two other families, with a common kitchen and facilities. They had two adjacent rooms: my mother-in-law occupied a walk-through—a small partition separated her sleeping quarters from the rest of the room, which served as a combination of living/dining room area—and Tatiana and her husband and their one-year-old daughter, Masha, occupied the other room. There were aah's and ooh's as the gifts were unwrapped, but the thing that sent Tatiana flying to me with hugs was a supply of ready-to-mix baby cereals for Masha, and baby multivitamins. I had not forgotten how it was to have a baby in Moscow.

"It's the best thing you could bring," she kept saying. "She is too young for adult cereals, and the baby cereals are so heavily sugared that she breaks out in rashes. And she throws up cod liver oil."

"So did I when I was a child," I said. "I still remember the taste."

Cod liver oil is still about the only source of vitamin D in the

Soviet Union. The only other one is caviar which, when available, is often purchased exclusively for children, but is too expensive to use as a source of the vitamin on a regular basis.

We stayed up late into the night. Inevitably there were questions about our life in Washington. But there was something else—for the first time in several months I felt completely at home, surrounded by real friends, able to talk about anything without worrying about whether I would be quoted later someplace or if somebody was listening to the conversation.

The next day I went out and faced Moscow reality—crowds everywhere, people elbowing each other to get through—in the subway, in the stores, on the streets. There was something strange and unfamiliar about the crowds, some persistent feeling that something was missing, until I finally realized—nobody was smiling. I was so used to smiling people in Washington—on the street, in the elevator, in a supermarket line. It's not that Russians are unfriendly—they are the warmest and friendliest people in the world—but only inside their homes. Out on the street, it's a fight for survival, you against the world.

And no color. Gray snow, mixed with smog, dirty buildings, drab clothes in subdued "practical" dark colors.

I was home.

———

I took Kitty to Leningrad, spent a couple of days with my parents, visited friends, left Kitty with adoring grandparents, and returned to Moscow to take care of the business at hand. Tatiana went with me to my new apartment.

It is very difficult for outsiders to understand the importance Russians attach to their housing. The apartment, or any living space, is any Russian's most prized possession, and people go to extraordinary lengths to obtain it or to protect what they have. It has a lot to do with the fact that Russians cannot move freely from one city to another—in order to do so they must have a residency permit to live in a particular city, which cannot be granted unless there is an available apartment and a ready job. For the government it is a way to control population growth in the large cities;

it is very attractive to live there because they have better supplies of consumer goods and a better choice of jobs. The population of Moscow, currently over eight million, would probably triple if people were permitted to move there freely, and the city's resources are limited. Some organizations are given preference in housing for their employees—it can be a perk of the job or a way to attract employees to industries experiencing severe manpower shortages, such as construction. This fact is not lost on some ambitious young people who often take construction jobs in Moscow, get an apartment, and then quit after staying the required two years on the job and go on to better jobs. Another way of getting Moscow residency is through marriage. A high percentage of students in Moscow colleges get married in their graduation year— they have a temporary permit in the dormitory while they are still in school, but after graduation they have to go back home. Marriages of convenience with substantial sums of money involved are also rather common. The danger in those arrangements is that after six months of sharing living quarters, the other party is entitled to an equal share of living space, and many divorces follow just after a residency permit and a job is obtained for the spouse but before any claim can be made on the apartment itself.

The housing situation in the Soviet Union is a major source of jokes, comedy plays, and movies, but in reality it is more tragic than funny. Countless families have been broken up by the fact that a newly married couple has been forced to live for years with their in-laws; family members become bitter enemies who wage all-or-nothing campaigns against each other, trying to gain precious living space; bribes, blackmail, and even anonymous letters to State authorities, declaring the political unreliability of former relatives, are not unknown. My own recollection of the Soviet phenomenon of the communal apartment goes back to my early childhood. The Air Force Academy, where my father worked, was evacuated from Leningrad during the war to a safer place close to the Urals, but was brought back shortly after the siege of Leningrad ended in 1944. Four-fifths of the city's housing had been destroyed by the German bombardments, and we were allocated one room in an apartment shared by fourteen families. There was one large kitchen, where each family had a small table and its own kerosene stove. The kitchen was about forty yards from our room, and my mother had to run back and forth all the time checking on the food. There was one toilet shared by everybody, but no bath or hot water. My father had several guns in our room because of his membership in the national marksmanship team, and my mother, who was also an Army champion in rifle shooting, never entered the toilet without a gun because huge rats lurked there. A couple of times she shot them.

A few years later we moved to another apartment, this one shared with only three other families, but our life did not get much easier. Sharing common facilities was a delicate task, and in the new apartment we faced a problem we had not had before—a neighbor on the warpath. After a while my mother did not even dare leave the food cooking in the kitchen unsupervised; a few times the stove was turned up and the food burned after she left the kitchen, and we started to find strange objects in our food. The explanation turned out to be that this neighbor had been hoping to get an extra room when it became available; instead, the room had been given to us and she vented her frustration by making our life as unpleasant as possible, hoping that it would force my father to ask for another place to live. Eventually we did get a separate apartment in 1952, where my parents lived ever after, but for many families even now a separate apartment remains just a dream.

In our particular situation in 1971, the only way Lev could have gotten a place to live after leaving Sonya was to exchange their apartment for two one-room apartments—such exchanges are permitted by law but left to the efforts of the parties involved. That would have confined Sonya and Xenia to sharing one room, however, which Lev did not want to do. We could afford to pay the price of private rental although we had to move several times— we were renting apartments from diplomats who were assigned abroad and had to move when the owners returned. His willingness to leave her the apartment also gave him leverage in another important matter—although he did not live there, his residency permit was for their apartment. I had finished my graduate study by then and my temporary permit had expired; in order to get me a permanent permit I had to be registered in his apartment, which required Sonya's consent. Even with his high position it would have taken him several years to get an apartment from the Academy of Sciences; finally, using all his connections, he managed to get us the place in a co-op I was about to inspect. Unlike getting an apartment from the State, which is free except for a nominal monthly charge, co-ops have to be paid for, just like buying an apartment in the West, and they are expensive—a typical down-payment is the equivalent of two and a half years of an average engineer's salary. The monthly cost to amortize the loan from the State is also high; however, co-ops are somewhat easier to get and the wait is only two or three years.

The visit was a shock, mainly because it was the first time I'd ever been in a brand-new apartment that came "as is." Although it was an "upgraded" design and a hard-to-get-into co-op, the apartment was not ready to be lived in. It wasn't just the aesthetics—I could put up temporarily with the horrible wallpaper and the dirty-gray plywood cabinet around the kitchen sink. It was the end of January, and despite all the heating the apartment was freezing cold. The heating elements were obviously inadequate, and the window frames did not fit, as they let cold air breeze through the apartment in all directions. We kept our coats on and heated some water on the stove to make instant coffee from the jar my mother had left on her previous visit to Moscow.

"You should have seen it in the beginning," Tatiana said. "Your mother was here when we received the key, and she stayed for several days after inspection. The heating was not working at all, the toilet was cracked, and there was almost an inch left between the entrance door and the floor. She found some men from the construction crew and had them fix it after hours—for extra pay, of course, but she could not stay long enough to take care of it all—it would take months."

One thing was clear—the apartment would have to stay empty for a while. Nobody would rent it the way it was.

We went to visit my friend Alana, who lived in the same building. I was curious to see how they had managed and wanted to ask her what could be done. When we walked into her apartment, we walked into another world.

Alana had had a crew of workmen working on her apartment nonstop for two months. Everything had been replaced—sinks, tile, heaters, stove. Parquet tile had been laid on top of the green linoleum that constituted the floors in my apartment. Alana was married to a young and talented psychiatrist who worked in one of the most prestigious Moscow hospitals and had a flourishing consulting practice on the side. Money was no object for her.

"How much did it cost you to have it fixed?" I asked.

"Three thousand," she said. Tatiana gasped quietly. It was the equivalent of her salary for two years. It was also almost as much as we had paid for a downpayment.

If all the energy and ingenuity Russian people use for bettering their personal standard of living could be channeled into State enterprises, the Soviet Union would have as high a standard of living as any European country. The problem is that people have no incentive to work for the State because their pay would not be any better if they worked more. Instead, they use their considerable energy and mental resources to make a living in addition to a State job. Any skill that can be used in moonlighting provides a nice additional income, as can—with lax supervision at State enterprises—the facilities of one's job and often State-supplied materials. Those who do not have marketable skills often take advantage of having access to certain facilities or goods to make extra money: store clerks habitually hide shipments of better imported goods and sell them to acquaintances for an additional gratuity; directors of large grocery stores are among Soviet millionaires. The pay of people in the service sector is so low that theft and selling of scarce goods for extra profits is almost built into the system. If all the supplies that the Soviet stores received were actully sold over the counter many of the shortages would be eliminated.

This "second economy" creates an additional circulation of money and goods of which the State has no part, and produces a lot of people with considerable buying power. It is almost standard for any foreigner who visits Moscow to comment on how shabbily people are dressed. However, what they see on the streets does not necessarily reflect life in Moscow. Moscow has over a million visitors and other people passing through it every day, and many of these people come from the provinces that do not have the same supply level as Moscow; they constitute a large part of the crowds on Moscow streets and of lines in the Moscow stores. Moscow has its share of mink coats proportionally probably the same as in New York, but the women who wear those coats are rarely seen on the street. They rarely use public transportation and almost never go to regular stores.

A good example was Katrina, my best friend in the apartment building where we had lived before leaving for the States. Katrina was a second-rate actress who had done one successful miniseries on Soviet TV, but she was married to Andrei Mironov—one of the top Soviet movie and television stars. Being a movie star in the Soviet Union is the same as everywhere else; although they are not paid anywhere close to their Western counterparts, the actors enjoy the same high level of recognition and adoration from their fans. Katrina never did any grocery shopping—Andrei usually stopped at one of the Moscow stores, where the director of the store, in exchange for free passes to popular theater performances and closed showings of Western films, and the mere joy of being able to drop Andrei's name among his acquaintances, always had all the choice goods packed for him in the back room. On the rare occasion when she ran out of milk, Katrina would simply call for a cab, ride two blocks to the shop, have the cab wait for her, and come back. One of the greatest favors she did for me was to introduce me to her hairdresser—a very valuable commodity in Moscow. He was working in the State-owned beauty salon, but had his own clientele that generously paid him extra for the privilege of having their hair done by him. He made about ten times as much in tips as he did in the salary paid to him by the State, and had three ex-wives, all of whom he left in possession of a co-op apartment.

Because of the position of her husband and his private practice, Alana had enormous connections, and she offered to help me with my problems. I did not have enough money to do the wonders she had in her apartment, but she would find the workmen to take care of the most immediate problems—windows, heating, and plumbing, supervising their work, and then finding a tenant. In return she made a list of things she needed from the States that even she, with all her connections, could not find in Moscow. The list was expertly made—Alana had spent her adolescence in New York, where her father had been attached to the Soviet mission. The things Alana wanted were not expensive in the States, but merely unattainable on the black market in the Soviet Union—it started with a supply of pipe tobacco for her husband and included quality cosmetics and skin-care products and baby toys. It was a fair trade.

I had to sell our collection of American jazz records that I had left in Tatiana's care, and some of my own clothes to raise the money. I figured that both were replaceable back in Washington. Before I left Moscow, I gave Alana a thousand rubles and was grateful that fate had placed her in the same building. Without her help, we could not even have come home for vacation and counted on a place to live.

There wasn't much left for me to do in Moscow. I returned to Leningrad to spend the remaining week with my parents. After two weeks of almost nonstop talking, I had practically lost my voice, but all major topics of conversation had been covered, and gradually I noticed that I was counting the days left till my return to Washington. Suddenly I was thinking of Washington as home. I wanted to go back there, where getting from one end of the city to another was not a major undertaking, where people were happy and smiling, back to my action shows, my car, my morning newspaper that would tell me what had happened in the world, to my embassy friends who would talk about upcoming Presidential elections instead of what was available in the neighborhood stores and the outrageous prices on the black market.

Why did it have to be that way? Russia is one of the richest countries in the world; its resources are almost unlimited, and certainly as great as those of the United States. The Russian people are industrious and hardworking—when they work for themselves. If all those resources and that industry were channeled in the right direction, if the system permitted them to be utilized to their full extent, the Soviet Union would be a genuine superpower, not a backward country with simply a large population and tremendous military power. With the exception of a few showcases—the space program, a few advanced clinics, a few collective farms that could be shown to foreigners—everywhere I looked I saw a country that was at least twenty years behind the West in its development. True, it had been devastated by the war, but so had Germany. No, the reasons were deeper than that, and the main problem was that the system actually discouraged the people from working. Why bother if there is no reward for better work? I've heard horror stories of waste, collective farms that grew vegetables which rotted in the fields because there were not enough trucks to take them out or not enough storage facilities to keep them.

I still remembered the shock we all experienced in the early seventies when, for the first time in Russian history, there was not enough grain to go around. Bleached flour was rationed and distributed through official centers by special coupons. A new kind of bread was introduced that quickly acquired the nickname "Nikita's machine gun." The flour used in baking this greenish-gray substance had been mixed with ground lentils, and therefore caused indigestion and gas. The nickname also implied the person responsible for the plight—Nikita Khrushchev. He'd become so fascinated with the versatility of corn during his visit to the United States in 1969 that he'd decided to make it a major crop grain in the Soviet Union. The orders from the top were followed blindly by the regional managers, who were anxious to please Moscow. Collective farm directors were not in a position to argue at all. As a result, collective farms in the northern regions abandoned their traditional crops and tried to grow corn in latitudes where it could never grow. The severe bread shortage was alleviated after a few months by massive grain purchases from the West, but remained in the consciousness of the people as the first sign of real trouble with the system. If Russia cannot feed itself, what else is left of the former breadbasket of Europe?

Of course I knew about the problems the Soviet system was causing for the economy, but took them for granted. That was the way it was and nothing could change it. Like many other people, I accepted it as a fact of life and made do with what was available. Living in Washington brought these problems into much sharper focus, because I saw with my own eyes what a country with similar resources could do when people had an incentive to work. I felt sorry for my country, and at the same time I knew there was nothing that I or anybody else could do to change it. All I could do was to escape it for a while and live for whatever short time I had in a brighter world.

And, despite the recent rift, I did miss my husband.

CHAPTER 5

WHEN I returned to Washington I found Lev at his wit's end. Natalie, his new secretary, could not handle the job. She could not type, her English was on a grade school level, and after a couple of months with the office she still could not, or cared not, to remember the names of our major publishing contacts, which was embarrassing. Letters piled up, and I spent the first several evenings redoing most of them simply because they could not be sent out the way they were. I spent most of the daytime cleaning the apartment—the kitchen counter looked like it had not been cleaned since I'd left, and several pots were burned beyond salvation.

After a while life returned to normal, but a troubling pattern started to develop. Lev kept asking me to review Natalie's work, and I ended up redoing most of it every evening. Finally I said that I was unwilling to spend my evenings covering somebody else's mistakes—I would rather take a paying job at the embassy or catch up on reading. Lev wrote several letters to Moscow, spoke to senior embassy officials, and finally got me back as his assistant—on condition that we would open an office separate from the apartment and keep normal business hours, with me working part-time either three days a week or half a day every day. We found an office on K Street around the corner from the embassy. The embassy did not have any space available in its building even to put in another desk, let alone an office, and the new embassy complex on Tunlaw Road was far from completion. Besides, we felt that our American visitors would feel more comfortable in a regular commercial office building rather than going through embassy security every time they had to visit us.

I had my own reasons for finding an office so close to the embassy. Lev still did not drive and had to depend on our neighbors for transportation. Since I would be working part-time, I would not always be around to drive him. Besides, I was planning to take another leave at the end of the year. After careful consideration I'd decided that I wanted another baby.

When Kitty had been born, I'd sworn that I would never have another child. The horror and pain of childbirth were so vivid for so long that I never wanted to go through it again.

As I got more acquainted with the people at the embassy, especially during our weekly outings to the embassy retreat on the Eastern Shore in the summer, I noticed quite a few young babies. Once, I commented to Alia that it was strange that Moscow would choose to send people with such young children on a foreign assignment.

"Most of them did not come here with children," she said. "They were born here. If a family wants to have a child at all, here is the time and the place to have it."

I talked to some of the young mothers. They were mostly wives of security men and maintenance workers, but all said essentially the same thing—having children here was easy, the medical facilities were incredible, and good nutrition could build a foundation for years of future health.

I could not consult any of my own friends—they were all in Lev's age bracket, with children at least of school age, and weren't planning any increase in the family. Because of my age difference with Lev and the fact that it was his second marriage, we were the only couple in our circle with a young child. But I did make my own comparisons when I visited Moscow and saw Tatiana's daughter, Masha, and Kitty together. They had been born one month apart, but raised in a completely different way. After taking maternity leave, Tatiana had gone back to work full-time. It had been a financial necessity—very few Soviet couples can live on one salary. With a full-time job and the time she had to spend after work scouting the stores for groceries, Tatiana knew perfectly well that she would have to leave the child-rearing to her mother, who lived with them. Had they lived separately, she probably would not dared to have a baby at all. She also wisely decided from the very beginning not to interfere with her mother's way of baby care. She was not very happy about it, but knew that two months later she would be completely dependent on her mother for help and did not want to create a conflict.

I had been determined to do things differently. Although a Russian translation of Dr. Spock's book was available, it was substantially abridged. Substantial parts of the information on child nutrition were missing for understandable reasons—things described in the book were not available in the Soviet Union. Other parts that were in disagreement with the ongoing theories of Soviet pediatric care were also substantially altered or missing.

Therefore when Lev took a trip to England a couple of months before Kitty was born, he had clear instructions—bring me an original edition of Spock's book and bring back as much British currency as possible to exchange for coupons so we could buy powdered baby formula in a diplomatic store. I anticipated a need for formula—nine out of ten nursing mothers in Moscow lose milk within two weeks of giving birth, some because of complications, but most because of the stress of child-rearing, and I did not think I would be an exception.

Tatiana was no exception, either. As soon as the need arose, we offered to buy formula for Masha. My mother-in-law did not believe in foreign substances, though. She preferred to get up at five o'clock every morning, walk to a special kitchen at the pediatric clinic, and get a prescription mixture of some kind of combination of milk and yogurt supposedly modified for a baby's digestion.

There was usually an hour's wait in line, and only one day's supply could be purchased; we kept offering the formula to ease the burden on her, but she stoically held the line.

Meanwhile I spent most of my time reading and rereading Spock. I was determined not to give in to tradition. When I came home from the hospital, my mother-in-law came to visit her new grand-daughter; she left in indignation, but not before she took Lev into the kitchen and vented her frustration.

"This baby is not going to live long," she said. "Look at her—she is lying on her stomach, face in the pillow. She'll suffocate! And if she doesn't suffocate, she'll scratch her eyes out because her hands are not bundled!"

Several days later I developed complications with high fever and had to ask her for help. She came and helped me with washing diapers and cooking for Lev, but refused even to touch the baby unless I agreed to let her to do it her way—to lay the baby on her back, as tightly bundled as a mummy. I was adamant. Finally, in exasperation, I summoned my mother from Leningrad, who came and followed my instructions to the letter. Two weeks later, Kitty was raising her head and moving around in her bassinette. Masha spent the first two months of her life flat on her back, with no opportunity to move her arms except for a few minutes a day while her diapers were being changed.

I knew I was taking chances. The pediatrician who came from the clinic did not hesitate to voice her disapproval of the way I was handling the baby. She also refused to take any responsibility unless we switched immediately from the formula to the clinic's kitchen concoctions. In response I hired a private pediatrician recommended by Katrina. Katrina was one of several friends with the mind and resources to deviate from the ancient system of Soviet child-rearing principles. The pediatrician she found me was also of the old school, but had treated enough of the Moscow elite's babies to let me have my own way as long as she could monitor the baby's progress regularly.

Now, a year later, I was looking at two children playing together in the playpen in Tatiana's room. Masha was still suffering from colic and broke out in rashes at the slightest provocation. She had developed a variety of allergies, and although she was one month older, her motor coordination was far below Kitty's. I was glad I had been so stubborn a year ago.

The only thing I had no way of verifying was that childbirth was easy in the United States. I would have to take the other mothers' word for it.

———

I enjoyed being at work again. At the same time my frustration with it was growing, too.

I often wondered why VAAP needed an office in Washington— the whole affair had been doomed from the beginning. Another agency existed to sell books printed in the Soviet Union directly to American booksellers. It was called International Book and had been in business for many years before VAAP. There was a market for Soviet art books, classics, and dictionaries in certain specialized bookstores. One such store was in Rockville, a Washington suburb. Most of the embassy personnel frequented it, because it was possible to buy all the rare books there that usually sold out in a matter of days back home. I suspect that Mme. Kamkin, the store's owner, went to extra trouble to make sure she had all the jewels of modern Soviet literature, in addition to the standard fare, because the embassy constituted a ready and reliable market for such books.

The Soviet people read a lot, and any book that's any good usually sells out instantly, despite huge print runs—a hundred thousand copies is almost standard for a first printing. Books are inexpensive, newspapers and television dull, and essentially there are very few things people can do in their spare time other than go to the movies and have parties with friends. Another factor that contributes to the high level of reading is the commuting distances and time spent on public transportation—a subway ride from the suburbs to the center of Moscow can easily take fifty minutes, and most people pass the time with a book in their hands. Good home libraries are a matter of immense pride, and easy access to rare books in Washington provided embassy personnel with an opportunity to build a library that would be the subject of envy back home.

With International Book taking care of books printed in the

Soviet Union, our task was much more difficult—we were supposed to sell manuscripts to be translated, published, and distributed through regular American channels, just like the work of any foreign author. Most technical translations were already handled by a small group of publishing houses that specialized in scientific works. They had a long established relationship with their Soviet counterparts, and only occasionally needed our help to resolve a minor contractual misunderstanding or to speed up paperwork. Our office was left with the most difficult and hopeless task—to sell Soviet fiction and research books in nontechnical areas to American publishers.

One of the problems was that VAAP sent tons of materials to its foreign offices without making any distinction between different markets: the same books that were promoted in Bulgaria were sent to us. We once had a good laugh when we received a large shipment of books written by Soviet agricultural experts on modern methods of growing crops. Given the fact that only three years before, the Soviet Union had experienced severe grain shortages and since then had continuously bought huge quantities of grain in the United States and Canada, I could only imagine how we would look if we offered those books to Americans! On the average, about 90 percent of the books VAAP sent us were so unsuitable for the American market that we often hesitated even to send the blurbs for review. In fiction, a lot of them were so similar that the blurbs sounded nearly identical: boy meets girl (at a factory, collective farm, etc.). Then a love triangle develops—a bad girl (boy) develops problems at work (family), then good friends straighten them out and the original couples live happily ever after, after they have become productivity leaders in their respective enterprises. I am sure the books themselves probably had some merit in them, but their descriptions, written in wooden English from a collection of standard phrases and then typewritten and mimeographed, were so unappealing that they did not stand a chance.

In rare instances, when we came across something really good, there were other obstacles. Most of the books we considered good, and had people in the embassy lining up to borrow, were deeply rooted in recent Soviet history, were psychologically subtle, and required a considerable knowledge of Soviet reality to be understood and appreciated. They were clearly not suitable for the American mass market, and although some were eventually translated and published for the sake of high art and good relations, most were money losers for their publishers.

A most spectacular flop was a monumental project undertaken by Macmillan—to publish an English translation of the forty-two-volume *Great Soviet Encyclopaedia*. The idea was that it presented a different view on the world and a different interpretation of world events that would be interesting to people involved in Soviet studies. Although the translation was done in Moscow, the cost of editing it into readable English, and of printing and distributing it, was so high that after selling 768 subscriptions at over a thousand dollars each and still losing over a million dollars, Macmillan tried to cut its losses and discontinue the project, or so I was told. Later, I heard that VAAP insisted on holding Macmillan to its contract.

We were not completely unsuccessful, though. Macmillan also decided to publish a library of Soviet science fiction—over a dozen books in all. Soviet sci-fi is generally very good, one of the reasons being that most talented Soviet authors can write unorthodox things in their books if they do it under the guise of events taking place in some distant future and on some undisclosed place on Earth. The best in the field were the Strugatsky brothers, Arkady and Boris, and two of their books were scheduled to be published first. The hitch was that Macmillan wanted the authors to come to the US for a promotional tour. With the first book ready for release, the publisher engaged in protracted negotiations with VAAP. VAAP stalled, clearly waiting for a decision in higher quarters, and finally the word came down—no tour. The science-fiction series was killed in its infancy.

Another glimpse of hope came when it looked like finally, after so many years, there was a real possibility that *Gone With the Wind* would be translated and published in the Soviet Union.

The Soviet Union is probably the only developed country that has not translated this international classic. The explanation always was that the book had a biased account of life in the South, and of the Civil War. Since persecution of blacks in the United States is one of the major topics in the Soviet propaganda war against the United States, and Soviet knowledge of the history of blacks is shaped by reading *Uncle Tom's Cabin,* Margaret Mitchell's account in *Gone With the Wind* clearly contradicted everything Soviet people read in history books. However, Macmillan, the original publisher of the book, was rapidly becoming our major trading partner, and VAAP finally agreed to consider publication. The translation had already been done years before by a very prominent Soviet translator, so it was only a matter of getting official permission to publish it, first in the magazine *Foreign Literature* and then in hardcover. Our hopes were high, although not for long. *Gone With the Wind* was shot down at the highest level.

One of the major frustrations of our work in the States was that Lev did not have real power to make any decisions on the spot. It was embarrassing to explain to our American contacts that everything we discussed with them had to be sent to Moscow for approval. Another related problem was that with VAAP it could take months to resolve even a minor issue. We knew that some major decisions could not be made even by the VAAP chairman but, being ideological matters, had to go higher up to be decided by the Party Committee on Propaganda. There were other minor things, however, that were perfectly within VAAP's power to resolve which still took us weeks just to get a reply. I lost count of how many times I had to tell publishers that we were trying to do all we could but, no, we did not have an answer from Moscow yet. Back in Moscow such a slow pace and inaction were a normal way of doing business, and we were accustomed to it. Here it was more difficult for us to take because we saw exactly the opposite in the way Americans did business. With the Americans, we always had a reply when it was promised, and if a delay was necessary, we were always told what had caused it and exactly how much more time the decison would require.

Some decisions Moscow made defied any logic at all. We received a letter from an American author Suzanne Massie, reinforced by a personal appeal from the president of Random House, to help her resolve the issue of her visa, which had been denied for no apparent reason. It took several months and an involvement on the part of the embassy to find out that Mrs. Massie, a renowned historian of Russian art who had made several prior trips to the Soviet Union, had been declared persona non grata. At first we thought it was because her husband's book *Nicholas and Alexandra* had been banned in the Soviet Union. The reason, however, turned out to be that on her last trip Mrs. Massie had been searched in Soviet Customs on suspicion of smuggling out a dissident manuscript. Although nothing had been found, she was blacklisted. The maddening aspect of the matter was that she was a person who genuinely loved Russia and the Russian people, and wrote wonderful books about Russian art. The purpose of her trip this time was most admirable—she was planning to write a book about the restoration of Pavlovsk palace. The restoration of this palace, which had been practically burned to the ground by the Germans at the end of World War II, is a matter of immense pride to the Soviet people. It took over twenty years and the best craftsmen in the country to re-create the palace's old splendor, and any American who wanted to bring the story of this great feat to the West should have been welcomed with open arms. Yet, because of some bureaucrat's decision, the project was put on hold for years because all the materials necessary for Mrs. Massie's research were in Pavlovsk.

So there we were, dutifully shuffling papers, sending mailings, receiving polite refusals most of the time, and producing no tangible results. Although we established good relationships with many major publishing houses, and were always received on the highest level whenever we traveled to New York to meet with publishers, all we could do was to recommend an occasional book that we deemed deserving of attention, maintain good public relations, and send everything to Moscow for a decision. I handled all the correspondence and sometimes accompanied Lev to New York. His English was fair, but sometimes, when he anticipated long discussions on important issues, he preferred to have me translate his conversations.

Life was not without diversions, though, and some of the most pleasant moments were visits from our acquaintances from Moscow. Only now did I understand why Eugene, a seemingly minor official in the Institute of International Economics, always had such a dazzling array of celebrities in his house in Moscow. At his parties we had met an astronaut, a prima ballerina from the Bolshoy theater, and other people with no relation to foreign affairs. They all had one thing in common, though—they had all visited New York when Eugene was stationed there as an administrator of the New York mission.

The situation of Soviet officials, and especially Soviet tourists, visiting foreign countries on short trips is deplorable. In order to control its foreign debt, the Soviet Union constantly tries to limit the outflow of hard currency such as American dollars. Since Soviet currency is not convertible—does not have a gold equivalent—it is not accepted by foreign banks. People who go on a foreign trip are issued a very limited amount of foreign currency in exchange for rubles before they leave Moscow. When I visited Iceland and Denmark in 1970, each of us was issued the equivalent of $22 for the entire two-week-trip. With the cost of a tourist trip equal to three or four months' of an average Soviet salary, people naturally want to bring some things home to offset the cost. Even on an official visit, when the trip is paid for by the State, the spending allowance is very small. Few people risk buying the currency on the Soviet black market at five to ten times the official exchange rate, since they can be caught with it in Customs and end up in jail. The people who are best off on such trips are those who have friends in foreign missions. Besides money, the visitors also need transportation and general guidance. The debt of gratitude is usually paid back home by means of connections or favors.

Therefore I was not surprised when I got a call from Andrei Mironov, the movie superstar who used to be our neighbor in Moscow. He'd divorced his wife, my best friend Katrina, before we'd left for Washington, but we'd maintained a friendly relationship. For several days, I drove him and his director, Eldar Ryazanov, around Washington and helped them with their purchases. For me it was a pleasure because I knew Andrei and liked him, and his director, famous for his comedy movies, was a delightful and witty man. I kept thinking, though, about the system that puts people like Andrei in this kind of dependence on strangers. In Moscow he could have had anything he wanted; all doors were open to him; he made tremendous amounts of money, and yet all his money was worthless here and could not even get him a few extra dollars to spend as he wanted. He could not afford to take a cab, and if I hadn't been in Washington, he would have had to depend on some other embassy official, somebody like Eugene, who would call in the debt back in Moscow.

I also found out that directors' gripes are the same everywhere. Like celebrities in American Express commercials, Ryazanov's name is known to practically every Soviet citizen, but his face is not. Late one afternoon we went to the embassy cafeteria to have lunch. The kitchen had run out of everything except beef stew. We already were sitting at the table when Andrei, who had stopped in the hallway to chat with Lev, went to the serving window and then joined us with a steak.

"Where did you get that?" Ryazanov asked. "They told us they were out of steaks."

"I saw it on the menu," Andrei said, grinning, perfectly well aware of the irresistible power of his movie smile, "and I just asked for it. I did not know they were out of it."

———

It was the summer of 1976, and America was celebrating its Bicentennial. I was glad we were here at that time—it was such a rare event to observe.

The way Americans celebrate their national events is completely different from the way it is done in the Soviet Union. The most amazing thing was that so many people wanted to *participate*. There are two major national holidays in the Soviet Union: May Day, which is the Day of Solidarity of All Workers of the World, and Revolution Day, November 7. There are other holidays—such as Women's Day in March—but only these two have a demonstration during which the populace is supposed to show its support for the system and its leaders. In addition, Revolution Day and V-Day (May 9) have a military parade on the Red Square.

Watched on television, the demonstrations look impressive—huge crowds pass the main square of each city for hours, waving placards and flags and carrying portraits of Lenin and current Politburo members. The problem is that most people would rather stay home. The attendance for the demonstrations is mandatory, not only for the members of the Communist Party, but for anybody who cares about his or her career, including students. A no-show can cause a reprimand and certainly goes on the record, indicating antisocial behavior.

Each factory or institution is given a designated gathering point and a time, depending on the sequence in which each district is expected to pass the main square. It can be tricky to get to the gathering point, since most ground transportation is cut off until the end of the celebration in the afternoon. The wait can be as long as several hours. Since most people know each other, a lot of socializing goes on. Somebody usually brings an accordion or a guitar; there are sing-alongs, impromptu concerts, and dances. Street vendors sell fake flowers, little yo-yos for the children, and food. No place sells or serves alcohol until late afternoon, although beer can be purchased. Some people bring vodka with them if the weather is cold, which is often the case in November. The mood really depends on the weather. If it is cold or raining, people often register with the party boss at the designated time, leave for a couple of hours to go to an apartment of a colleague, if one happens to live nearby, and then return closer to the time when the crowds actually start moving.

The placards, flags, and portraits of the leaders are officially distributed to each organization, and no hand-painted or unapproved signs are permitted. The sequence of events is well programmed. It is known how much time is required to walk from the designated point to the main square, and every column starts moving at the predetermined time, usually silently. At the square itself, there are large loudspeakers through which an official announcer shouts slogans such as "Long live the Communist Party—the leader of all the free people in the world!" and a few dozen others. The crowds respond with a loud "Hurray!" The demonstration usually ends late in the afternoon; then people go home and have parties with friends and families. Official or not, it is a holiday, and no Russian would ever pass up an occasion for a party.

In all probability some people would still go even if attendance were not mandatory. Loyalty to the State, especially among older generations, runs pretty high, and some people would consider it their civic duty to attend. Russians are no less patriotic than Americans. They love their country, and in a critical situation, such as war, they would rise to defend it without hesitation. The problem is that the government does not really trust its own population. They know that official slogans leave most people cold. The authorities do not want to leave anything to chance, or to concede that they cannot control the weather that would make many people stay home on a blustery day. They must have uniformly huge crowds to show the world that the Soviet people's support for their leaders never ceases. As a result, most Russians consider attendance at national celebrations to be just another bit of drudgery they have to put up with, dispense with, and forget about. By making it a duty rather than an expression of human feelings, the system takes away whatever joy some people may have left in feeling united with their country.

Even the crowds greeting the foreign dignitaries on the streets of Moscow are usually conscripts. Not that the people mind—they are given time off work to go to the streets and wave little flags of the visitor's country, also supplied by the State. The size of the crowd is carefully controlled. In fact, the streets along the route are usually sealed off for security reasons, and only designated "greeters" can get through. This method also allows the Soviet media to show carefully calibrated "mass support": the number of people sent as "greeters" depends on the current state of relations with the visitor's country. That explains how Fidel Castro always draws larger crowds in Moscow than, for example, General de Gaulle did.

Therefore, the Bicentennial celebration was overwhelming to me because it was such a novelty. We did not go to see the parade—a visit to the Cherry Blossom Parade had already given me an idea of what to expect. Instead, we stayed home and watched the colorful bands and floats on television. But the uplifted mood in the city was hard to miss. People really *cared*. It was their country, and everybody was celebrating its birthday. Nobody sent people to the streets or to the Mall; they went because they felt they were part of this country; it was their celebration. I particularly remember the big gala televised that evening. When everybody in the audience rose to join the chorus singing "God Bless America," I felt tears in my eyes, and, to my surprise, noticed that I was silently singing the words along with them.

Gradually, the Bicentennial went away. The city returned to its normal summer life. Most Washingtonians leave the city in August because of the weather. So did we. In the middle of August we went on our first official vacation: first to Moscow and then to the Black Sea.

CHAPTER **6**

WE returned to Washington in the middle of September. Lev was in a depressed mood. The visit home had affected him more than I had anticipated. Some things had been predictable, such as a quarrel with Sonya. A less predictable discovery had been Lev's disenchantment with his own friends. In a way, he too had seen home with different eyes, just as I had on my first trip to Moscow, but with him it was on a much deeper and more personal scale. He had visited all his friends—people he had always considered to be the brightest and most talented in the social sciences, and that, of course, they were—and then he had discovered that there wasn't much they could talk about. Obviously the news of who was where, who was fired, who was promoted in the institute was interesting. And then—what? Suddenly he discovered that he had little else to talk about with his friends of some twenty years.

Peter smiled understandingly when Lev mentioned his confused feelings at our welcome-home party in Washington.

"Welcome to the club," he said. "You have just joined an exclusive fraternity called Soviet Americans. We all went through that stage and by now are resigned to the fact that we are different and will never be the same people we were before we came here."

"It's as if we were talking a different language," Lev said. "We could not understand each other."

"Exactly," said Peter. "And in a way you *were* speaking a different language. Your perspective has changed because of your exposure to all this information; and by being a part of the embassy you got used to thinking about things in more global terms. Your friends cannot understand you because their concerns are confined to their own local world of internal politics in Moscow, and it bothers you because you know there are more important things in the world. They don't understand many things you mention in your conversation because they don't know what these things are. Unfortunately I cannot offer you any consolation. Your change is permanent. When you return to Moscow, you will continue to socialize with people you met here at the embassy, rather than with your old friends, because we know the same things, we think the same way. You will feel like a foreigner in Moscow for many years to come, and the only people you will be comfortable with are those with the same experience."

I knew that what Peter was saying was true, because I had gone through the same thing with my friends. For me, however, the blow had been softened by the fact that with my women friends I could always find things to talk about—practical, everyday things: children, romances, relationships—things that were, in a way, more universal, because human relationships are the same wherever people live.

I was also wondering how Lev would go back to doing what he had been doing for the past ten years—writing books about modern American philosophy. Even before our arrival here it hadn't been easy—a lot of material that he had orginally included in his books he later took out because he knew it would never pass the standards of ideological suitability, and even after that the censor always found more things that had to be deleted. All of that was when he was relying mostly on printed sources, most of them American but always highly critical of American society. Now that he had actually lived here and seen the reality that was different from what he had read in the books, how much self-censorship would he have to impose on himself, and how much inner conflict would it create in him?

My own professional future did not concern me very much at that time—our second child was on the way, and after that I had almost two more years here. Why worry now?

By the beginning of December we had found a secretary to substitute for me in the office. Regina was competent and energetic, and I felt that Lev was in good hands. I took a maternity leave. After the sonogram my obstetrician insisted that the baby would be born before Christmas, but I disagreed.

"I do not expect a baby until the end of January, doctor," I reassured him.

"That is impossible," he said. "The sonograms are very precise. They are based on thousands of statistical observations."

"Doctor," I said, "we do not have sonograms in Russia, but I can assure you that it is wrong. Maybe Russian babies are different from American ones."

He did not believe me and insisted that I check into a hospital by the middle of January. He firmly believed I was overdue and insisted on induction. It did not work, and I was released the next day. I was not worried—for once, old-fashioned Russian methods beat American science.

The doctor was nice and knowledgeable, and by then I had become used to his examinations. It was uncomfortable at first, because I wasn't used to a man examining me, but I finally got used to the idea, figuring that other women in the embassy must have gone through the same thing. He finally became resigned to the fact that the sonogram was wrong, but insisted on checkups every two days and finally decided to put me in the hospital at the end of January.

The morning I was due to go to the hospital, I got up early and packed my suitcase. I was going to drive to the doctor's office, have my examination, and then go to the hospital one block away.

As I was getting ready to leave, I suddenly felt a familiar sensation.

"I think my plans are changing slightly," I told Lev. "I am going to have the baby today. Maybe you better go with me."

"I can't," he said, "What am I going to do there? I'll be stranded with the car, and what am I going to do with Kitty?"

"You can call the embassy pool. They'll have to send somebody to pick up the car anyway—it cannot stay in the hospital parking lot for three days. Then you take Kitty to a babysitter and go to work."

He was still hesitating. "You don't really know for sure. It could be just a cramp."

"I do know for sure." I was getting impatient. I was also scared and wanted to get to the safety of the doctor's office as quickly as possible. I had had a so-called accelerated delivery with Kitty; she had been born in just one and a half hours, and it could happen again. "What if it starts for real while I am driving?"

"Nothing happens that quickly." He finally made up his mind. "It's only a half-hour drive."

I gave up. He saw me downstairs to the garage, kissed me good-bye, and went back to the apartment.

I drove to the doctor's office by myself. An hour later I was in the hospital. A couple of hours later I called Lev and told him that I would have the baby before the evening.

"Great," he said. "I'll stop by later in the afternoon."

"You know," I said, "you can come anytime. It's not like in Moscow—you can be with me here while I am waiting."

"What am I going to do there?" His bewilderment was genuine.

"What other husbands do!" I shouted into the receiver. "They stay with their wives to make them feel better. Only by now I am beginning to think I would really be better off without you!" And I slammed the receiver.

It was a useless outburst. If he had to ask, he would not understand anyway.

I had plenty of time to kill. The room was comfortable. I was surrounded by some monitoring equipment. I recognized only one apparatus—I had seen it before in Moscow.

Like so many other things in Moscow, the choice of the hospital there was a matter of connections. When I'd had Kitty, I hadn't wanted to take chances in the regular district hospital—Tatiana had told me some horror stories about careless handling and unsanitary conditions there. My mother had substantial connections in the medical world in Leningrad, and so I was able to register in the maternity ward of the Institute of Gynecology of the Academy of Sciences in Moscow. It did not have the amenities of the Kremlin clinic, but it did have the best specialists and the best equipment. The women who are accepted there are either very difficult cases with some abnormalities of interest to science or, like myself, got there through connections.

It appeared to be clean, and the nurses checked on me regularly. Finally, things started to progress, and I was strapped to some kind of machine—I never learned its name—to measure the progress, I was told.

The strange thing was that although I had six doctors around me, nobody paid any attention to me. Everybody was fascinated with the machine. From their conversations I gathered that it was brand new, just arrived from Europe, and the hospital was one of the few in the entire Soviet Union to get it. I fully expected them to start clapping their hands at the performance of that wonderful machine, but my immediate concern was to get them to pay some attention to me. Finally somebody noticed what was happening, and I was rushed to the delivery room in the nick of time.

That was the same machine that was a piece of standard equipment in every room in this rather average hospital in Washington!

I fully understood what other women in the embassy meant by saying "It's easy here" when I was given an anesthetic. It's not that Soviet doctors are admirers of natural childbirth—I was given some kind of gas mask there that did not do much good—but they simply don't have such a modern marvel as epidural injection. "My God," I thought, "it's almost fun having a baby here!"

Lev finally showed up shortly after five. Our friends drove him to the hospital and waited in the car. My doctor came to my room to meet him.

"Well, you have about ten minutes together," he said. "We'll be taking her to the delivery room after that. I'll leave you alone now." He shook Lev's hand and left the room.

"In half an hour you will know whether you have a son," I said. I knew that he wanted a boy. He often complained that he was constantly surrounded by women at home: his mother and sister and two daughters, and that he wanted a boy whom he could take fishing. I was not angry anymore—after my outburst in the morning I had had enough time to think, and right now I just wanted him to be there. His reply caught me by suprise.

"I can't stay," he said. "You know that Victor and Laura are going home next week. They planned to spend the whole evening shopping. They will bring me back after the stores close at nine."

I said nothing. The thought that he could stay and Victor could come back for him had not occurred to him, and I was not going to suggest it.

Half an hour later, when the doctor took off his gloves and said, "Well, congratulations—you've got quite a guy here. I am going out to tell the happy father," I only said, "He is not there, doctor."

He looked as if he were going to say something and then changed his mind. Finally, he said, "Well, I'll see you later, then."

Mercifully, I was left alone in the recovery room. Two other women were there, separated from me by partitions. I could hear their voices as they talked quietly to their husbands while I lay there, crying. I was so happy to have a son. He was a big boy, over nine pounds, and if newborn babies have personalities, this one already showed determination. I wished I could share my joy with somebody. Finally, in an hour I was transferred to my room. Lev's arrival later in the evening went almost unnoticed—I said I was tired and needed rest.

The next three days in the hospital were the most restful days I'd had in a long time. To me it felt as if I were on vacation in a luxury hotel. The TV, the phone next to my bed, visitors at any time, my baby whenever I wanted him, the nurse who answered the ring almost instantly, and, most important, privacy—all the things I had not had in Moscow.

The hospital in Moscow had twenty-four beds in each room. Next to each bed was a small cabinet where we could keep our possessions and food brought from home. Not that there was much food—although nobody believed that we could survive on hospital food, the list of items we were permitted to have was restricted to fruits and some dairy products. The hospital stay is seven days' minimum, sometimes longer if complications develop, and no visitors are permitted—male or female. The only contact with the outside world was through the telephone—two pay phones for each floor. The first two days we were not even permitted to get up, and therefore could not get to the phone, so the only means of communications were written notes. The notes and food packages were accepted for only two hours a day at the receptionist's window downstairs.

I am sure there were reasons for these regulations—the fear of infections, food allergies, and the desire to give us maximum rest during the time of recovery. The results were, of course, the opposite—we all suffered from anxiety and the lack of contact with our families, and none of us cared for the health foods that were permitted in the food packages—we all wanted to gorge on fancy foods to reward ourselves for the terrible experience we had just been through. Worst of all, we could see our babies only when they were brought in for nursing three times a day—the nursery in the ward was off limits to mothers.

As it always happens, the inbred Russian ingenuity won. Generations of women in Soviet maternity wards had learned by word of mouth what to expect, and both we and our families were prepared to deal with it.

Maternity wards in Soviet cities are instantly recognizable by the number of men standing on the sidewalks and peering into the windows, trying to catch a glimpse of their wives. The lucky ones who have wives in rooms below the third floor can even shout a few phrases to each other. Most of the time, however, it's sign language.

The hospital did not have a ventilation system. To clear the air in the room, the windows had to be opened twice a day. Because of that necessity, the windows are not sealed, even during the winter. They were our lifeline to the outside world. Each room had a roll of long string with a weight attached to it, more or less like a fishing line. It was passed from one generation to another, and somebody in the room was always assigned to hide it in the clothing during cleanups. The husbands "belonging" to a particular room were quickly identified and memorized by everybody able to walk to the window. If a woman could not walk yet, a description was given until the identity was confirmed. From there on, the team took over.

When one of the husbands appeared on the sidewalk and signaled that he had something to send, a lookout team would go to the door to watch for hospital personnel. We knew the scheduled procedures exactly, and the husbands were notified of the best times for contact. Then the string was lowered out the window, the package tied to it, and it was pulled back into the room. Thank goodness our room was only on the fourth floor, so it did not take long. I was told by experienced women that in other hospitals with more than six floors the women on the lower floors usually volunteered to help and then passed the packages to the floors higher up. The spirit of camaraderie was unbelievable, although the presence of so many people in one room made rest quite elusive.

We all wanted to get out as quickly as possible, partly because of boredom, but mostly out of concern for our babies. They were not well cared for. If the baby was fidgety during feeding time, it often went to the nursery still hungry, and more often than not received no additional feeding. Diapers were not changed often enough—practically all mothers told me that they brought their babies home with severe diaper rash or even sores. I was anxious to get home, but kept running a mild fever and stayed in the hospital for ten days. I would have been kept there longer if I had not cheated by watching the thermometer and shaking it down to normal temperature before the nurse came to collect the readings. The trick backfired later, when I developed high fever three days after release, but by then I was safely home and could at least take care of my baby.

Now, amidst the luxury of a private room, all of that was just a fading memory. It was definitely easy to have babies in the United States.

Three days of relative solitude also gave me time to think, and the thoughts were not always pleasant. I was deciding what to do with my marriage. My mother always told me that women should give more to a marriage than men because they have more at stake. I thought about where it had gotten her, and where it had gotten me, and questioned the whole concept.

Both my mother and my father were students of architecture when the war started. My father was about to graduate, but Mother was only a second-year student. She never finished her education—the year I was born she contracted tuberculosis from my grandfather, who died from it the same year. That she survived at all was a miracle—antibiotics did not exist yet, and the only cure was a change of climate and better nutrition. She spent a better part of the next several years in sanitoriums, and often said that only the thought of me gave her the will and the strength to survive. However, she was never well enough after that to hold a regular job. Continuing education was out of the question. She became a housewife.

Being a housewife in the Soviet Union is a stigma. Most women work out of necessity to support a family that cannot survive on one income; those who are not in dire need of extra income work out of tradition. Although my mother had a valid reason for not working, it made her feel guilty about not making a contribution to the family income: we were better off than many other people after the war because my father was in the military, but there were still many things we could not afford. Out of that guilt, she threw her considerable talents and energy into her family and her husband's career. Our home was always immaculate; my father never had to lift a finger; she even shined his boots.

It was she who talked my father into writing a book after he left his sports career and was depressed over it—the idea had not occurred to him. She put up with his moods and shouts when the work did not progress very well; she spent countless nights developing films and working in a darkroom to print the twelve thousand photographs included in the book. And it was she who did not even get her name mentioned in the acknowledgments until the book editor insisted on it—my father felt too embarrassed to thank his wife publicly.

I grew up in an atmosphere that placed the man of the family on a pedestal, his slightest wish catered to immediately. He was *working,* I was told, he was bringing the money home, and we depended on him. But it was my mother who could play the piano, knew how to use the darkroom, sewed my dresses and knitted my sweaters, drove and fixed the family car, and fixed things around the house. I took a snapshot once when we were stranded on the highway during a vacation—my mother lying under the car fixing it and my father standing on the road shoulder and smoking. She was the one who taught me all those things, and with it, instilled the feeling that it was a woman's job to do everything and to leave her husband free for serious things such as *work.*

I do not know when her disenchantment started to settle in—I was too busy growing up. Perhaps it happened when she found the receipts for expensive gifts to other women and then discovered a large sum of money hidden behind the books in the bookcase. The money was for the second edition of his book—the one he said was classified as a reprint and therefore not paid for. She did not tell him that she found the money, and did not take any of it, but as soon as I finished high school, she went to work.

I remember the argument that ensued when she announced her decision. "What can you do?" Father was yelling. "Who is going to hire you? You have no education, you don't know how to do anything, you've been a housewife, a burden on my shoulders all my life."

She was adamant. She found a job as a secretary in a research institute. A year later she took a job as an editor at a youth magazine, and two years later she was writing her own stories and was accepted as a member in the Journalists' Guild, the only professional organization of journalists in the USSR.

Finally she asked for a divorce. He would not give it to her. He told people that it was a silly idea and of course he could not leave the poor sick woman even if she went temporarily insane with this idea of divorce. She did not want a messy scandal and stayed, living her own life, having her own friends—and her own money that she could finally spend on herself.

As I went through my own life and my own marriage, I suddenly saw with alarm how perilously close I was coming to following that pattern. True, my situation was different. My mother, always fearing that she would not live long, had raised me to be self-sufficient and independent from a very early age. She'd always said she wanted me to be able to take care of myself if she died and my father remarried. I worked from the moment I graduated from the university, obtained an advanced degree, and was fairly independent financially; although I was much better off being Lev's wife, he was not the only breadwinner in the family. Yet, with all the differences between my mother's situation and my own, I was falling into the same trap. It was always my husband who came first—his moods, his wishes, his favorite things, I was doing everything possible to make his life carefree and happy, and what did I get for it—driving alone by myself to a hospital, already in labor, to have his baby?

As a sociologist I was aware that the reasons for this trend were deeply rooted in Soviet reality. Soviet men rely heavily on women to take care of their needs practically all their lives because they seldom have an opportunity to live alone. Because of the housing shortage a young man often continues to live with his parents long after he is out of school, working, and financially independent, while his mother continues to provide all domestic services. When he marries, his wife takes over the housekeeping duties. Thus, many men go from childhood through advanced age without ever having to cook their own meals or do their own laundry. In addition, Russian men are rather macho in their own peculiar way and consider helping around the house unmanly. This attitude is reinforced by the fact that women can handle anything by themselves, an idea which the women themselves are in no hurry to dispel. They work in construction jobs that require lifting heavy objects, they sweep streets, they drive trolleys. But there is still a substantial disparity in earnings—most women are confined to lower-paying jobs, their earning power far below that of men.

All those factors made perfect sense in theory, but I found it difficult to accept them in my own situation. And the more I thought about it, the more I thought about Sonya. I had always believed without questioning what Lev and Tatiana had told me—

that she was a gold digger, a poor provincial girl whom Lev had married out of pity and because, after he had lost Irina, he had not really cared about anything anymore.

Suppose she really loved him? That suggested a different scenario entirely, one that suddenly made a lot of sense. I knew that she was attractive, bright, and well respected professionally—many of our friends in Moscow had told me that. There were stories of her social life, but not until after Lev had started seeing Irina again. I imagined myself, with a newborn baby, finding out that my husband was seeing another woman—wouldn't I run to somebody else for comfort? I remembered an incident Tatiana had told me about, in which Sonya had not even tried to hide her infidelity. One day she had simply told Tatiana: "I finally found a *real man*." Tatiana, completely devoted to her brother, had gone straight to Lev and told him the news. Even Sonya's love for material possessions could be seen in a different light in this new scenario. Sonya came from a poor family, and financial security was important to her. Good clothes are a valuable investment in the Soviet Union, and if Lev was the same tower of Jell-O in his first marriage as he was in his second, she simply felt better surrounding herself with expensive things that could be her protection against a rainy day.

Was the same thing happening to me? Was it possible that Lev was still chasing the moon and lived in that adolescent dream about his true love, Irina, and that he had married me on the spur of the moment because he could not accept that I was walking out on him? He mentioned Irina once in a while, mostly when he disapproved of my actions, and would sometimes say, "Irina would never do that," or even, "Irina had the class and upbringing to handle that better." I usually dismissed such remarks, but perhaps there was a deeper meaning to it.

There are lessons to be learned from ex-wives. I wished I had given it more thought earlier. Meanwhile, what was I going to do with my own marriage?

One thing was clear—I had to stay in it at least until our term in Washington expired. I owed it to my children to let them get as much as possible out of this wonderful country—good nutrition, medical care, colorful toys, a comfortable place to live. Therefore I had to continue living as if nothing had happened, and to leave any scenes and explanations until our return to Moscow. I also needed to continue working on my English and my knowledge of this country—both would be an invaluable asset when we returned to Moscow, where I would have to start a life of my own.

For all practical purposes my marriage was over. From now on it was just a waiting game.

CHAPTER 7

FOUR months had passed since my stay in the hospital. I returned to work in March, but changed my schedule from three full days a week to five mornings because of the babysitting arrangements. Regina had kept the work up-to-date during my absence from the office, and I was able to maintain it without extra exertion. In the morning I dropped Kitty and Konstantin off at the embassy compound on Tunlaw Road, where the wife of a security guard took care of them, drove to the office, and then left after lunch. Lev stayed in the office for the rest of the day and caught a ride home with one of our neighbors. In fact, I did not always go straight home—Maria only asked me that I pick the children up before her husband came home at six o'clock, and I often ran errands or did some shopping in the afternoon before going home.

That particular day I stayed at the embassy longer than usual. My business there had been finished an hour ago, but I lingered in the dark, cool cafeteria, sipping my third cup of coffee. I was in no rush to get home. The apartment would be unbearably hot that afternoon—Washington was suffering from one of those heat waves that regularly strike it at the end of April, when the air

conditioning in apartment buildings is "under spring maintenance." I always suspected that since the landlords were not required to turn the air conditioning on until mid-May, "spring
maintenance " was a euphemism for lowering their utility bills.

It was past two o'clock in the afternoon, and most of the embassy
staff was back at work in their offices. The only people left in the
cafeteria were the embassy pool drivers who were on call, waiting
for assignments. The topic of the conversation was a recent incident
in which the trade attaché had been stopped on the New Jersey
Turnpike doing ninety miles an hour. We all knew the details, but
it was recounted again for the benefit of a new driver recently
assigned to Washington.

"You see, it is not the matter of getting a ticket," one of the
old-timers was saying. "We don't pay tickets anyway, and the
turnpike police know that. What they do now is to escort you to
the nearest exit and get you off the highway, which is a real problem, because then you have to take a different route than the one
you filed with the State Department, and State always makes an
issue out of it."

"Oh, come on," said another driver. "They guy should be given
a medal for getting ninety miles out of that tin can. Still can't figure
out how he did that."

The car in question, irreverently referred to as a tin can, was
the Soviet-made Lada, one of the five cars the embassy was permitted to have here although they did not meet emission and many
other American standards. They were brought in for "promotional
purposes" and assigned to embassy officials to drive. There were
some nasty rumors that to avoid that "privilege" one of the high
officials had procured a certificate from the embassy doctor stating
that because of arthritis, he had to have a car with power steering.
With power steering, obviously, came air conditioning and other
amenities the Soviet-made cars did not have.

"We'll never sell them here anyway," continued the driver. "Last
time the Americans checked, they said that the cars required sixty-
seven modifications in order to meet their standards. If we accept
that, these cars will cost more to modify than we can sell them
for."

I thought lovingly about my own "ocean liner"—an Oldsmobile Delta 88, with all its comfort and gadgets. Only two years ago just reading its manual had been a puzzle full of unknowns. Speaking of comfort—"By the way, guys," I said, "my max switch on the air conditioning is blown again. The service station has tried to fix it three times already. The car feels like a sauna on a day like this, and it takes forever to cool."

"That's all because you took it to the wrong place to fix," laughed Oleg, who was still with the embassy, going on his sixth year there. "Bet you took it to that dealership in Chevy Chase."

"Where else? It's only half a block from where I live."

"Serves you right," he said. "Always take the car back where you bought it. Never mind it's out of your way—we buy so many cars from them that we always get good service. Go to Derek, he'll take care of it."

I vaguely remembered Derek, who had sold me my car—a very tall and handsome man in his fifties. Probably even older—unlike Russian men, Americans always look at least ten years younger than their age, so I stopped even guessing. "You mean every time I have a problem I will have to drive all the way to Arlington?" I complained. "Well, you want to have that car fixed, don't you?" said Oleg patronizingly.

I did not mind his patronizing. The embassy drivers had sort of taken me under their wing since the day we had bought the car; by now I was the only woman in the embassy permitted to drive alone—Lev still did not know how to drive, and since it was obvious that we could not conduct our business without transportation, the embassy had made an exception for me a year ago when new rules prohibiting women to drive alone had been introduced, ostensibly for security reasons. I knew I was not the only person wondering what excuse my husband had offered to the ambassador to explain why he could not learn how to drive in our two years in Washington, but whatever it was, the special request had been granted. The drivers were always very friendly and helpful to me, and I certainly appreciated their advice.

"OK." I sighed. "I'll go."

I left the cafeteria, quickly crossed the street, silently cursing

Washington weather, picked up an inevitable parking ticket from the windshield, gasped at the hot air that hit me from the air-conditioning vents, and drove to Arlington to fix my car and to change my life forever.

———

The dealership in Arlington was only a few miles away from the embassy. After two years in Washington, I was fairly familiar with the central part of the city and the Chevy Chase area, but I had little opportunity to go to the Virginia side very often. I pulled out a map to check the best route. It was a routine thing by now— my struggles with the American road system were over.

It had not occurred to me to call Derek for an appointment before I'd left the embassy, but fortunately he was in. I introduced myself, told him that Oleg had sent me, and explained my continuing problem with the car. He took my keys, moved the car to the service area, and came back. "They'll check it right away," he said and offered me a cup of coffee. In a few minutes the service department called and said that a wire was shorting in the air-conditioning system, which caused the fuses to blow, and they would need half an hour to fix it. I settled down to wait.

"Do you mind if I ask you a few questions?" Derek said. I did not mind, although I already anticipated the standard boring questions about life in the Soviet Union that Americans liked to ask so often. In a way I understood their curiosity—the press accounts were often selective and biased, although not as much as those published in the Soviet Union about the United States. People wanted to hear from a real person whether life over there was really as terrible as the press described it. I had standard replies for most of the questions that were most often asked, and a conversation, even a dull one, was more preferable than reading *Sports Illustrated,* which seemed to be the only publication in the dealership's waiting room.

"I was puzzled when you came in," Derek continued. "You do not look like an American, but I did not think you were from the Soviet Embassy either, because I've never seen a woman from the embassy bring a car in for service. It's always men."

"My husband does not drive."

"Oh, I see." He looked at me quizzically. "But you have been here for quite a while by now, haven't you?"

"Yes, almost two years now," I said curtly and quickly changed the subject. Lev's reluctance to drive was the last thing I wanted to discuss with a stranger, because it was such a sore spot for me. Since Konstanin's birth, being the only driver in the family, on top of working in the office and caring for the children, had placed quite a burden on me. I could not count on Lev's help even for a run to the grocery store. Quite a few times he had been called to the embassy in the evening or on the weekend to read an urgent message from Moscow and I had had to drop everything, take the children, and drive him downtown. The pressure had been building up since I had returned to work in March, and lately I had started to point out to him in not so gentle terms that it was about time to come out of his nirvana and start driving. Our friends had backed me up by telling him that his dependence on me was causing raised eyebrows at the embassy. The latest round of criticism had been triggered by a visit from an official delegation from our Moscow office. I had been in my last month of pregnancy and officially on leave, but during their five-day stay I had been constantly driving them from one official function to another. Apparently they'd also asked a few questions at the embassy about our transportation arrangements and discovered that no reason was ever given as to why my husband was incapable of driving. Our combined efforts finally brought results, and Lev agreed to pay one of the embassy drivers for private lessons, but the progress was slow and he was still a long way from taking a driving test.

Derek apparently sensed my mood and shifted easily to general questions about women in the Soviet Union—do most of them work? Are they paid well? How do they combine the demands of job and the family? Standard fare. He was pleasant and listened attentively, and I found myelf involved in the conversation more than I had expected.

Finally my car was ready. He brought it back to the entrance. "By the way," he said, "your car needs a tuneup and the brakes feel sluggish. When was the last time they were inspected?"

I knew he was right. The car had had nothing but routine changes of oil and filters in two years, and it was probably time to do serious maintenance. "How long will it take to do it?" I asked. The prospect of being without a car even for a day was not very attractive.

"Oh, a few hours," he said. "I can drive you back to the embassy," he added hastily. "Or"—he paused—"we could have lunch and talk some more. I really enjoyed talking to you, and the Soviet Union is such a fascinating country."

I promised to bring the car for maintenance. Somehow the thought of getting away from home and having a long lunch was not all that unpleasant.

———

During the next few months I probably had the best maintained car in the embassy. Every little thing that had not been checked and fixed during the first two years suddenly required a special trip, and since the repairs were minor, it was always "we'll do it while you wait." Fortunately the charges were also minimal, but I sometimes wondered what our Moscow office thought about the quality of American cars that, for all appearances, started to fall apart after only two years of use. The embassy did not pay any attention to my trips to the dealership since our car was not part of the embassy pool, and my husband, who happily failed his first driving test in July, did not question my judgment as to what needed to be done as long as the car was in good running condition and I was around to drive it.

Derek worked alternate morning and evening hours, and I always scheduled my car maintenance to coincide with his shifts. Whenever I came, he took time off and we went for a cup of coffee and my favorite cheesecake at a nearby Lum's restaurant, or took a ride in his car to a little park on the Potomac for a walk along the river. After a while I started feeling guilty about taking so much time from his work, but he reassured me that, being a senior salesman, he worked by appointment only, and when he knew I was coming he simply did not schedule any appointments.

Our conversations had long since shifted from general interest in the Soviet Union to what seemed to be a genuine friendly concern about my problems. Since the incident at the hospital, I had become more withdrawn and felt completly isolated; I could not mention my problems to anybody in the embassy for fear that the information would be passed to the security officer and we would be sent home as a security risk. I called my mother often enough, but could not discuss anything of that nature over the phone; besides, I did not want her to worry about me since there was nothing she could do to help me. The few American couples with whom we had developed friendly relationships were also business acquaintances, and I tried to maintain a happy façade in front of them. It was no secret to anybody in or outside the embassy that Lev continued to drink. More than once I intercepted a sympathetic glance from my American friends when he had had a drink too many at a party, but at least I could pretend that everything was fine otherwise. Our friends did not want to pry into my personal affairs, and I did not volunteer any comments.

Derek seemed to be an ideal person for a confidant. He was over thirty years older than I was, happily married, a good listener, and full of interesting and funny stories about his own life. In many ways he was what I had always wanted my father to be—a warm, understanding man who was genuinely concerned about my well-being. Had he been younger, I probably would not have dared to start such a friendship for fear that it would develop into something more romantic, but as it was, I felt completely safe.

From what he told me, the early years of his life had been full of adventures. He'd worked as a stuntman doubling for Gregory Peck—the resemblance was indeed striking—and as a disk jockey, and had gambled quite a lot some years ago. One day he showed me his Paramount ID card, but it had a different first name printed on it.

"How do I know it's yours?" I said. "It has a different name and no date. And anyway, wasn't Gregory Peck at MGM at that time?"

I was just teasing, but he suddenly became defensive. "Everybody in the movies used assumed names in those days."

"You weren't an actor,"I pointed out."Stuntmen have no need

for assumed names. And what exactly were 'those days'? The card is not dated."

"I was hoping to get into acting. Anyway, if you don't believe me, so be it."

"I do, I do." I felt that maybe I'd gone too far. "Although some of your tales seem pretty farfetched, especially your hints of your connection with the mob."

"I have no connections with the mob," he said. "Where in the world did you get that idea?"

I was referring to his vague and somewhat hard-to-believe stories about his cardplaying business. As he told it, he was a very good poker player, and often played for other people. He hinted that the stakes were very high, and he regularly played with other people's money, for which he got a commission on his winnings. Those "friends," as he called them, were very rich and powerful, and if he had named them, he said, their names would be so familiar to the American public that it would create a scandal. For that reason, and because he was such a valuable "investment," they maintained some sort of security around him and kept an eye on his comings and goings. That's why he always met me in the same restaurant, he said, so "they" would not get concerned about his whereabouts.

Most of the time I dismissed his ramblings about his "friends" as a ploy to impress me, although once or twice I had an uneasy feeling that he was testing me to see if I would become curious and ask him about the names of those "very important people." I never did. I had enough problems of my own to worry about, and one of them was how long my lame excuses about car maintenance would last before somebody in the embassy started asking questions. My only concern was that if somebody was watching over *him*, did that mean any danger to me?

One episode in particular got me worried. It was already August, and by then there was absolutely nothing my car needed for the foreseeable future. Besides, I was concerned that other people in the dealership were beginning to notice our frequent get-togethers. Therefore I changed tactics—instead of coming to the dealership and leaving from there with Derek, I started calling Derek and meeting him at Lum's. After a while, however, I began to worry that the waitresses at Lum's had also seen us together too often, and one day I asked Derek to meet me at a little French restaurant across the street from Lum's. As we were sitting there drinking espresso, a man suddenly stopped by our table. I almost jumped— it was late afternoon and the restaurant was empty. I had been facing the front door and yet I had not seen him come in. Since he could not have materialized out of thin air, he must have come in though the back door.

"Hi, Derek," he said. "Just wanted to remind you that we'll pick you up at eight." He gave me a cursory glance and walked out.

"I have a game tonight," Derek said. "He works for those people I told you about."

"But why did you tell them where you were going?" I asked. All of a sudden I felt angry. "I have told you many times that, being with the embassy, I am in a rather delicate position meeting with you like this. I do not want some shady characters to know about our relationship—if they are the kind of unscrupulous people you described, they can use it against me someday."

"I did not tell them," he said. "They must have followed me here from the dealership."

For the first time I did not believe him. I had not told him the day before, when we'd been planning our meeting, that I was going to change restaurants. Instead, I'd called him about ten minutes before the meeting and told him where I was. It seemed unlikely that somebody would go to the trouble of keeping a guard on him round the clock. That left only two possibilities, neither of them very pleasant: (a) his "friends" were expecting us to be at Lum's and he'd called them about the change of plans, or (b) somebody was following me. If it was the former, then the message was clear: "Derek will not go against us, don't try to change the rules of the game." The latter opened a whole range of possibilities that I did not even want to contemplate.

In the back of my mind, all the inconsistencies and evasions that had puzzled me in our conversations started to surface, and I knew that I had to make a choice. I could keep asking him questions until I was certain that he was lying, and by doing that destroy our friendship, or I could dismiss the whole thing and pretend that nothing had happened. I chose the second option. I simply could not lose the escape valve he represented and go back to the hopeless loneliness of the existence I had felt before. Whatever he was doing, whoever his "friends" were, I would deal with that later. He'd become too much of a lifeline to me to give it up because of one incident. As long as the embassy did not suspect me of any wrongdoing, the situation was manageable.

CHAPTER 8

THE summer of 1977 was coming to an end. Lev was in Moscow—he and Kitty had left in the middle of August. My parents had been begging for a chance to have their granddaughter for a while, and so he was going to leave her with them in Leningrad and take Xenia on a vacation trip to the Black Sea before the beginning of the school year. After that he had to spend two weeks in consultations with the VAAP staff. I stayed in Washington with Konstantin and in charge of the office. Business was slow as usual. VAAP had not changed its pace or procedures.

I wondered how long this could go on, and whether the "consultations" for which Lev's presence had been requested had anything to do with our lack of progress. We had one more year to go on our three-year assignment, and the embassy had requested an extension of our stay—a fairly standard procedure for many people assigned to Washington, since the common wisdom was that it took at least two years for most people on their first assignment to get acquainted with the country and become functional in their area. Peter kept reassuring us that our extension was inevitable.

"Things are not as bad as you think," he kept saying. "You

have accomplished what could be expected within the given frame of time. You have a good personal relationship with your American counterparts, your opinion is trusted, and with a little luck and some improvement in promotional materials, you can get results. To send somebody else now would disrupt the process—the new man would have to start from scratch, and it would take him another two years just to get going. It just doesn't make sense, and we will fight for you."

All that made perfect sense for anyone thinking in terms of another literary representative.

What nobody took into account was that somebody might want the position for a different purpose.

When Lev came back from Moscow, there wasn't much to cheer about. Boris Pankin, his boss, was still fighting to keep his foreign representatives "clean," but he was under a lot of pressure to send a man with double duties—an intelligence operative. The case was being made that, business being the way it was, we were not over-loaded with work, and so somebody could easily handle our direct duties and still have plenty of time to do something else. The cover was too good for the KGB to pass up without a fight.

The decision was not final. An extension request from the embassy was not something to be taken lightly, and among high-level VAAP officials there were supporters for both sides.

"Meanwhile," said Lev, concluding his recital of events in Moscow, "we better be prepared to leave next September. It is time to start saving a little and making provisions for our future in Moscow." He wasn't referring to his professional future—that was assured. He was referring to the practice of "taking a piece of America home with us" which was prevalent among Soviet diplomats. It wasn't necessarily a question of making money, although it is quite possible to make a small fortune by buying things that are in demand in the Soviet Union and reselling them on the black market. Everybody does it to a different degree—some just to make a little extra for an unscheduled vacation trip, some to build their financial future. In our case, as it was with many of our friends in the embassy, the financial side was not critical—all of us would have well-paying jobs upon our return to Moscow. It was the

American life-style, the things that make life bright and comfortable, that most people wanted to bring home with them. It is almost impossible to go back to the drab Soviet environment after living in the US for a period of time, so the solution was to re-create the American environment in your own little world in Moscow—your home.

We had already taken care of some major things such as wall-to-wall shag carpets—thankfully, Soviet apartments are small—and major appliances adapted for European current—I was taken to a special appliance store in New York that caters almost exclusively to the Soviet community. Small everyday household items had been shipped home in quantities sufficient to last for several years. But I had another dream—or folly, according to my husband. I wanted to keep my American car. Although it officially belonged to VAAP, the embassy practice was to replace cars after three years of service and sell them for the salvage value. Quite a few embassy drivers bought their cars, unable to part with their mechanical friends after years of taking care of them. The problem, of course, was spare parts and maintenance. I brought up the question in my next meeting with Derek.

"I think it's crazy," he said. "You cannot take all the parts with you, and too many things can go wrong with a three-year-old car."

"We can do a thorough maintenance before we leave."

"It will cost you a fortune," he pointed out. "Besides, you said yourself there is no unleaded gas in the Soviet Union. You'll ruin the catalytic converter, and the next thing you know the whole exhaust system will go."

"There must be a way," I insisted. "Other people do it."

" 'Other people' are professional drivers and mechanics. They can handle it. You will have nothing but a nightmare. Anyway, I have another solution for you."

"Which is?"

"Which is—why not leave the car here and stay with it to drive it?"

"You are out of your mind. I could never do anything like that."

"Why? You like living here, don't you? You said it yourself many times."

"Of course I do." I could not understand why he was pursuing such a dead-end subject. "As a diplomat, not a refugee. I have a home in Moscow, my family, my friends. Besides, I have my children and their future to think about."

That was a mistake. Mentioning the children gave him another opening.

"Precisely. You said yourself that this country is a much happier environment for the children, and that you would not have had a second child if you weren't here at the time."

"This conversation is not leading us anywhere. What you are suggesting is utterly impossible, and I do not want to discuss it any further. Now, given that your solution is unrealistic, what can I do about my car?"

"It is unrealistic," he said, pointedly using the same word. "Forget it."

I was quite upset over the unexpected turn of the conversation. It was true that I had often said I enjoyed life in Washington. But to jump to the conclusion that I would leave my country was preposterous. I had heard of people who defected to the West— some even from the Soviet mission in New York. They'd usually been people with serious personal problems that threatened their future jobs or their status—or spies. I was neither. So what made Derek think that I would even discuss it?

An uneasy recollection of the incident in the French restaurant stirred in my memory. Did this whole thing have something to do with his "friends"? Did they have photographs, had they recorded our conversations? Our relationship was innocent enough, but even close friendship with the Americans was taboo for us. Besides, I was very open and often critical of the Soviet system in my conversations with him. Did they intend to blackmail me? But for what purpose? I had absolutely no access to any sensitive information in the embassy, and if Lev did, he was not telling me. So what would anybody gain by ruining me except maybe some marginal political advantage? And why would businesspeople whose ostensible interest in Derek was his ability to play poker be interested in me, anyway?

I went home and got on with my plans of building a nice nest in Moscow. The embassy request had apparently been shelved in the Ministry of Foreign Affairs. We were going home next September.

———————

Life went on without much happening until the end of October. Then I received a jolt that shook me out of my complacency. It was Tuesday night, and Lev came back home about six in the evening, as usual. He had finally learned how to drive and turned out to be reasonably good at it, except that he had no sense of direction. However, after several trips to the embassy with me next to him, he had memorized the route and could manage getting there and back by himself.

"You are going to a meeting at the embassy tonight," he said matter-of-factly. "Why don't you call Tamara—Peter will appreciate the fact that he won't have to drive her."

"There is no meeting tonight," I said. I thought he had gotten mixed up about the days of the week—Wednesday was a regular night for the embassy women's meeting, often with a showing of a recent Soviet movie or an educational lecture.

"It's a special meeting," he said. "Mandatory attendance. Better get ready—I'll feed the children." His voice was calm and it was obvious he was treating the request as nothing out of the ordinary.

I tried to find out whether he knew what was behind it. "Do you know why they are calling it on such short notice?" I asked, trying to sound casual.

"Have no idea," he replied "Probably another campaign started in Moscow, regular briefing."

"Did you have a briefing today?"

"No," he said and cut the conversation short. Even if he knew, he was not going to tell me.

When Tamara and I arrived at the embassy, I found with surprise that it was not a general meeting—only about thirty women, wives of counselors and first secretaries, were present. Nobody had any idea what was going on. Even the wife of the embassy party boss was there. It was usually her husband who conducted ideological briefings—surely he could have spared her the boredom of two hours of slogans, but she was sitting there, engaged in a guessing game just like everybody else.

What was going on? All of a sudden I felt cold.

The cold feeling grew into panic when I saw the embassy security officer walk into the room. Why him? In more than two years I had never seen him conduct any meetings, at least not with women. I knew very well that his duties were in the realm of counterintelligence—Vitaly's job was to watch over embassy personnel for any kind of deviations and prevent them from becoming recruitment targets for American intelligence.

The room quieted, and Vitaly started to speak.

"You all know," he said "that life here has its difficulties. Although it is easy to forget, we do live in a hostile environment. We are constantly watched by American intelligence services who stand ready to use the smallest human weakness, a minor failure, or a deviation from expected behavior to turn it to their advantage.

"We've been fortunate in that our embassy here has been relatively immune from regrettable incidents that sometimes take place in other Soviet missions." This was a not so subtle reference to the Soviet mission in the United Nations, which had had several unpleasant incidents in the past few years. The relationship between the Washington and New York communities was not unlike that between real-world Washingtonians and New Yorkers. People at the New York mission were considered to be arrogant backstabbers, no notion of manners or civility, who would cut your throat to get ahead. The New York mission considered the Washington community to be provincial and stodgy, lacking the flair of a truly cosmopolitan city like New York.

"We are not completely immune, however," continued Vitaly. "It appears that our enemies recently changed their tactics. That's why this meeting is with you and not with your husbands. It appears that they found a weak link in our defense—our women."

I froze. What was he talking about?

"We know that most of you make a tremendous sacrifice by being what you are. You are all well-educated professional women. Most of you have advanced degrees. When you come here, you abandon your careers in favor of your husbands' and for the good of your country, and have to settle for little more than being housewives, with nothing more than part-time clerical jobs available for you in the embassy. We appreciate this sacrifice, but we also understand that it places a strain on you, and some of you apparently cannot handle this stress as well as the others. And this is a weakness our enemies are ready to exploit. They play on the loneliness of a woman whose husband has to spend most of his time doing his job at the embassy, on the isolation and the lack of companionship. Most of you are friends and keep each other company. But some are loners and do not fit very well into the specific environment we have here, or do not understand the importance of being on guard against enemies.

"The regrettable incident I am going to tell you about came to our attention only recently," he continued. "One of our women became very friendly with an American who, for all we know, may be working for American intelligence. The amazing thing is that this has been going on for quite a while, and while some embassy people knew about it, they failed to bring it to the attention of the proper embassy authorities."

He went on, describing how the woman had been seen taking walks with her American friend, engaged in long conversations. "We hope that nothing of value was passed on," he continued, "but eventually it would be. Relationshps like that are started with the sole purpose of putting the victim in a compromising situation, and eventually of demanding information in return for a cover-up."

He still did not name the woman. He was talking, pacing in front of the front row, occasionally stopping and looking at one of us. Why did I have the feeling he was looking at me more often than others? Was he building up tension for a dramatic scene where he would finaly say, "And this woman is one of you. Here she is!"? I wished there had been a mirror in the room so I could see my face—was my horror plainly written on it or had I managed to keep calm?

The only discordant note in the whole affair was the timing. It was Tuesday night. Surely, with a serious incident like this they would put the guilty party on the first plane home. But there was only one plane a week from Washington to Moscow, and it had departed at seven o'clock that evening. Maybe they just had not found out in time to put me on that plane. And, of course, there was always the Thursday plane from New York.

I was so lost in my thoughts that I missed part of Vitaly's speech. I came back to reality when I heard a collective gasp.

"What did he say?" I asked Tamara. "I've had a long day; I lost my concentration for a moment."

She repeated the name of the woman who was already on the plane that had departed a couple of hours earlier. She was the wife of a second secretary in the embassy.

Vitaly continued with the details. The woman's neighbor in the apartment building spoke Russian reasonably well, and he was an avid reader of Russian literature. She used to be a teacher, and they'd struck up a friendship which had grown into a full-blown love affair. Amazingly, all the Soviet families in the building had known about it and covered up for them. Who says that love does not conquer all? The affair had continued for quite a while, and the couple had gradually gotten so carried away that they forgot to exercise caution at a house party attended by some embassy employees who did not live in that building. It was then that the affair was reported to Vitaly.

"Of course," Vitaly was saying, "it is no coincidence that a Russian-speaking American suddenly surfaces in the building where a dozen Soviet families live. What is amazing is that apparently her Soviet neighbors did not think enough about it and did not report it, so we did not learn about it in time."

"In time for what?" I thought. "What would you have done differently if she had just taken a few walks around the building instead of falling in love? Her life is ruined, her husband's career finished. What would you have done if you had learned about it earlier? Had a fatherly talk with her and told the poor little lamb not to get in trouble anymore? She'd be on her way home all the same, only a little earlier."

Gradually, the horror of my own situation started to come back. In the relief of hearing another name I almost forgot that mine was next on the list. It was only a matter of time till somebody found out about Derek and me. I was taking an incredible risk, and for what—just because I was lonely? Vitaly was right—we all had our problems here, and most women were obviously handling it better than I was. I had to stop seeing Derek before it was too late—or was it already too late?

———

I knew I had to find a way to see Derek and tell him about the meeting, then tell him I could see him no longer. It wasn't anything I could do over the phone, but I didn't dare go to the dealership openly anymore. I had to arrange a meeting in the evening, which presented another problem—what excuse would I give my husband for leaving home in the evening? All my legitimate activites were confined to the daytime.

It was almost two weeks before an opportunity presented itself. Gennady was returning home from a short business trip to Moscow. Alia had already returned to Moscow permanently. Their older son was starting eighth grade—the Soviet equivalent of high school—and the Soviet school in Washington had only seven grades. Since Soviet teenagers were not permitted by the embassy to attend American high schools, many families with children of that age had to resort to living separately—the wife in Moscow, the husband in Washington. Gennady had one more year to go on his assignment, and although he missed his family, he did not have much choice.

I'd driven Gennady to the airport when he'd left for Moscow and promised to meet him when he returned. I knew it would be seven before we got to his apartment in Arlington, and it was its proximity to the dealership that gave me an idea. I called Derek from a pay phone and told him that I had to meet him urgently, and I needed to do it after the dealership closed at nine o'clock. He promised to wait for me in the parking lot.

All embassy people returning from Moscow get a lot of visitors the night of their arrival. As with our first day in the country, people come and go, making it an impromptu welcome party, although the reasons are very practical. The traveler usually brings letters from home and little packages of goods from relatives. The contents were usually food—black bread, homemade pickled mushrooms, salamis, and other delicatessen fare. Bread is usually the heaviest, and we often joked that it was the most expensive bread in the world—although it cost pennies in Moscow, the excess luggage charges brought it to about five dollars a pound. It was decidedly better than any American bread, but more importantly, it represented a symbol, a piece of home which we all missed to a certain degree. The sausages—any meat that wasn't canned— were prohibited by Customs from being brought into the US, but nobody searched our diplomatic luggage, even though some of the suitcases emitted a teasingly appetizing smell that could be detected even through the suitcase covers. It was unlikely that the Customs people did not know what we were doing, but they probably did not want to create an incident over a trivial matter. With all those goodies requiring immediate refrigeration, the packages were picked up as quickly as possible to relieve the carrier from any responsibility for their contents.

Equally important were letters from home. We all served as letter carriers both to and from Washington. Of course we could send letters through the diplomatic mail, which we did, but very soon after our arrival I was told not to write anything important or personal in those letters, because they could be opened by embassy security. In fact, everybody knew better even than to drop those letters into the airport mailbox in Sheremetyevo—being an international airport, everyone presumed the contents of the mailbox was examined by the KGB before being sent on its way. The common thing was to drop the letters off in some inconspicuous mailbox halfway between the airport and home.

Therefore I was fairly certain that the party would go on for a few hours, and being one of Gennady's closest friends, I was expected to stay. Lev would stay home with the children—we did not use a babysitter in the evening except on very rare and urgent occasions. In the middle of the party I told Gennady that I had forgotten to pick up medication for Kitty and had to make a run to a drugstore in Rosslyn before it closed. As it happened, it was an all-night drugstore, but if anybody ever checked the validity of my excuse, I could always say I'd thought it was a regular store.

I drove to the store, picked up some cough syrup, and then drove to the dealership, ignoring most of the traffic signals to save time. Derek was waiting for me in the parking lot at the back of the dealership. I quickly told him about the scare I had received at the embassy meeting and said that I could not see him anymore, at least for quite a while.

I was ready to leave when he stopped me.

"I have to tell you something," he said. Suddenly his face had a serious, almost drawn look. "Leave your purse on the hood of your car and come over to my car."

His request was so strange that I laughed. "I don't want to leave my purse," I said. "What if somebody passes by and picks it up while I am sitting in your car? And what is this whole thing about, anyway? Do you think I have a tape recorder there?"

I was joking, but he was serious. "Leave it," he repeated. "Nobody is going to pass by, and we can see anybody approaching your car from here."

Reluctantly, I obeyed. There was something urgent in his tone, and I knew he was dead serious. I left my purse and walked over to his car.

"Don't panic," he said. "What I am going to tell you is unpleasant, but you have nothing to worry about."

I already knew. All the suspicions I had had before suddenly came together and made sense. "You are an intelligence officer," I said flatly. I was surprised that I could still talk, but my head was clear. The shock that came with the sudden realization left me drained of all emotion. The only thought left was: there must be some way out of it. Nothing is final except death.

"No, I am not," he said. "But I was approached by intelligence agents after our second meeting. It appears they had some interest in you, and they asked me to encourage this relationship. I did not know you very well then and I agreed, although I knew it could hurt you. We were not friends yet, so it did not matter."

"What difference does it make now?" I said bitterly. "I trusted you and you set me up. That's all there is to it."

"Not quite. In the beginning, yes, I did set you up. But as I got to know you I began to like you very much, and our friendship became very real. I did not pretend to be your friend—I *was* and I *am* your friend. And I am not going to let anybody hurt you. You have to believe that."

"What can you do now? With your 'help,' they already have enough pictures and recorded conversations to bury me."

"Remember my friends I told you about? The ones I play cards for. They are very powerful people. They owe me some favors, and I can ask them to interfere. They have enough influence to close the matter and make everybody forget it ever existed."

"I don't trust your friends, or anybody for that matter from now on. I'll face whatever comes when it comes, and I'll figure some way to get out of it."

"Just remember," he said, "if you decide that you want me to do something about it, or if you need help—any kind of help— call me."

"Your best help would be staying away from me."

I walked over to my car and drove back to Gennady's apartment. Forty-five minutes had passed since I'd left—far too much time for a trip to a drugstore half a mile away, but nobody at the party asked what took me so long. I stayed for another hour and then went home, replaying my conversation with Derek in my head and trying to find some ray of hope that would indicate the whole thing was just a big joke. I knew it wasn't. All my life I had had incredible luck that had pulled me through seemingly hopeless situations, but I knew that every lucky streak had an end. That night it ended for me.

CHAPTER 9

*F*OR the next two months I lived in a strange dual world. On the surface I was the same person to everybody around me, but the thought of my conversation with Derek remained constantly in the back of my mind. I thought about it at home, in the office, at parties. A couple of times Lev remarked that my mind seemed to be wandering somewhere else when I talked to him. I blamed it on my tiredness, but I knew that sooner or later the change in my behavior would begin to show to others. My mind seemed to live a life of its own—no matter how I tried, I could not stop thinking about my situation and its potential consequences.

Derek said that the intelligence agents had approached him because they were interested in me. That was the part I could not figure out. I had no affiliation with the KGB and, to the best of my knowledge, neither did my husband. Of course Lev was required to file reports on all his contacts with the Americans, but so was everybody else in the embassy. It was so routine that it certainly did not qualify as an involvement with intelligence. So, assuming the whole thing had been started with the purpose of blackmailing me, what could anybody possibly gain? I remembered the time Derek had brought up the subject of defection. Was that the ultimate goal? What purpose would that serve? Besides, I was inclined to think that his remark had not been a part of a preconceived plan. I had heard my other American friends say more than once that they were amazed how easily I fit into the American life-style, and that it was a shame that I had not been born here. I'd always regarded it as a compliment and had no reason to interpret it as an attempt to recruit me. Still, the possibility of defecting as a final solution to my problem had occurred to me more than once.

I went through my conversations with Derek hundreds of times, trying to recall every word and every possible hidden meaning in everything he had said. Finally it was clear that this brooding was getting me nowhere. I simply did not have enough information to make a decision.

Finally, in early January 1978, I called him.

"Those friends of yours," I said. "I want to meet them."

"Why?"

"Because you said they could help me," I reminded him. "Somebody out there is sitting on a lot of compromising material about me, and I just cannot live like that. I want to know what my options are."

"OK. I'll arrange for a meeting."

I did not hear from him for a week. Then suddenly he called and said that the meeting had been arranged—that very night, at nine, I was to come to the Holiday Inn in Rosslyn. It was already seven.

"I can't do that," I said. "Lev is in Chicago and there is nobody I can leave the children with."

"It's tonight or never. I'll wait for you on the first level of the Holiday Inn underground parking lot until nine-fifteen. If you don't come, I won't be able to do it again. My friends are very busy people—I can't ask them twice."

I thought feverishly of what to do. I almost never asked my friends to babysit, and certainly never on a moment's notice. What kind of excuse could I offer?

I finally came up with an outrageous lie—a New York publisher had just called; he had been planning to be in Washington for a couple of days and to meet with Lev, but his plans had changed suddenly and now he only had a short stopover in Washington on his way to Europe. He had hoped to meet with Lev for a couple of hours at the airport, but since Lev was away, perhaps I could meet him and pick up some important papers? With that, I called Peter and Tamara and asked them to take the children for a couple of hours. At such a late hour, both children would go to sleep instantly and would require little supervision. I hated to lie to my best friends, but my excuse probably sounded plausible enough, and Tamara graciously agreed to help me out. I brought the children over to their apartment, stayed with them until they fell asleep on Tamara's bed, and left.

I barely made it to the Holiday Inn parking lot in time. Derek was waiting for me near the entrance.

"Park your car," he said. "We are going upstairs. My friend is waiting for you in a hotel room. I will take you there."

A hotel room? In all the incidents with Soviet diplomats that I had heard of, hotel rooms figured prominently. God knows what they can do to you there when you are alone—drug you to unconsciousness, and then what?

"I am not going to any hotel room," I said. "We are going to meet in a public place—a hotel restaurant will do fine."

My resolve probably showed—he did not argue. We went to the restaurant and ordered coffee.

"How will your friend know we are here?" I asked. "You were with me all the time, so I know you did not call him."

"I am not going to call him. I took you here so we could talk, and to give you time to calm down. After that we will go upstairs. Now, what's the problem?"

I told him why I wanted to meet in a public place.

"In other words," he said, "you still do not trust me. Well, that's only fair after what I did to you. However, let me point out that if somebody wanted to compromise you, we did not have to arrange this meeting. They already have enough material in their hands. I am trying to help you. If you don't trust me, you can leave and go home right now."

"I still do not see why he cannot join us here," I said. "What's the difference?"

"Because he is a very important man and cannot be seen with you," Derek said. "And by the way, right now he is wasting time in that hotel room, and if I do not show up with you before ten o'clock, he will leave. So make up your mind."

I looked at my watch—it was a quarter to ten. "All right," I said. "I don't know why I trust you, but I'll go."

I recognized his friend instantly—it was the same man who had stopped by our table at the French restaurant several months before. He was in his late thirties and introduced himself as John.

Derek launched into a long speech explaining my plight and how much I needed John's help. John interrupted him rather briskly and sent him downstairs to have a drink at the bar. Derek meekly complied, and John and I were left alone.

"So what's on your mind," he asked, "and how can I be of help?"

I explained my predicament. I said that, granted, I had acted foolishly, but it was an innocent thing that could be blown out of proportion and ruin my life. What I wanted, I said, was to make sure that whatever American intelligence had on me would never see the light of the day. Could it be done?

I was very nervous and, strangely, he seemed to be nervous, too. I noticed that he broke several matches trying to give me a light for my cigarette.

"Yes, it can be done," he said.

"How?"

"I have certain connections. We can put some pressure on the people at the top, and they will tell their underlings to forget it. It would simply be archived, never to be used again."

"There is no guarantee of that. Somebody can dig up the archives a year from now, when we all think that the whole incident is over and forgotten. Besides, the underlings, as you call them, may get angry and deliberately blow the whistle to the embassy. These things happen."

"Why do you think it can happen?"

I said that I had been told on more than one occasion that our embassy security people had a good relationship with their American counterparts and sometimes exchanged mildly sensitive information to keep a favor-for-favor relationship. If somebody was pressured into dropping me as the subject of an investigation, it would make an ideal opportunity for that somebody to do a quiet favor for his Soviet counterpart and to get even with me.

"That's highly unlikely," he said dryly. "There is no such exchange of information."

I was not convinced.

"By the way," he continued. "how come you attracted attention in the first place? Are you working for Soviet intelligence?"

"No." I laughed. "I honestly do not know why anybody would think that.

"I was told you move around quite freely," he said cautiously. "That would certainly suggest that you have some out-of-the-ordinary privileges or some other duties."

"Aha," I thought, "you've been better briefed than I thought."

I explained that it was not by my choice, but because my husband had been unwilling to drive, so that I ended up being the only driver in the family.

We talked for a few more minutes. Finally he called downstairs and asked the bartender to give Derek a message to come upstairs.

"Don't worry," he said. "I will help you, just as Derek has promised. You are in no danger. Nobody is going to bother you."

We shook hands. Derek, who by then had reappeared looking rather tipsy, took my back to my car. As I drove out of the parking garage and made a U-turn, I noticed another car making a U-turn behind me. I drove home, keeping an eye on my rearview mirror. The car followed the same route, sometimes falling behind and then reappearing. It was not difficult to keep an eye on it—with all the different car models in the States a car could be easily identified by the shape of its headlights. I realized that it was probably much more difficult for American diplomats to keep track of their tails in Moscow, where only three basic car models exist. Finally the car passed me as I approached my building. It was a Volkswagen with diplomatic license plates.

By then I realized that I had driven into my own building's garage without remembering that I had to pick up my children. As I backed out, I also remembered something else. My building was the last apartment building on the street. The next block was occupied by several stores which were closed at this time of the night. By passing me, the unknown car had headed straight toward Wisconsin Avenue. But if that was its original destination, it should have made a turn four blocks before—going to my building had been a considerable detour.

I had been followed. The only question was, by whom?

I did not get much sleep that night. With Lev out of town, I was alone and had all the time I needed to think. And the more I thought about the meeting that had taken place earlier that night, the more it did not make sense. Something was very, very wrong. Mostly small details, but because of them the whole thing had a false ring to it.

It started with Derek and his attempt to explain my situation to John. That had obviously been unneeded. If he had convinced John to come and meet me in the first place, he must have given him the reason for it. So why repeat it? To impress me with the seriousness of my situation? To give John an opportunity to show his authority?

Then, there was something about John himself. He did not look, or behave, like a wealthy businessman, or any businessman for that matter. There was something military about him—maybe his haircut, maybe the way he was dressed. I could not put my finger on it, but I had met enough American businessmen by then to sense the difference.

And the telephone call John had received minutes after our meeting started—it had been from a "General Simpson's assistant." The conversation had been brief—John simply said to tell the general that he would see him the next day. Again, it had appeared almost staged for my benefit—nobody is that important that he would get calls late in the evening in a strange hotel room. And why would a general call a mere businessman? A reinforcement to make me believe in his status and influence?

And finally, Derek coming back upstairs, ostensibly tipsy after a couple of drinks at the bar. That was an impossibility—Derek did not drink at all, and he played the part of a drunk very unconvincingly.

The whole thing seemed to be so unprofessionally theatrical that it bordered on the circus.

Strangely, despite all the pretense, John seemed to be a nice person. He'd listened attentively, asked the right questions, and appeared to be understanding. There was something about his eyes—honesty? kindness? concern? I could not exactly define it, but for some reason, in spite of all the theatrics, I wanted to trust him. He just did not seem to be the kind of man who would be associated with the mob or some shady power brokers.

So who was he?

If my instinct was right, and lately I was beginning to doubt my instincts about people, the only logical conclusion was that he was an intelligence agent. A minor point in favor of that conclusion was that he had gotten visibly upset when I mentioned the exhange of information between embassy security and American intelligence. If he was an agent, then why the meeting? Was it because they had finally discovered that I was of no interest to them, after all, and wanted to close the matter and to reassure me that there would be no repercussions? Or was it a part of some plan to get me in deeper than before? Deeper into what? If they wanted to blackmail me, they already had all they needed.

I was back where I had started—I had no idea what was going on.

I shifted to another part of the conversation. Just to cover all possible ground, I had asked John what would happen if I decided to stay in the States. I still did not think it a viable possiblity, but I had wanted to cover all the options.

His answer had surprised me.

"You should not think about it because you think you are trapped," he said "because you are not. As I said, you have nothing to fear; everything will be taken care of. However, I do think you should consider it for your own sake and for the sake of your children, simply because you would be happy here."

"I can't be happy in a strange country, away from home. Everything I know, everything I love is there, in the Soviet Union."

"I do not agree with you. You love your children, and they are right here with you. You love your husband, and he could stay with you too. But most importantly, you should do it for yourself. You are the kind of person who would do very well in this country because it was built by people like you—people who were not afraid of the unknown, who were not afraid to take chances. They took the risks and prospered. You would do well in American business."

"Why are you saying I am not afraid to take chances? I am here, with you, precisely because I do not want to take any chances with my future, because I want to be reassured that I am safe."

"Maybe. But you have been taking quite a few risks by not following the embassy rules, and I am not just talking about your meetings with Derek. You like to do things your own way, and if the rules do not make sense to you, you break them."

That was true. I'd broken several embassy regulations, starting with opening a checking account and getting a credit card, but to take a chance of such magnitude—that was something different. And yet, the thought kept returning, not just that night, but for days afterward. "What would it be like," I wondered, "to live in this country—as one of them? What would my life be like?"

And always, another thought: "What would my life be like if I went back?"

CHAPTER **10**

*N*o matter which aspect of my life I considered, returning home with divorce on my mind did not look very promising.

First, the divorce itself. I knew I would face a long, protracted battle with Lev, who would not want to give me a divorce in the first place, since he obviously did not suspect there was anything wrong with our relationship. I doubted very much that I would ever be able to explain to him convincingly why I felt so put down by his attitude. I was also afraid he would talk me into staying in the marriage—with his background in positivist logic, the man could talk anybody into anything. I'd seen his reasoning power too many times before, when he had talked me out of or into something directly opposite to what I'd wanted. My decision to marry him had been a classic example—I'd come to the airport to see him for the last time, and within hours my resolve had been crushed.

Assuming that I got him to agree to the divorce, I doubted I could talk him into moving out of our Moscow apartment even temporarily; the only way to break up would be to take the children and move in with my parents in Leningrad. It would be terribly crowded in their two-room apartment, but I knew they would be happy to have us. Moving there, however, would present the immediate problem of finding a job. I would not be able to get anything even close to the job I had had in Moscow. My choices would be limited—to go back to sociological research or, using my newly acquired proficiency in English, to become an interpreter again. I'd enjoyed doing that when I was ten years younger, but conducting guided tours was no longer appealing. Besides, an interpreter's job often required substantial travel, and with my mother's poor health, I could not burden her with child care on a full-time basis. I could not take another job teaching Marxism— those positions required membership in the Communist Party, which I did not have. To acquire membership, people must be with the same organization for at least two years in order to obtain recommendations from co-workers. The only place where I could get such recommendations almost immediately was the Leningrad branch of the Institute of Philosophy, where I had worked before and where my previous stay would count toward those two years.

That meant going back into research or teaching, neither of which I particularly liked. I'd always wanted to be in an administrative position, and my work here in the States had only reinforced my conviction that it was something I liked and could do well. I liked the challenge of dealing with different things every day, of solving problems, getting things done. That avenue, however, was practically closed to me. Other than secretarial work, administrative positions in scientific institutions are held by senior scholars who must first have an established record of professional achievement.

There is no such thing as a professional manager in the Soviet Union. In fact, there is not even a word in the Russian language that translates as "manager." Most of the purely administrative jobs are held by professional Party "apparatchiks"—people who rise through the ranks of the Communist Party. Once they are established within the party apparatus, they are considered capable of directing organizational activities, no matter what those activities might be. This party bureacracy, called "nomenklatura," is rotated among jobs, and that is how somebody with a minimal education in agriculture, or a former graduate of a pedagogical institute, might easily end up being the director of an auto factory. The assumption is that there are always engineers to run the factory, but that the director is there to inspire the people and "lead" them. Of course, with the director often having only a vague idea of how the factory operates, the "leadership" is often reduced to passing along orders from the party's higher quarters and to conducting general meetings. Not that it matters—no factory director in the centralized Soviet economy has the authority to decide how the factory should operate and what it is going to produce anyway.

However, even if I somehow managed to get my party membership quickly, it would take years to move up to a level in which I could be in a position of authority. People who have that kind of career in mind usually start very early by being active in the party organization when they are still in the university. And even if I could defy the odds, it was not the kind of career I wanted. From living here, I had become too spoiled about being able to pick up the phone, reach a person in a position to make a decision, and have the problem resolved in a matter of minutes. Things do not work like that in the Soviet Union, and thinking about going back to deal with the bureaucracy, where everything sinks as if in quicksand, gave me jitters.

No matter where I turned, a divorce meant going back to a mundane and tedious job. I was not worried about my financial position—I knew Lev would not use money as leverage once he realized I had left for good. Neither was I worried about my social position—it did not really matter since I was not going to stay in Moscow. Back in Leningrad I would get right back in the literary and artistic circles of which my mother was an established member. Having an interesting career without Lev's support, however, was next to impossible. It is a common miconception that women are equal to men in that workers' paradise. It is not so. Maybe they have an equal opportunity to get heavy-duty construction jobs, but when it comes to professional life, very few women rise to a position of significance and power by merit alone.

It is partly due to the general conditions of life. Proportionally, more women graduate from Soviet colleges than men. The inequality begins after that. Men are offered better positions since it is assumed that a woman will eventually get married. Then she would be entitled to a maternity leave which, if the time off without pay is included, can last up to fourteen months. After that she is basically finished. Because of the tremendous time required to keep up with even the basic household chores—Soviet women still spend five times more on household duties then men—inadequate child care that keeps children at home off and on, and the nonexistence of babysitters, which results in mothers often having to take time off, women do not get the same chances for promotion as do men. In many organizations, promotion also depends on active participation in party activities, which are usually conducted in the evening—something few mothers can afford. As a result, ten years after graduation from college, a husband usually earns 1.5 times as much as his wife, even if they had the same head start together.

Even women who are not burdened by family, or have older children who put less demand on the mother, have difficulty establishing themselves professionally because of the ingrained macho mentality of Soviet society. Connections help tremendously, because then a man simply does a favor for a friend by hiring the friend's wife; he doesn't have to admit that the woman is better qualified for the job. I have met quite a few women doctors of philosophy; somehow most of them also happened to be married to older, well-established male doctors of philosophy or to party apparatchiks, or were daughters of the high-level officials. The Soviet Union functions on nepotism and connections. I had no illusions that I would have had my prestigious job in Moscow, despite my unusual qualifications, if I hadn't been Lev's wife at the time.

Another set of thoughts revolved around the children. I really did not want to bring them back and let them grow up in the Soviet Union. Of course, they were young and they would adjust. After all, children grow up there. They are not as healthy as American children, growing up on a Soviet diet that is practically devoid of fresh fruits and vegetables, especially in the winter, but other children survive there, and so would mine. I could bring back a supply of vitamins, toys, and clothes to last them for several years, and then maintain it with the things Lev brought back from his foreign trips, provided we stayed on friendly terms. He always brought things for Xenia, and I had no reason to believe he would not do the same for our children.

The main adjustment would have to be my own. The children were too young to know the difference yet, but I knew. Unlike my mother, who'd stayed at home until I finished high school, I would have to work. That meant the children would have to attend kindergarten, and thus would be exposed to the Soviet system of propaganda from a very early age, rather than from the age of seven, as I was. I remembered Katrina flying into my apartment once in a smoldering rage.

"What happened?" I asked. "Had another quarrel with Andrei?" They were heading for a divorce, and it was not unusual for either one of them to come over to our apartment to complain about the other. We never took sides, just listened, and they both knew it.

"No, it's Maria," she said. Maria was their four-year-old daughter, who'd just started kindergarten. "You won't believe what happened. She is making a present for her grandfather."

"So what?" I said. "She loves her grandparents, you know that, even though you don't like your in-laws."

"You miss the point," Katrina said. "Her grandfather's birthday is several months away. She is making a present for grandfather Lenin's birthday! She was told in kindergarten that she had two grandfathers, and grandfather Lenin was the more important one. Just like in *Animal Farm*! I am going to take her out of that place."

"No, you won't," I said. "These days children are expected to attend kindergarten, whether they need it or not. Pulling her out would label her as antisocial."

Now, thinking back, I wondered how I would have reacted in Katrina's place, seeing my child being brainwashed at the age of four. Actually, I knew I would have been in the same rage, maybe worse. If I went back, my children would be exposed to that, too. What's more, I would have to encourage it if I wanted them to have any normal future in Soviet society. They would have to be taught, gradually and carefully, to read between the lines; they would have to learn that there were two truths—the official and the unofficial—to learn doublethink, and I would have to be the one to teach them to lead that life of lies if I wanted them to succeed in it. I could not even hope for the sanctuary of another foreign assignment; opportunities like the one we had had were extremely rare for nondiplomats, and it would mean staying with Lev in any case.

Of course I would miss Washington. I would miss its carefree life, the *Washington Post, Time* magazine, television, movies, smiling and friendly people. But I would readjust to the Soviet pattern of life. I'd always been adept in dealing with the Soviet system, separating the official from the personal. Maybe I could even adjust to my life with Lev. It had been almost a year since the memorable day in the hospital, when Konstantin was born, and I was more or less used to living in my new state of mind. After all, it would not be the first marriage to exist without love—people stay married for a variety of reasons, and love is quite often not one of them.

Question was, did I have to?

Two months earlier I had read a book published by Svetlana Alliluyeva. Like everybody else in the Soviet Union, I'd known about Svetlana's defection years ago from foreign radio broadcasts. Even in the Soviet Union it is impossible to keep news about somebody as well known as Stalin's daughter quiet. I even met a woman who used to be Svetlana's best friend in Moscow, a black woman who was the daughter of a former secretary of the American Communist Party. She'd come to study in Moscow, gotten married, and stayed there. She did not like to talk about Svetlana, though.

"Imagine," she said once, "Svetlana called me from Switzerland after she defected. Didn't she realize how much damage it could do to me here?"

I knew that Svetlana had published *Twenty Letters to a Friend*, a book about the Soviet Union, even before she had defected. On our recent trip to New York, however, we'd had dinner with the editor from Harper & Row who'd edited Svetlana's second book, *Only One Year*. I asked to borrow the book, and read it with great interest. Svetlana described in detail how, fed up with the system, she had arrived at her decision to defect, how wonderful were the people who had helped her, and how happy she was to feel free for the first time in her life in her first year in the United States. Many thoughts in the book echoed my own feelings. I also knew that her family back home had not suffered any ill consequences, although they had had to sever all ties with her. That, of course, would be true in my case as well. The Soviet Union has a long-standing policy that no relatives of defectors are ever allowed to emigrate. The policy has never been violated and serves as a serious deterrent to would-be defectors.

The main problem was, how would I feel about myself if I defected? There was something distasteful about defection, even the word itself suggested something defective, inferior, *wrong*. I did not feel that I would be betraying my country—I did not have any big secrets to tell, and the system itself was certainly not something to feel loyal to. What was at stake was my loyalty to my friends—but even that could be handled if I explained my motives carefully, presented them as purely personal, and kept things quiet, avoiding any public statements. I already felt guilty even thinking about it, but Svetlana had had the same mixed feelings and had obviously managed to overcome it after a while.

Yes, I could go back and adjust, but was it worth it? I had very little doubt that I would be happier staying here, that the opportunities this country presented were immense and that the things I could do here with my life and work were unlimited. I could finally *choose* what I wanted to be, what I wanted to do. I had little doubt that, even alone and with two children on my hands, I could manage to handle both my work and my family in a way that was impossible back home. And what a wonderful way to avoid a messy divorce—provided, of course, that Lev decided to return home.

That was an unpredictable factor. Lev liked living in Washington, and there was no question that he could find a teaching job in a college or an institute engaged in Soviet research. On the other hand, he would have to sacrifice his established position and prestige in Soviet society, and to accept the fact that he would never see Xenia, his mother, or his sister again. I knew I would also have to give up any chance of ever seeing my parents, but Lev's feelings for his mother were special. Since his father's death he had assumed the role of the man in the family, and considered his mother and sister his responsibility.

I knew of course that taking the children with me would present him with a difficult choice, but deep inside, I knew what his choice would be. He'd never wanted us to have children together. When I'd gotten pregnant for the first time, he practically forced me to have an abortion. At first he hadn't said it openly. He just became very irritable and difficult to put up with. Then, gradually, he started to advance arguments about how having a child would interfere with the life we were just starting together and how inadequate our living accomodations were, and finally he suggested an abortion. By then I was so tired of his constant irritability that I gave up. His mood improved immediately, and later, when he was drunk, he confessed that he'd been afraid that another child would take away some of his love for Xenia, who, he felt, had already been dealt a harsh blow by his divorce.

I did not give up hope, however. I was nearing thirty and I desperately wanted a child. The next time I made sure that he could not interfere. Soviet law prohibits an abortion after twelve weeks of pregnancy, and I simply did not tell him until it was too late. He was outraged, but finally resigned himself to the fact that there was nothing he could do about it. When Kitty was born, he became attached to her, and was a good father, but I knew that deep down inside, Xenia would always remain his favorite child. Everything being equal, he would choose her. For my purposes, it was an advantage now. If he decided to return to the Soviet Union, he would still have Xenia, and I doubted very much that he would fight very hard to take our children from me.

Finally, after two weeks of agonizing vacillation, I called Derek and requested another meeting with John. It was quickly arranged. Derek did not even go with me to the hotel.

It was apparent that John expected some serious talking. After all, why else would I ask for a meeting? I had gotten all the assurances about my safety the time before. I noticed that he had ordered a bottle of my favorite Amaretto from room service and plenty of coffee to make me feel at ease. We chatted about this and that for a few minutes, while I gathered my courage to get to the point.

"I've been thinking seriously about the defection," I said finally. "But I have a few more questions. First of all, what will I live on?"

"You'll be given a living allowance from the government," John said. "We will also help you find a job." He'd obviously expected my question and had a ready answer.

"I don't want just 'a job' and I don't want to live on welfare for the rest of my life. The main reason I want to stay is because I want to do something different with my life; to become what I always wanted to be—a businesswoman. My degrees are useless here. I will need an American degree in business."

"I don't think that would be a problem," he said, smiling. "After all, it will be a bargain for the government—once you get your education, you'll support yourself, and I have no doubt that you will be able to do that. Next question?"

"I would want no press coverage. I don't want to make any statements. I want to handle it as a strictly personal decision; I don't want to hurt anybody, and if I keep quiet there is a better chance that the Soviet government will leave me alone."

"I can't promise you that if your husband decides to stay with you. With somebody of his status we simply won't be permitted not to capitalize on it. If it's just you and the children, we can handle it."

"That brings up an interesting point. As you said yourself, on my own I do not present as much interest to you as my husband would. So, what's in it for you?" Unspoken, the question on my mind was—would they ask me to spy for them while I was still with the embassy? That was one thing I did not think I could ever handle.

"I told you the last time we met," John said. "It is our duty to help anybody who seeks freedom in our country. You don't have to do anything."

I decided to let it go at that. If there were strings attached, I was not going to find out now.

"There is one more thing," I said. "I don't want to do it right now. I want to stay at the embassy as long as I can, until it is time to go home. And I need to make another trip to Moscow to take care of a few things."

"This could be very dangerous. The longer we keep it a secret, the greater the chance that something will go wrong. And the idea of a trip to Moscow is sheer lunacy. If somebody suspects you, you won't be able to return to Washington. We can provide protection here, but out there you are on your own."

"I'll have to go. My parents want to see their grandson. I need to take care of some financial matters to provide for my parents and for Lev's family in case he decides to stay here. And it will be my last chance to see my mother."

"OK," he said finally. "If you insist. But I still think it's crazy. Call me when you get back."

CHAPTER 11

I flew to Moscow in early March 1978, but first I made a couple of adjustments to our life in Washington. The first was to move from Chevy Chase. Our lease had expired, and the rent was going up in excess of our rental allowance. I jumped at the opportunity to move to another building where no other Soviet families lived. John approved of the idea: we could not continue meeting in hotels where I had absolutely no business being and where I could offer no reasonable explanation should anybody from the embassy see me going there; on the other hand, John didn't dare do anything in a building where other Soviet families lived. Lev was surprised at my choice of residence, but was finally sold on an enchanting backyard patio that came with a ground floor apartment in a building in Arlington. The embassy did not mind.

Another change I implemented was to put Kitty in an American day-care center. I checked with the embassy, and it was not unprecedented although rarely done: it was the least expensive day care I could find, run by a Baptist church several blocks away from our new home, but even with that the fees were roughly equal to what I was being paid as Lev's secretary—$120 a month. My argument was that it would give Kitty an invaluable head start in

English which I could then easily maintain in Moscow. Lev believed in early language education in the native environment—something he had unsuccessfully tried with Xenia—and did not argue. I did want Kitty to have a head start in English, but for her new life in America.

My official excuse for a trip to Moscow was that, with our return scheduled for September, I needed time for a major remodeling of our apartment before we came home with the children. I did in fact intend to do exactly that. There was a good chance Lev would indeed return there, and it was the least I could do for him. Kitty stayed in Washington, but I took Konstantin with me to show him off. My father was tremendously proud that he finally had a male heir in the family, and took to his grandfatherly duties eagerly. I returned to Moscow almost immediately, planning to hire the workers to work on the apartment and then to come back to Leningrad again.

Alana had been as good as her word, and the most glaring problems with the apartment had been fixed. One room was filled with stuff I had shipped from Washington: a washer and dryer, carpeting, wallpaper, boxes with books and records. What I needed was a team of workers to repaint the walls, hang the wallpaper, lay parquet floors, replace the linoleum in the kitchen, replace all plumbing fixtures, and install the new appliances. I immediately went to see Andrei Mironov; I knew that he and his new wife had recently redone their entire apartment—he had proudly shown it to me on my previous trip to Moscow.

"It's impossible," he said after I explained my problem and he had made a few calls. "It's not even a matter of money; it's the time. It would take at least two weeks just to get the team together, and then about a month to do the job. These are the best moonlighters in Moscow and they are always busy."

"What about somebody else?" I asked. "Surely your man knows other people in the business."

"I already asked," Andrei said. "Anybody who is good enough will take time to get, and besides, if my man says he needs at least a month, nobody can do it faster. You should have called me from Washington in advance."

I knew he was right. I'd underestimated the flexibility of the

Soviet second economy. Even though it was ten times more efficient than the official economy, lack of proper tools and the difficulty of getting local supplies even on the black market added to the time needed to do so much.

"Don't worry," said Andrei. "Let me know a couple of months in advance exactly when you are going to return, and we will have all the materials ready for you. Then the job can be done while you are living in the apartment, room by room. It will work out fine."

I thanked him for his help and promised to call him from Washington. If he only knew!

With the apartment problem beyond my control, I set out for the main task I had come to accomplish—to get together as much cash as possible and give it to my mother.

I did not want to dispose of any of the household items we had shipped from Washington; I still believed there was a greater chance that Lev would return rather than stay, and those things were our common property. He was entitled to keep them if I left. I did take one precaution: I moved everything that was easily movable to Tatiana's apartment and shipped some of the small items to Leningrad. I was afraid that if we both defected, our apartment would be sealed and possibly confiscated by the State, and all the contents would be lost. This way at least some of it could be kept by our families, who could claim that whatever they had in their possession was a gift.

The only things I could dispose of freely were books, records, and, for obvious reasons, my own clothes. I also brought a few things I had purchased specifically for resale. American paperbacks are accepted without limit by official Soviet secondhand bookstores at an equivalent of eight to twelve dollars each. Records are also very valuable and go for about fifty dollars for jazz to ninety dollars for pop and rock. Not many people can afford to buy many of them at once at such prices, and I did not want to dabble openly in the black market. I had two wholesale sources for selling records, though. One was a friend of ours, a musician by the name of Igor, who had given us a long list of jazz records he wanted; we'd agreed on a fixed price per record in advance, regardless of the prices we paid for them in the States. That way he was protected from any surprises, and I had a guaranteed market. Another source was my old friend Anatol, whom I had almost married years ago.

Anatol was running a booming private enterprise typical of the entrepreneuring Russians. Officially, he worked as an electrical engineer. However, the bulk of his substantial income came from his private recording studio. He invested in Western records, of which he had an enormous collection, and semiprofessional Western stereo equipment, and made taped copies of his records for his clients. Having the music on tape cost them about a quarter of what they would have had to pay for the original records. In addition, it eliminated the risk of buying sealed records without listening to the contents. Dealing with Anatol, they got high-quality recordings chosen exactly to their tastes; he got a return on his investment plus a tidy profit—a record paid for itself after four or five copies.

He'd gotten married a couple of years after we had broken up, and I'd maintained a friendly relationship with him and his wife. Anatol was always on the lookout for new records for his collection, and I took all the records I had left to him. The price he offered was lower than Igor had paid, but on the other hand, he took them all off my hands, and I did not have to worry about them anymore. For clothing, I brought everything I had to sell to an old acquaintance named Olga, who had a lot of friends interested in buying Western clothes. I named my price and left everything with her. What she got for it was her business, and she was entitled to make a profit for being an intermediary. Then I went to visit Katrina. We spent several hours together, catching up on her news. She said that after the dust had settled from her divorce from Andrei she had dated several eligible men; her latest beau was an art collector who used to be married to a Finnish girl, still traveled to Finland very often, and was very wealthy. She proudly showed me a mink coat he'd given her and insisted that we get together for a little party later in the evening.

I was rather tired, but promised to come. However, that afternoon I went to visit Anatol, and stayed there longer than I had expected. I called Katrina to cancel, but, almost in tears, she begged me to come, saying that they would wait for me. They did, and although I was more than an hour late, we drove to her friend's apartment. It turned out to be a party for four—there was only one other man besides Katrina's friend. The table was laid lavishly with the rare delicatessen fare only very privileged people, or people with hard currency, could get; the host played the records by Sinatra and Ella Fitzgerald, but I felt uneasy. Perhaps it was because I was tense or just plain tired, but all of a sudden I started wondering why I was there, and why Katrina had insisted on this party so much. I had already met her boyfriend earlier; if she'd wanted to show him off, there had been enough time for that during the day. I dismissed the thought that she was trying to pair me off with somebody—although I mentioned during the day that there was a rift in my relationship with Lev, I hadn't said anything that would have warranted such a swift action.

As the evening progressed, the men started to ask me questions about my life in the United States; there was nothing unusual about their interest, but the questions indicated that both of them were well informed about life abroad. Everybody asked me questions, and I was usually sincere with my friends, but these two were strangers. Without any particular reason I felt uneasy. Katrina's boyfriend, who, according to her, frequently traveled to Finland, talked with admiration about the Western way of life, occasionally asking my opinion as if he expected me to agree both with his adoration of the West and his critique of the Soviet system. It could be that he felt that way; on the other hand, if they were KGB informers, it was a good way to ferret out my own opinions.

I remembered all too well another acquaintance of ours in Moscow—a man with the unusual name of Tankred. He had been born and raised in Hong Kong, where his Russian parents had emigrated before the war, and then decided to return to the Soviet Union on his own when he was nineteen. He was very charming, the life of the party, completely bilingual, and had easy access to the latest Western periodicals. He also had friends among dissident writers and was accepted in the homes of the most interesting and liberal artists and writers. He often complained bitterly that because he was Jewish and not a member of the Communist Party, he could not get a decent full-time job and had to exist on occasional trans-lations. We liked him very much and he was one of our best friends until I ran into an old acquaintance who had known Tankred for several years back in Novosibirsk. It seems that Tankred was a KGB stoolie, who'd endeared himself to many people there—not really dissidents, just some scientists who had been a bit too liberal for the KGB's taste. There'd been a crackdown, several people had been arrested, and Tankred had quickly moved to Moscow to avoid the wrath of his former friends. I never told Tankred what I had learned about him, but I did tell Lev; we did not ban Tankred's visits, partly because his wife was a wonderful woman—and my gynecologist—who probably did not know about his activities, but since then we had been very careful about what we said in Tankred's presence.

Much as I hated the thought that Katrina might have turned into a female Tankred, I decided to play it safe with her friends and resorted to innocent doubletalk: yes, that's true, but, on the other hand, etc. Finally I pleaded fatigue, and Katrina and her friend drove me home.

Within a couple of days I had completed all my wheeling and dealing and was ready to go back to Leningrad. I'd also closed my savings account in the State bank. Then I faced the last, and most difficult, task I'd come to accomplish there—I had to get some papers out of the Soviet Union. My diploma and my birth certif-icate were no problem—they were in Leningrad. But the marriage certificate, which I knew I would need if I were to get a divorce in the United States, and Kitty's birth certificate, were in my mother-in-law's safekeeping.

I kept delaying this mission because for once I did not have any excuse at all to ask her for the papers. Finally, as the day of my departure for Leningrad approached, I came upon an idea. I told her that the management of our building needed to update some records for our apartment, and I needed to make the copies of both documents. Then I went to Leningrad, and when I returned to Moscow ready to fly back to Washington, I told her that I had forgotten the papers in Leningrad. I wondered whether she would check with my mother but decided it was unlikely.

My stay in Leningrad was the most traumatic time of my visit.

I hated to lie to my mother, but I had to do it for her own protection. I gave her all the money I had and told her that I was considering a divorce and wanted her to stash it for me for a rainy day. She was not particularly surprised; she knew I had been growing unhappy in my marriage; my father, had he heard, would only have been delighted—he'd never liked Lev, mostly because he despised Lev's inability to control his drinking. Nor was she shocked at my request: after she'd gone to work she'd kept some money in her own account, building some reserves for the time when she could finally persuade my father to give her a divorce. What was unusual was the sum and the fact that I had come back from Moscow with practically nothing to wear—I had not been known to go to such extremes in the past. I did not have to ask her for my papers because I knew where she kept the family archives; all I had to do was remove them when she was out shopping. We talked a lot, staying up late at night when my father was asleep, but even then I had to be careful in what I said in order not to alarm her unnecessarily.

Besides, she needed to talk to me even more than I needed to talk to her. My parents' marriage was deteriorating rapidly; she'd asked for divorce twice, but my father had always refused. She wanted my advice about how to deal with it. She could not write about the details of her personal problems in her letters to me, and there were a lot of little things that had accumulated in the year and a half since my last visit. I was glad she had so much to tell me because it steered the conversation away from my own affairs. Or maybe she sensed with that sixth feeling that only mothers possess that it was better for both of us not to ask too many questions.

To this day I do not know whether she had figured my plans out, but all of a sudden she decided to go to Moscow with me to see me off to Washington. That was surprising. She usually did not feel well in the wintertime, when the damp sea winds in Leningrad exacerbated her asthma, and there was no need for her to take the trip since we were supposed to be coming back in a few months. She insisted, however, and I did not protest; I wanted to be with her as long as I could.

As I packed my suitcase, I faced another dilemma. Igor had given me a beautiful old icon in lieu of some of the money for the records. I wanted to take it with me because it would probably fetch a nice price in an antique store in New York. It was wrapped in black paper to protect it from sunlight, and I did not know what kind of devices were used at Moscow's international airport to look through the luggage; it was also possible the baggage might be opened for inspection after it had been checked in. Although I had a diplomatic passport, and nobody would open my luggage in my presence, nothing could be ruled out in Moscow Customs. It might be just part of a routine check to catch foreigners trying to smuggle something out. In any case, if for some reason the icon was discovered, my purse would be searched as well, and if I were caught with my papers in it, I would be finished. It is a criminal offense to take Soviet identification papers out of the country; when people travel they are issued an external passport. An internal Soviet passport—the most important document in the life of every Soviet citizen because for most of them it is their only identification, something constantly required in everyday dealings with the Soviet system—must stay inside the country.

Finally, I decided not to take any chances. Much as I wanted to have a little reserve cash after defection—the icon was probably worth close to ten thousand dollars—the papers were more important. I left the icon with my mother without even mentioning that I had considered taking it with me to Washington, and asked her to keep it, together with the money I'd given her.

I'll remember the scene at the airport as long as I live. I lingered until the last moment. Finally I had to leave. When I got to the upper balcony reserved for international departures only, I looked down. Standing there on the ground floor, my mother looked smaller than she was; I saw that her eyes were filled with tears, and I suddenly realized how much she had aged during the three years I had been in Washington, and how much I would miss her. From now on I would only see her in photographs; our telephone conversations would have to be carefully controlled because somebody would always be listening. I knew it was the last time I would be seeing her—she would not be allowed out of the Soviet Union, and I would never be able to go back and visit her. And I wondered again—had she guessed? Did she know it was the last time, too?

———

My return to Washington was almost routine. Everything was fine at home, and there was some good news: VAAP had decided to extend our stay for one more year.

"That's just the beginning," Peter said. "The first extension is the most important one, because that's where the issue is decided in principle. After that, it's almost automatic—another year, then another year. Look at me—I wanted to take a break after eleven years here, but they wouldn't let me."

I met with John, gave him my papers, because I was afraid to keep them in our apartment, and told him that I would be staying with the embassy longer than I had thought but that my intention was unchanged. For about a month nothing happened, until an event near the beginning of April changed the situation dramatically.

It was April 7, 1978. Lev was out of town, and I was home alone with the children, when suddenly I heard a knock on the door. It was close to eight in the evening, and I did not expect any guests. As I opened the door, I saw Vladimir, a young diplomat who was the ambassador's special aide. I'd met him earlier that day and reminded him of a long-standing invitation to come and listen to some of our records; the best part of our collection was in Washington, and Vladimir was an ardent jazz fan.

"Just thought I'd take you up on your word," he said. I fixed him a drink, asked him what he wanted to listen to, and put the record on. He did not seem to listen, though. He looked very tired, his face was almost ashen, and I wondered what kind of a grueling day he had had. When I'd seen him earlier at lunch, he'd been his normal energetic and cheerful self.

"Did you have a bad day?" I asked. "You look awfully tired."

He did not answer right away, but first fixed himself another scotch. "Something terrible has happened," he said. "It won't be in the newspapers until Monday, but we already know. One of our highest-ranking diplomats in New York, Arcady Schevchenko, defected."

I was stunned. I knew practically nobody in the New York community, and the name meant nothing to me, but the significance of the action could have serious repercussions in Washington.

"Did he know much?" I asked, trying to sound sincerely concerned. "Know" was a commonly understood euphemism for "Is he going to blow a lot of covers?"

"Did he!" Vladimir said. "We spent the entire afternoon trying to figure out who is going to be expelled and how soon. Quite a few people are still at the embassy and probably will stay there half of the night. I'm going back early in the morning."

We talked a little more. Fearful of ever present bugging, he did not say much except the bare facts that would be in the newspapers later anyway. He did manage to relax a bit after a few drinks, and soon he went home feeling better. I stayed up late, trying to think about what this new development could mean for me. First of all, there would probably be increased security checks; then, probably, increased surveillance from our own counterintelligence to make sure that everything was OK in Washington. I did not want to call John—although the number he'd given me was manned twenty-four hours a day, the situation was not critical.

On Tuesday the story broke on the front pages of all the newspapers, but there was little talk about the event inside the embassy; most people behaved as if nothing had happened. Admittedly, it was an unpleasant topic; in addition, I figured everybody was afraid to comment on it for fear that they might be misinterpreted if they showed too much interest. The only person to whom I talked about it was Peter. He was bitter and angry.

"It did not have to happen," he said. "The s.o.b. would have been back in Moscow a long time ago if he weren't Gromyko's protégé. Everybody in New York knew he had family problems and was drinking heavily, and the New York security section requested three times that he be recalled, but every time Gromyko covered for him. At least nobody will lose a job because of this bastard—those reports are on file, so nobody here can be blamed for what happened." Other than that, the picture was bleak—Schevchenko was the highest-ranking Soviet diplomat in the U.N. secretariat and knew the identity of many KGB agents who worked there under U.N. cover. I wondered if that was why John had never asked me any questions pertaining to intelligence matters; if they had a guy like this, they had all the information they needed.

I also saw a disturbing glimpse of what my friends would say about me after I left. No matter how personal my motives were, I would be thought of as dirt for the rest of my life.

———

John had a few more points to add to my worries; the most important one was that, with Schevchenko's prior history and increased security checks, Lev might be identified as a security risk because of his drinking, and our stay in Washington could be shorter than I had thought.

"I want you to meet somebody else who is in a position to discuss the details of your resettlement," he said. "I think it's time to get from general discussions to detailed planning."

We were scheduled to meet the next Saturday in the apartment that he was now renting in the same building. It was certainly safer than meeting in hotels: however, it did not solve my logistical problems. I could not bring the children with me. Kitty was old enough to talk, and later could have told Lev that we had visited another apartment; therefore, the children had to be taken to the babysitter. Lev was still out of town; I planned to take the children to the babysitter in the morning, leave them there for a couple of hours, then pick them up again and drive directly to the embassy's summer retreat on the Eastern Shore.

As I got ready to leave, I looked through the patio door and saw to my horror that the car had a flat tire. I had no idea how to change it, and I did not know anybody in the building except the elderly lady next door.

It was still half an hour before the meeting, but I went upstairs, hoping that John would be there. He was, but he was not alone. I was so upset that I started explaining what had happened even before I was introduced to the other man. At that moment I forgot how nervous I'd been just a few minutes before: it was to be the first time I would meet somebody other than John, and I was scared, but right now nothing mattered except that unless I had help, I could not make it to the meeting.

"I can't help you," said John. "I cannot be seen with you. Why don't you call the service station?"

Several frantic calls brought no results. It was Memorial Day weekend, and although the gas stations were open, garages were not. In two places people laughed at me when I said I needed somebody to come and change the tire. In one place they said they could send a truck, but it would take at least three hours of waiting.

"Look, it's real easy," John said. "I'll explain it to you and you can do it yourself."

By then my nerves had given up. I was away from my apartment, where I had left the children alone, and everything was going wrong. "I am not going to do it," I said. "Either one of you comes out to help me or I am staying home to wait for that truck."

"OK, I'll do it," the other man said, whose name turned out to be Jim. "Go to your car and pretend you just discovered it, just in case somebody's looking."

I went downstairs, made sure the children were still playing quietly, and went outside. As I stood next to my car, looking at my flat tire with an expression of total despair, Jim walked into the parking lot, whistling a tune. Then, as if he had just noticed my predicament, he stopped and asked casually, "Need any help, lady?"

"Oh, yes, thank you," I said eagerly, almost laughing inside now. At least I wasn't scared of him anymore; he seemed to be a nice, down-to-earth guy and certainly handled the situation with humor.

Half an hour later I was back in the apartment upstairs, and we got down to business.

"Jim is a relocation expert," John said. "He will discuss with you the paperwork we need and the details of future arrangements."

A relocation expert? Who was he kidding? Even if John himself was who he said he was—a businessman—surely by now American intelligence was involved. Why was he still playing that game? Didn't they trust me?

"John," I said, "I've known you for some time and I trust you. Please don't insult my intelligence by referring to some 'relocation expert.' Why don't you level with me and tell me that Jim is an intelligence agent from the CIA."

"As a matter of fact, it's the FBI," Jim said. "Don't you know that the CIA cannot operate inside this country?"

"No," I said, quite surprised. Everybody in the embassy always referred to the CIA when mentioning surveillance. "I thought the FBI was like the Soviet militia—to catch criminals." Jim explained to me that all counterintelligence inside the US was FBI business.

The first thing he wanted me to do was fill out some forms and write a formal request for asylum. He explained to me that the application for US citizenship was a complicated and lengthy process, and I would have to be sponsored by a congressman to have it approved on an exceptional basis. They wanted to have the paperwork ready as soon as possible. It was a standard government form, an application for permanent residency: name, age, address, parents, and so forth. The request for asylum took a little longer— it had to be written in my own words, and I had to give a reason for such a request. Finally, after several drafts, we settled on a short statement, about half a page long, with a fairly standard wording—that I did not agree with the ideology on which the Soviet system was based and wanted to live in a free country.

Both Jim and John were concerned about the Schevchenko affair and its possible repercussions in Washington. We agreed on a signal by which they would let me know when they needed me to contact John. I was always supposed to take the same exit from the parking lot. At the intersection, there was a stop sign. The signal was a piece of metal tape wrapped around the stem of the sign.

"But I only drive there in the morning," I said. "What if you need to contact me during the day?"

"If there is an emergency, we'll find you," Jim said. I understood the implication; no more "rotating surveillance"; they would keep an eye on me around the clock.

A couple of hours later I was on my way to the Eastern Shore, knowing that I had made the first irrevocable step. By now it was not just conversation; I had signed the official papers requesting asylum. If the papers fell into the wrong hands and made their way to the embassy . . . Was it really such a good idea to insist that I wanted to stay with the embassy as long as possible? The longer I stayed, the greater the risks I was taking.

One good thing the Schevchenko affair did for me, however, was to provide me with an opportunity to open the subject with Lev. I kept wondering what his decision would turn out to be, and decided to test the waters. In the middle of June, Lev and I went to Baltimore to make a presentation at a meeting of the Association of American University Presses. It was a perfect opportunity—I knew Lev would be more comfortable talking openly in the bar of the Baltimore Hotel than anywhere in Washington. I suggested having a drink before heading home, and carefully brought up the subject. His opinion of Schevchenko's actions was the same as the embassy's.

"Actually," I said casually, "you remember how often our American friends said how well *we* fit into the American environment?"

He looked at me in astonishment. "What's the connection? Are you saying that you took those compliments seriously?"

There was something else in his face, some other expression that I could not define but did not particularly like. "Of course not," I said lightly. "I was only trying to say that he'd been here for many years and probably had quite a few friends who had told him the same thing, and that's probably how it started." It was dangerous to continue the conversation, and I quickly changed the subject. It was clear that Lev would have to be told only at the last moment.

———

The events of the next two months proved that my worry was not unwarranted. First came a minor incident, insignificant on its own, but ominous in the context of my current situation. I got a telephone call from Katrina. That was not unusual; she was very impulsive and had called me a few times before when she felt low. Eight hours of time differential made me conveniently available as a shoulder to cry on when it was the middle of the night in Moscow. This time, however, she sounded strained and her voice was almost artificial.

"Are you still having problems with Lev?" she asked, almost without a preamble.

"No, everything is fine," I managed to say. For a moment I almost lost my capacity to speak. Katrina was a streetwise woman who knew better than to talk about personal matters over international telephone lines where every conversation was recorded on the Soviet side. There was only one explanation; she must have been asked to. I remembered her "friends" in Moscow.

So my instinct had been right—she had set me up for a KGB "checkup" and now she'd been told to follow up. It also meant that the security check in the embassy was going on for real.

My suspicions were confirmed in a few days. Out of the blue, we received a telegram from Moscow terminating our extension and ordering us to return to Moscow as originally planned, at the beginning of September.

"This does not make sense," Peter said when we told him about the telegram. "The VAAP delegation is coming to the States on the ninth of September. It would be a logical thing for Lev to accompany them on the trip and use the opportunity to introduce his successor personally to his American counterparts. Yet they want you to return to Moscow on the third."

It may not have made much sense to him or to Lev, but it made perfect sense to me. We were being recalled to Moscow; our original date of return was the earliest they could get us out inconspicuously; the only consolation was that if the KGB had thought the situation was serious enough, they would have ordered us to return earlier.

Apparantly the FBI was also concerned. One day in the middle of July I got a call from Derek while I was in the office.

"I have a buyer interested in your car," he said. "Why don't you give him a call? Here is the phone number."

There was no need to write down the number—it did not mean anything. Although I was replacing our old car with a new one to spare our successor the hassle of dealing with it immediately, I intended to trade in the old car. What Derek was saying was that John wanted me to contact him—immediately.

Lev was in the office, but paid no attention to the call. He'd left the shopping for the new car to me, and I'd spoken to Derek on the phone several times during the past week. Since I'd started talking to John, my relationship with Derek had become strictly official and I did not go to the dealership unless it was absolutely necessary.

A few minutes later I left the office, ostensibly for the ladies' room. Instead, I ran downstairs to the pay phone. John answered immediately.

"Don't go to the airport today," he said.

Our friend Peter was flying to Moscow that afternoon, and had asked me to accompany him and then take his car back.

"How do you know—" I started to say, then realized that they obviously knew all about it. "Why?" I asked instead.

"I can't explain. Just don't go. We have a reason to believe that the KGB may want to put you on that plane to Moscow."

"I can't do that. Peter is our best friend. His wife is in Moscow. He is going to drive his car to the airport, and he asked me to take it back to town. I have absolutely no reason to refuse."

John thought for a few moments. "You have a point," he said finally. "Well, go, but under no circumstances go near the moving lounge at the Aeroflot counter. Stay in the middle of the waiting area. If you see or hear anything suspicious, take off your glasses and wipe them with a handkerchief."

I tried to joke. "I don't have a handkerchief."

"Use a Kleenex." He laughed. "Seriously," he added, "be careful. There will be people there watching you, so don't take off your glasses just because your nose is itching or you'll have a shootout on your hands."

I did find a handkerchief at home and put it in my purse. As we entered the airport, I kept looking around me, trying to see if I could spot the FBI people. No such luck. Nobody was sitting on a bench pretending to read a newspaper and darting his eyes furtively over the edge; nobody was pretending to be asleep and occasionally opening one eye; I went through all the scenes I had seen in spy movies, trying to remember the techniques used in tailing. Nothing. If the FBI people were there, of which I had no doubt, they had made themselves invisible.

I did follow John's advice to stay away from the lounge. In addition, I tried to steer clear of any group of embassy people whom I did not know well and who could be a part of the embassy security staff. Fortunately Peter did not seem to want to join any groups either. We went to the airport bar where Peter and Lev had a glass of beer and I ordered a cup of coffee. Then, final hugs and kisses, and I left at the earliest opportunity. Lev stayed behind—I was taking Peter's car home and he was going to get a ride to the embassy with somebody else.

I crossed the parking lot; still nobody in sight. Finally I got into Peter's car and breathed a sign of relief. Then my anxiety disappeared completely—Peter's Buick had a markedly different ride and handling from our Olds, and I had to concentrate on getting it back safely. The last thing I wanted was to damage somebody else's car.

I never learned what made the FBI think I was in danger on that particular day. Neither did I know until much later that the agents had an executive order signed by the President to hold the plane in case I was put on it against my will. But although the airport scare turned out to be a false alarm, it did bring to all of us a realization that my double life could not continue much longer. How many times could they send a dozen armed agents at the airport? Another growing concern was that, if I did have to run away in an emergency, I might not be able to keep the children. Kitty was in an American day-care center, and the FBI could get to her quickly enough, but Konstanin still spent half a day with the Soviet babysitter at the Tunlaw compound. There was no way we could get him out of there in case of an emergency.

Two days later, when I met with Jim and John, the decision was made. It was too risky to wait till the last moment. They were pulling me out on August 2.

CHAPTER **12**

*N*ow that the date was finally set, I could feel only one thing—relief.

As long as I could remember, I'd always hated uncertainty. My mother had noticed it early on after I'd gotten hysterically angry at a nurse who'd offered me candy and then had sneaked an inoculation shot into my behind. I could not stop crying—not from pain or fear, but from the humiliation of being made a fool. "Why didn't you tell me?" I kept asking between sobs. "I was not afraid of it. I was not going to give you any trouble." Ever since, my mother had always told me in advance if something unpleasant was going to happen. It was easier for me to cope with whatever was to come as long as I knew what to expect. Later in life, that attitude spilled over into my personal relationships. A sixth sense usually told me when I was being fed white lies by men whose philosophy was "what she doesn't know won't hurt her." The problem was that I usually picked up little bits and pieces of information that made me wonder, and it was always the uncertainty that was the worst. It never lasted long, though—people who were unwilling to give me a straight answer were usually dismissed from my universe with speed.

Knowing that the plan had finally been set into action gave me a new burst of energy. I looked forward to that day, at the same time trying to use whatever time I had left to get my affairs in order. I made sure that all my bills were paid and no new charges made on my credit cards; spent extra time in the office making sure that all the working files were in perfect order and that our office bookkeeping was completely up-to-date. That was particularly important, because Lev never knew how our accounting was done, and any shortage in VAAP's money could exacerbate his problems, of which he would have plenty if he decided not to join me. I did feel guilty about doing it to him, but there was no way to avoid it; I could only hope that the questioning would not take long and that he would be cleared soon. Meanwhile, all I could do for him was eliminate any possibility of secondary charges that could make things worse.

I also tried to make the evening before the big day into something special, knowing that it could well be our last night together. I cooked his favorite dinner and set the table for two with candles and music. He did not sense the mood, though. He ate his dinner quickly, had a few drinks, and went to bed early. I stayed up late doing last-minute packing; when I finally got to bed, he did not wake up.

The next morning he went to work, and then all the hectic events of the next few hours followed: rushing back and forth between the apartments, between the house and the motel, signing the papers, leaving the children in the care of the FBI agents, waiting in the parking lot. Then they were all behind me. I was walking slowly toward the patio of my apartment, still holding John's hand. This was the final uncertainty that had to be resolved—was my marriage to continue or would I be a single woman from now on?

Whether from the tension, or the heat of the hot August afternoon, I was beginning to feel light-headed. I kept holding John's hand as though afraid that if I let go I would wake up and realize that it was all happening not to me but to somebody else, somebody in my dream. This was not reality—it was something from a novel I'd read a long time ago or an old B movie I'd seen on TV. Was it really me, hiding in a getaway car out of sight, surrounded by armed agents and the crackle of portable radios? The fifty yards that separated me from the apartment door seemed like an eternity. Then I came to my senses—Lev was standing on the patio, waiting for me to approach. He looked sad and angry.

"I want to talk to you alone. Let's go inside," he said simply. Then he repeated it in English. I looked at John—he shook his head. Once inside the apartment, Lev could lock the door and refuse to open it, invoking his diplomatic immunity, until the embassy representative arrived.

"We can talk in Russian," I said. "Nobody will understand."

We stayed on the patio. What he said was predictable: I must have lost my mind, this was all a mistake, I should come back before the embassy found out—if *they* would let me. And why, why had I even thought of it in the first place??? He was cool and controlled. He took it better than I'd thought, or maybe the presence of other people restrained him from showing his emotions.

"You've read my letter," I said wearily. "I like this country. I want to stay here. I want the children to grow up here."

We went on for about half an hour, pacing the parking lot. He finally insisted that John and Larry leave me alone with him. They fell back a few paces, but followed us closely enough to prevent me from being pushed or dragged into the apartment. Finally John caught up with us. "We have to go," he said.

"What are you going to do?" I asked Lev. "I can't stay any longer. Are you coming with me?"

"I don't know," he said. "I need time to think. How can I get in touch with you?"

I looked at John. "I'll call you," I said. John nodded. "May I speak with you for a moment?" he asked Lev.

I went back to the car with Larry; John and Lev stayed behind. I could see Lev talking angrily. Finally John gave him a small piece of paper and returned to us.

"What was that?" I asked.

"Some phone numbers he can call if he wants to." I assumed he'd left Lev some instructions about how and whom to contact in case he decided to stay here. I knew that the embassy had to be notified before the end of the day. That did not leave Lev with much time.

I looked back as we turned the corner. Lev was still standing on the patio looking at me. He was a handsome man, I thought; his tan jacket and light blue shirt contrasted nicely with his tanned face and gray hair. Would I ever see him again? And did I really want to see him again?

We went back to the motel to pick up the children. Linda, the babysitter, who turned out to be an FBI agent, was playing happily with them and they obviously liked her. Kitty had learned some English in the day-care school, and although she could not speak it very well yet, there seemed to be no communication problems. Our two-car cavalcade took off again, heading west, and an hour later we were registered in a suite at a Sheraton hotel in Virginia, some fifty miles outside of the city—and outside the twenty-five mile zone to which Soviet diplomats were restricted. Everybody seemed to be happily exhausted. We ordered some food and drink from room service and toasted our success. Finally Larry went downstairs to make a call.

"He is still in the apartment," he said when he came back. "Has not made any calls. Just sits there."

"How much time does he have?" I asked.

"You'll call him at five. Three hours should be enough."

"You don't know my husband." I laughed. "Lev does not like to make quick decisions."

I was right. When I called at five o'clock, Lev simply complained that he needed more time to think. I had to promise to call later. Larry talked to somebody on the phone and finally said that they could keep it quiet till the morning. I called Lev back and said I would call him later in the evening.

I called him again at ten o'clock. To my surprise, he was sober. He did not want to talk about himself—he wanted to talk about me. For twenty minutes he went through our marriage, reminding me of all the good things we had had together and how it could be great again if I returned. John ran to the restaurant, brought a handful of change, and kept feeding the coins into the telephone. Finally the pressure Lev was bringing on me started to show, and I began to cry. I told him I would call him early in the morning and hung up. We went back to the suite. One glance at me told Larry what had happened. John confirmed it, and we all settled in for a long, sleepless night.

By six o'clock in the morning none of us had had any sleep, except Linda, who had been sent to bed because she had to get up early when the children woke up. Larry got several calls from Washington—Lev was still in the apartment, no outside calls, the light had been on all night. Finally we went downstairs to the pay phone again.

"I cannot go through it again," I told John. "I am going to ask him for yes or no, that's all. I cannot take this pressure."

"You're doing fine," he said. "You said all the right things last night. Just take control of the conversation and press him for a decision. We cannot keep it a secret forever."

I looked at him in surprise. Last night I'd been talking to Lev in Russian, which John did not speak. They must have recorded the conversation and had it translated already.

"Yes, of course," he answered my unspoken question. "We must have a record of everything in case there are some accusations of unfair play later."

The call did not bring any results. Lev told me that he had had a sleepless night, too, and although I managed to keep him from tearing me apart with reminiscences, he was still not ready for a decision—he needed more time.

"I don't like it," Larry fumed when we returned to the suite. "With all the time he has had, anybody is capable of making up his mind. He's just stalling for time and putting pressure on Elena, that's all there is to it. We'll have to notify the embassy."

We talked about it some more, and I assured him that the worst pressure had been during the night before and that by now I could cope with it. "He's always been that way," I said. "Give him more time. Meanwhile, what I need is some sleep."

The day went fast. John drove to Washington and returned in the evening. I caught a few hours of restless sleep. I hoped that Larry and Jim were also able to take a nap—we were all exhausted—but I wouldn't have been surprised if they didn't. Late in the afternoon I called Lev again, and I could tell by his voice that he was still sober. He was still hoping that I would come back and the whole thing would disappear like a bad dream.

"I am not coming back," I said. "I planned this for several months, and I am not going to change my mind now." I finally told him that Larry had gotten the final extension—at ten o'clock the next morning a formal letter would be delivered from the State Department to the embassy. He had until then. We both knew that after that he would have no chance—somebody from the embassy would be with him all the time until he got on a plane to Moscow, and if he changed his mind afterward, there was nothing anybody could do to help him out.

The second night was not as tense as the first. We'd already talked endlessly about all the possible considerations that might have been going through Lev's mind, and generally agreed that the odds were he would go back home. In any case there wasn't anything else any of us could do. John did not want me to make any more calls; he thought it would be useless by now and too much of a strain for me. Lev had all the information he needed; he did call the phone number John had left him and asked a few questions. He was told that if he wanted to join me he was to drive to the phone booth three blocks away from our home by ten the next morning and make a phone call. Somebody would come to pick him up.

Finally the morning came. We were all up by seven. Larry got several calls from Washington during the night—no change.

"You know," John said, "as a human being I hope he will stay—it is terrible to lose a family like that. But as your friend, I hope he won't. You will be much better off without him."

All the months I had been seeing John I'd been awed by his seeming ability to read my thoughts. True, he was a trained agent and we had had enough time for him to get to know me well, but his way of saying exactly the thing I was thinking at the moment was uncanny.

Suddenly, a few minutes before ten, the phone rang. Larry answered quickly, and a look of pleasant surprise came over his face.

"Well, what do you know," he said. "We were all wrong. Lev loaded his things into the car and left the apartment. I guess you'll be seeing him soon."

I thought about something else. Just about then, the embassy would be receiving a letter from the State Department; the finality of my action suddenly took shape and became real. I'd burned all the bridges—there was no return.

"Well," John said, "now that it's all over, we might as well have a good breakfast. Frankly, I am sick and tired of the room service. Let's go downstairs and have a decent meal. Maybe we'll get decent cups, too."

We all laughed. The first night, room sevice had sent us Styrofoam cups with our coffee. John had called the restaurant management and, with all of us giggling, explained at length that a hotel like the Sheraton should not even have things like that around, let alone send them to the Presidential Suite.

"I hope you realize," he'd said with a straight face, "that when people choose to stay in your best suite, they expect adequate service." We'd all rolled with laughter. The choice of the suite had not been based on luxury of accommodations, but on the fact that it was the only one with two bedrooms so that Linda and I could have privacy at night. John slept on the couch in the living room, and Jim and Larry had to contend with the cots.

The incident was a standing joke among us and prompted the speculations that by now the hotel personnel might think that Jim was some kind of mob brass. He was not very tall and rather stocky and had checked in using an Italian-sounding name; and with my dark hair and accent, we could easily be mistaken for an Italian family traveling with a nursemaid. John and Larry, both tall and powerfully built, were everybody's image of bodyguards. Fortunately the people in the hotel did not know that the men indeed carried guns in their shoulder holsters. If they had, though, I somehow had the feeling nobody would have been surprised.

We went downstairs in a cheerful mood. Everything was going well; we'd gotten over the first hurdle. The children finished their breakfast quickly and Linda took them upstairs; the four of us stayed, lingering over coffee. We had several days before us with practically nothing to do except take care of some formalities— the final meeting with the Soviet representatives at the State Department, the final papers, and so forth. Now that the tension was over, we could relax.

"You know," Larry said, "I've learned more about you in these past two days than I have in all these months of watching you. But I still have one unresolved question in my mind."

"Go ahead," I said. "Ask your question." I expected something along the lines of "So, after all, why did you decide to stay here?" I was totally unprepared for what came.

"Are you a KGB agent?" he said, deadpan.

"Of course," I replied, keeping an equally straight face. "And you guys are under arrest for kidnapping me and creating an international incident with the purpose of embarrassing the Soviet Union."

The roar that followed made people in the restaurant turn their heads in our direction. Finally Jim managed to say: "Hey, guys, if you don't stop, we will *all* get arrested for public disturbance."

Still laughing, we went back to our room. Larry stopped by the phone to call Washington. When he came upstairs five minutes later, he was not smiling anymore.

"You won't believe it," he said. "He went back to the apartment."

In a few minutes we knew the story. There wasn't much to tell. Lev had left the apartment shortly before ten. He'd driven to the phone booth, gotten out of the car, gone to the booth, stayed there for a couple of minutes as if lost in thought, then returned to the car and driven back to the apartment. I knew that by then he had run a full balance sheet of pros and cons in his head and come up with the conclusion that the pros outweighed the cons. What happened at that last moment I would never know for certain; I could only guess that some emotional thought had overcome all his careful calculations and driven him back: love for his family, fear, or just that mysterious Russian soul that keeps its people emotionally tied to their land.

Suddenly, for the first time I clearly realized the dimensions of my own loss. Not only had I lost my husband and would never see my own family again; I had also lost something of myself, the identity that had been a part of me all my life. I would have to become a different person, with a different name, a person without a country and without a past. Was what was left enough to get me through? Only time would tell. I started to cry.

Wisely, they let me go to my room and cry it out. When I came back, everybody still sat at the table, talking quietly. John handed me a drink.

"Don't think about the past," he said. "Think about the future—yours and the children's. That's what you told me the first time we met—that you wanted a different future. Remember?"

I remembered. Except that I could not stop thinking about the past.

———

Gradually I began to feel more relaxed, though. All the fears that had been on my mind constantly during the past few months slowly started to dissipate. Nobody had found out about my plans; I was safely away from the embassy; my children were with me. I called my mother the very first day and told her that I was staying here permanently, and asked her to take care of the things I had left in her care. I knew she would understand that I meant the money, and that the amount I left her would easily take care of her needs for several years. There wasn't much else I could say—I had to be extremely careful in what I was saying so it could not be used against her later. Lev was going home, and I had to start thinking about myself in terms of being a single mother. It was time to sort things out and to start to plan for the future.

Ironically, my own idea of my future in this new country was fuzzy beyond this point. Other than a general desire to go to business school and eventually to make my own living, I had not contemplated the details of my future life. Perhaps it was because there were so many other things going on that the future seemed too distant and uncertain to plan for; perhaps it was because of the old Russian superstition against planning too much in advance. Whatever the reason, I had to face reality now, and the first thing I learned was that after all the formalities were completed, I would be turned over to the CIA, where a special relocation office would take care of my new identity, a place to live, and job training.

I was very surprised. It did not make sense to me that an agency whose primary purpose is foreign intelligence, rather than a domestic agency such as the FBI, would be undertaking a job search for me. But those were the rules, that was the way the government worked, and, as I knew from my Soviet experience, governments often work in mysterious ways.

Larry reassured me, though, that there would be no abrupt transition, and that some of the FBI people would stay in contact with me until I got used to the CIA people. Meanwhile there was one more formality to take care of—an official meeting with the Soviet representative at the State Department. Such meetings are almost routine, and their main purpose is so the other side can ascertain that its citizen is acting on his or her own free will. I was told that the embassy had requested the meeting but that I did not have to go if I felt it would put too much strain on me. However, John said, the State Department would appreciate it greatly if I agreed, because, like so many other things in the Soviet-American relations, it was a reciprocal agreement, and if I refused, Moscow would have an opportunity to refuse the American embassy a similar privilege sometime in the future when an American citizen was in trouble and needed help. I also wanted to go for my own reasons. The embassy had already filed a protest in which they had said that according to Lev I had been confused and appeared drugged during my last meeting with him, and that he had almost talked me into coming back when the FBI agents had taken me away by force. Whether he'd actually said that, or the protest had been concocted by the embassy, was immaterial: the Soviet Union never admits that any of its citizens would want to leave voluntarily, and the receiving side is always accused of some foul play or coercion. I wanted to set the record straight and also, as much as possible, to leave my husband and my family out of it.

However, I did not particularly look forward to meeting my former compatriots. Although I was taken on a brief tour of the State Department to meet the American who would be present at the meeting and to see the conference room where it would take place, I knew that the embassy would try to put a lot of pressure on me. In such situations it was not uncommon to bring the relatives in from the Soviet Union to make a personal appeal. Although I doubted very much that they would bring my mother, it was possible that Lev would be there, or that the embassy would be represented by one of my close friends. What I needed was reinforcement, and, like many other women, my reinforcement was to dress to kill.

The problem was that most of my clothes were still back in the apartment the FBI had been renting. We'd had enough time to move my things upstairs, but there'd only been so much space in the two cars that had taken us to Fredericksburg. All I had with me was the bare necessities, mostly for the children. I told Larry about my dilemma.

"I need my white linen suit," I said. "I will feel much more comfortable and confident wearing it."

"It's impossible," Larry said. "We can't go even near the building. The KGB is all around the place, Lev is never alone, and I'm sure they are watching the entrance as well. Why can't we just buy you another suit?"

"I do not want another suit," I said. "I never feel comfortable in new clothes." I knew I was being unreasonable, but with all the familiar things around me crumbling by the minute, the suit was the last bastion of comfort I could cling to in a stressful situation. He probably understood how I felt, because the next day the suit was delivered to me. Apparently, Craig, who was relatively new on the force and therefore faced less chance of being recognized, had volunteered to smuggle the suit out of the building.

The meeting was set for Tuesday, the eighth, and there was little we could do but wait. We went to the only movie theater in town; I had some of my favorite tapes with me, and Larry procured a tape recorder somewhere so we could play them. There were some laughs when I played a tape of some music I'd recorded from the radio sometime ago because I'd thought it was pretty—it turned out to be Christmas music, and I wondered how many other American customs I was ignorant of because of my sheltered life in the embassy, and how much more I would have to learn.

I could not make any phone calls in case the listening equipment at the embassy picked up the conversation and traced the call; neither could I visit any of my American friends—they were all known to Lev and their houses could be watched. Since, as I'd requested, there were no press accounts of the incident, officially it had not taken place, and the embassy was free to try to find me and get me back. Everybody was certain that was exactly what they were doing. Larry had even been reluctant to let me call Moscow that first night, but I had been adamant, and since the embassy had not been notified yet, the likelihood had been that even if they had listened to the call on the Soviet side they would not have had enough time to turn around and trace it through the American telephone system.

At least one thing the FBI men learned from me in those several days was how to play canasta, and we passed the time playing cards or, occasionally, Monopoly, which Linda had brought from home.

Finally, Tuesday came, and we went to the State Department. Security was tight—I noticed several FBI cars strategically parked in the streets leading to the State Department; there were probably more I did not notice. We went straight to the underground garage that was off-limits to foreign diplomats, and then to the elevator upstairs. We came about fifteen minutes early so we would already be in the conference room when the Soviet representatives arrived. I was beginning to feel panicky again. The FBI could not be present in the conference room—it was against the rules—but I knew I would feel much better if there were somebody I knew in there with me. Finally, a compromise was worked out: John, who did not work for the FBI, was permitted to stay in the room as an observer, although not at the conference table itself. Just knowing he was there, however, made me feel better.

The two representatives from the Soviet embassy were a man named Kavalerov, the head of the consular section, and a younger man from the consulate whose name I did not know. They did not bring Lev with them, and I wondered briefly if they were afraid he would ask for asylum right there at the meeting. Kavalerov was a portly, soft-spoken, middle-aged man who was well liked in the embassy. He sat across the table from the official interpreter, who sat by my side. The State Department official was at the head of the table; the younger man from the consulate was right across the table from me. I could not see John, who stayed in the chair near the wall behind me.

As soon as Kavalerov started to speak, I understood their game plan. He talked almost nonstop; in the most fatherly manner he told me that nobody held a grudge against me; that I had probably gotten upset over something, but that whatever it was it could be straightened out, and the embassy stood ready to help me with any problems I may have had. The translator was busy translating Kavalerov's speech for the record, and the State Department official, who did not speak Russian, listened to the translation. Meanwhile, the younger man leaned over the table and, with an impassioned face, talked directly to me. He did not have much time: Kavalerov would not talk forever, and soon he would start asking me questions, thus involving me in a dialogue. But in the short ten minutes the younger man had, he packed a big punch.

"Do you really think you can get away with it?" he said. "We'll find you anywhere, provided you do not starve or end up on a street corner first. You think you can spit on us, you spiteful little bitch? You are pathetic. Cold-blooded, too—don't you know what will happen to your parents? Remember, they are still there, and will be there forever. We can do whatever we want with them. And just remember—we never forgive traitors. Sooner or later you will get what you deserve." He called me all the dirty names that existed in the Russian language. Some of them I had never even heard, but it was not difficult to figure out that they were not meant as compliments. It was a typical bad cop-good cop routine, and a brilliant ploy: with Kavalerov keeping the interpreter busy, nobody could catch what the man was saying except me. Finally Kavalerov finished his speech and started asking me questions. I answered most of them and reaffirmed my decision to seek asylum. I also said that I had nothing against the embassy or the country itself; it was a personal decision, and I was not going to make any political statements to the press. To his credit, he never changed the tone of his voice or his manner; when we rose to leave after the meeting, he only said how much he regretted the mistake I was making by ruining my life like this.

"Your main mistake is that you think you know this country," he said. "But you don't. You looked at it through rose-colored glasses from behind the embassy walls. Right now you feel like a hero, because the people around you tell you so. But soon you will be useless to them, and they will throw you out like a used rag. You will never make it here on your own, and this country is not a heaven for people who have no means of supporting themselves. When you find that out, come back, and we will still take you, because Russia is where you belong."

I was disturbed by what he said more than I wanted to admit to myself. I had no idea what my future held; all my assumptions were based on the premise that what John had told me was true, and that they would keep their promise to put me through school. What would I do if they did not keep that promise?

We waited until the Soviet representative left the building and then went back to the car. As we drove out, Larry waved to the other cars; they took off and followed us.

"Boy, you were real cool in there," Larry said. "John told me what was going on. And now let's celebrate."

The "celebration" turned out to be lunch in a fast-food place in McLean. People from the other cars joined us; there were about twenty people there, and I recognized some of them, including the "cabdriver." Everybody was congratulating me, shaking my hands, hugging me. The mood was exuberant: finally it was *officially* over.

Except for one last thing I wanted to do. It was Tuesday, the day of the Aeroflot flight to Moscow, and I knew Lev would be on it. I wanted to say goodbye to him for the last time.

"Go ahead," Larry said. "He is in the office. Just don't let him upset you."

A stranger's voice answered our office number. I was not surprised; I knew Lev would not be alone until he was on the plane to Moscow. I was surprised, though, that they called him to the phone. The conversation was short—everything that could be said had already been said during my calls from Fredericksburg. I also knew he was restrained by the presence of the stranger, who was certainly listening on another extension.

"I just called to say goodbye," I said. He said nothing. "When are you leaving for the airport?"

"In two hours."

"I just finished the meeting at the State Department," I said after a pause. "It's final now."

"Nothing is final." Suddenly he was speaking rapidly. "You could still come back. I was assured there would be no repercussions. We could be on the plane together and forget this whole nightmare."

"No," I said. "I am not coming back."

"What about the children? Did you think about them?"

"Yes. They are one of the reasons I am staying."

"Do you think it is fair for you to deprive them of their father, of their homeland, just because they are too young to speak for themselves?" His voice got more animated. "And what are you going to tell them when they grow up? That their father did not love them and left them?"

"I will tell them that we got a divorce," I said. "Millions of people get divorced; there is nothing unusual about it. And whatever you may think about me, nobody ever accused me of not being a good mother. Besides, it's a free country. When they are old enough to make their own decisions, they may decide to return to the Soviet Union. But at least they will have a choice."

I hung up and went back to the table. I'd already separated myself mentally from him, and the conversation had not upset me. It had simply been a last gesture of goodwill; I felt that our seven years of marriage entitled him to it.

After the lunch most of the FBI people said gooodbye to me, and I realized that for them it was the end of the assignment. They would go on to other things they had to do, and I would start a new stage of my life, of which the FBI would no longer be a part. The thought was slightly disconcerting—in the past few months I'd grown accustomed to the idea that they were always somewhere near, ready to stand by me and protect me from any unpleasant surprises. How would it feel to know that from now on I stood alone? Would the people about to take over be just as nice, as caring, and as protective, as they had been? I thanked them all for everything they'd done for me, and drove back to Fredericksburg with "the Bunch"—Jim, John, and Larry.

It was our last evening in Fredericksburg. We went out for dinner and spent most of the time reminiscing about funny episodes from the past few months, talking about my future and just having a good time. I knew I would miss them tremendously—they'd become almost a family to me, and at that moment there was nobody in this entire country closer to me than those people. I only hoped that they would not fade out of my life like everything else had.

The next morning we packed and left the Sheraton to meet my new hosts—the CIA.

CHAPTER 13

THREE people were waiting for us in the car in the Marriott parking lot: two men and one woman. During brief introductions I learned that the men's names were Paul and George, and the woman's name was Barbara. Both men were in their late forties, medium height; Paul was rather distinguished-looking, with reddish hair and a small mustache, and smoked a pipe; George had dark hair and a slicked-back haircut that I thought had gone out of fashion long ago. His face was not typical for an American, and I later learned that he was indeed a second-generation East European. He was down-to-earth and friendly, while Paul had a more remote look that suggested authority. Barbara was a woman in her late twenties. She was taller than both men, and was apparently aware of her height because she wore flat-heeled shoes.

We returned to our car and followed the CIA car to a residential area in northern Virginia. I'd read enough about defectors to know that the first few months they usually lived in a safe house—a place that was secure and where the defectors were well protected.

My safe house turned out to be an ordinary two-level townhouse, with three bedrooms upstairs and a comfortable living/dining room and a small kitchen downstairs. The woman who met us there had a simple lunch ready for all of us; I learned that she was a house-keeper and was supposed to come daily to do the shopping and cook, but would not stay there overnight.

After lunch, during which there was mostly small talk, Paul outlined the plan my life was to follow for the next several months. Barbara was assigned as my "case officer"; she would take care of all the paperwork, coordinate debriefing activities, schedule my time, and familiarize me with American life. Besides debriefing I would take professional aptitude tests and meet with a job coun-selor to determine what was most suitable for me. She would be with me on a daily basis. George, her supervisor, would take care of the paperwork Barbara prepared for him and see it through channels on the agency level. Paul was the boss; he was not directly involved in day-to-day activites, but if I needed him I could request a meeting and he would come to see me.

The biggest, and most pleasant surprise, was that the Bunch would stay with me for the next couple of weeks. They had to conduct the debriefing anyway, and instead of coming and going every day, they'd volunteered to provide my protection as well. Linda would stay with me most of the time, with John and Larry taking turns in overnight stays. How they'd managed to do that I did not know, but I was certain that it had not come about by itself; they'd figured how lonely I would be without them and wanted to ease me into the new pattern gradually, for which I was eternally grateful.

The meeting went on for about three hours. Finally Paul rose to leave. "I'll leave you with Barbara so you girls could get ac-quainted," he said. "Is there anything you want to ask before I leave?"

"Yes," I said. "I am not used to having somebody cook for me, and the children are used to their own kind of food. I'd rather take care of the household chores myself. It would also feel more like home to me."

Donna, the housekeeper, did not seem particularly pleased, but Paul was unperturbed. "No problem," he said. "Donna will come twice a week to do your shopping. The rest is up to you."

"I'd like to do my own shopping as well," I persisted.

"That might be difficult," Paul said. "Donna only works during normal day hours, and you will be busy during the day. Just give her a list of what you need."

The conversation was clearly over. Paul and George left. Barbara, whose car was parked outside, stayed "to get acquainted," but the conversation did not seem to hold together. She asked a few polite questions that showed she was familiar with my background. Then she told me she would bring Social Security applications the next day and left.

"You did not like her very much, did you?" John asked. As always, he was perceptive. "We did share you psychological profile with the agency, and one of the things on it said that you get along better with men than with women. I don't know why they still decided to assign a women to work with you."

"That's not really true," I protested. "I get along with Linda wonderfully, and I have a lot of women friends."

"Let's agree that it's half true." John laughed. I knew he was right. Although I did have some women friends, there weren't many, and they were generally older professional women who were secure enough in their jobs, their families, and themselves to let other people be themselves. In my life in the States, however, I had discovered a certain category of women for whom I had little tolerance: those who did not know how to handle their newfound liberation and still felt insecure dealing with the world outside of their home; their desire to assert themselves in a position of even minimal power resulted only in their bossing everybody around them, from their husbands to their colleagues. I did find it much easier to work with men who were generally secure enough not to mind my independence. It's not that I was against women building their careers—hardly!—it's just that I preferred to stay out of their way while they were doing it.

Interestingly enough, however, I had encountered that syndrome more often in older women returning to the marketplace after staying at home, and Barbara did not fit that description: she had worked for the agency since she had finished college and belonged to the new generation of women who should have felt less handicapped by past inequalities. It's just that she was . . . sort of cold. I'd found out a long time ago that the Americans were very different from the Russians in regard to their personal "space." The Americans are nice and friendly, but they don't let other people get too close to them. Perhaps it is a result of growing up in spacious houses where each person can have his or her own room and be left alone. The Russians do not have this luxury; they live in close quarters where their life is open to other people. Because of difficult economic conditions, support networks are important, and the Russians normally develop much faster, and deeper, emotional ties to each other. It is also true that in Russia friends are the only source of comfort and advice: there are no ministers, no shrinks, no counselors—and who would trust them anyway if they worked for the State? Therefore relationships between people in Russia are almost by necessity far more personal than they are here. Even in the embassy, with all the restrictions we had, we found true friends with whom we were really close.

Of course it was unfair to compare Barbara to Linda. Linda was "one of the bunch," a totally professional and well-trained FBI agent who at the same time maintained the sincerity and the warmth of a country girl. She was wonderful with children, and had more than once told me about her desire to get married and to have children. I knew she would be a wonderful mother, but at the same time she firmly intended to stay with the bureau, the job she openly loved. She did not call it a "career"—she simply loved what she was doing and intended to continue doing it for a long time, doing the best for her family when the time came. No, I did not have any problems getting along with Linda, and maybe with time, Barbara would turn out to be nice, too.

The next two weeks were uneventful. Barbara showed up every morning with various forms, and set up some appointments for me. Larry and John came every day for a few hours for what they called debriefing. There was little that we had not discussed during our stay in Fredericksburg, but they had to make some official records. The questions revolved mostly about practical details of embassy life and life in the Soviet Union. We usually brought sandwiches from a nearby deli for lunch, and in the early afternoon they left, leaving me with enough time to attend to practical details with Barbara; then one of them returned in the evening. Linda stayed overnight almost all of the time. I could not figure out how she managed to get by with so little sleep—she frequently got calls from her boyfriend sometime after midnight and stayed on the phone for a good hour. From what she told me, I gathered that he was attached to one of the protective services and rarely got home before midnight. By five in the morning she was up and running, always in freshly washed and ironed clothes, her long blond hair always looking as if it had just been done. I wished I had her energy—I seemed to be falling into some kind of relapse after months of high-strung living, and began to suspect that I was developing an ulcer. A visit to a doctor did not reveal anything serious except excessive stress and some heart palpitations, probably related. He prescribed a tranquilizer and told me to avoid worrying. It was good advice but unfortunately hard to follow.

My name was changed from Yelena Mitrokhina to Elena Alexandra Costa, and both my and my children's green cards were issued with our new last name. I told the CIA that I did not want cosmetic surgery, but I did want to change my appearance somewhat. The easiest way was to replace my glasses with contact lenses; I'd always wanted them but they hadn't been available in the Soviet Union. For occasional shopping trips I bought a blond wig, which changed my appearance dramatically. Barbara took me to see her optometrist, and for the first time I got a glimpse of how the agency operated. While we were waiting, the nurse came out and reminded Barbara about her appointment.

"Why did she call you Judy?" I asked Barbara. She seemed embarrassed but quickly recovered her composure. "She got me mixed up with my twin sister," she said. "We look very much alike."

I mentioned the episode to John, and he laughed. "I don't think she has a twin sister," he said. "The truth is, agency people never use their real names dealing with defectors. Too many people go back, and some are simply sent to learn about our procedures and return. It's a reasonable precaution."

"But why couldn't she just tell me that?" I asked. "Certainly I can understand that there are rules and restrictions they have to follow."

"Well, they are just not in the habit of telling people like you anything beyond what is strictly necessary."

"You always answered my questions," I said. "If you couldn't, you just said so, and I did not ask anymore."

"We work differently," he said. "Thank goodness," I added silently.

There was another disturbing thought on my mind that I did not mention to John. Clearly it was prudent on the agency's part to exercise caution this early in the game. But what about later? Would I ever be trusted? Or would the stigma of the person who betrayed her country stay with me forever?

All good times come to an end. In two weeks the FBI debriefing was completed and my friends had to leave. We had a final party and they went back to their jobs. The agency took over.

———————

I did not have much time to feel lonely. After a brief break, the agency started sending their own people for debriefing. They began asking the same questions as the FBI, and I finally called John and asked him why they couldn't share notes rather than repeating the whole thing.

"They like to ask their own questions," he said "Bear with it, it won't last forever."

The agency certainly did things their own way. Two people came to go through my biography, which took several days; two different people came to ask about Moscow life; and so on. Some of them spoke passable Russian, but I preferred to conduct the conversations in English—first because I needed the practice and second because I felt it was less strain on me to speak English than for them to speak Russian, and that way we could accomplish things faster. I especially liked one woman named Anna. Her Russian was fluent, and she was very knowledgeable about Soviet culture and literature. A couple of evenings she stayed on after debriefing and we had long talks; when I complained that I had left all my favorite books in my apartment, she showed up the next day with the best selection of modern Russian literature I'd seen in a long time. She was also well informed on many other areas of Russian life and seemed to be interested in my opinions on a variety of subjects. It was a welcome change from the other people who came and went with their lists of questions from which they never deviated, and I became quite attached to her.

One of my minor problems was that although I had finally insisted on doing my own grocery shopping, I was still rather immobile. I did not have a car, or money, for that matter, because Barbara took me shopping and she paid at the checkout counter. This complete dependence on her began to get to me. Formally I was free; nobody stayed with me overnight anymore. I did not mind staying alone at night—it was a nice break after a long day of talk, and occasionally Larry or John still dropped in after work for a couple of hours' visit. In case of emergency I had a number to call where people would know how to locate Barbara or George. Informally, however, I could not move—without money or a car, I was completely homebound.

Just how precarious the arrangement was became clear during the Labor Day weekend. Everybody was off; there was no work scheduled. Barbara left late Friday afternoon to go out of town with her fiancé. I faced a long, long weekend.

Friday evening and Saturday went by without incident, but by Sunday afternoon I found myself running low on milk and diapers. I'd never had a habit of stocking up on things, because the nearest supermarket had been only a few minutes away, and that habit backfired now. I also began to feel lonely. It was the first time I'd been completely alone for more than a day since the day of the defection. Everybody was having a holiday; everybody was having fun going to picnics and visiting friends. I missed my friends, both Russian and American. I'd been told not to make acquaintance with my neighbors next door so they would not get curious about my accent and start asking questions I could not answer, and I still was not permitted to call my American acquaintances I'd known before the defection. Was this the way I was going to spend my future life, hiding from everybody? The future looked bleak and hopeless, and it felt like the debriefing was never going to end. What was I doing here, anyway?

Perhaps I would have come up wth a surprising answer if I had spent another day alone. Fortunately I did not get that chance. Linda called to say hello, and when I mentioned that I was alone and needed groceries, she came over within half an hour. She stayed through the evening and managed to cheer me out of my silly thoughts; Larry stopped by for a couple of hours the next day, and by the end of the weekend I was wondering why I had become depressed in the first place.

Anna was furious when I told her about my weekend. "That's how we lose people," she said. "Everybody gets depressed after a while, practically without exception; the only difference is the time it takes to get to that point. You should not have been left alone, and it's amazing you did not turn to the embassy in that state of mind. Quite a few people do, you know." She told me about Victor Belenko, a former Soviet Air Force officer who, after almost a year here, had become so homesick while traveling cross-country that he had driven back almost nonstop for two days and almost ended on the doorstep of the Soviet embassy. Fortunately he'd stopped to see his former case officer first and talked things over. He was still living happily in this country now.

"The embassy is almost ten miles away and I don't even have a stroller," I joked. The crisis was over. I had not really considered going back—even if I had not ended up in jail after returning home, I had no illusions about my future and the fact that I would be declared an unfit mother and my children taken away from me. No, whatever I was facing here—the reality was not quite what I had expected—I would have to cope with it the best I could. There was no way back.

Anna was a senior officer and she apparently voiced her disapproval; so did Larry. The next time I saw Barbara, she was tight-lipped and colder than usual. I knew by then that it was her first assignment with the relocation office; before that she had had mostly secretarial jobs in foreign missions, and this was supposed to be a promotion. Now, apparently, she felt that I was blowing her chances for career advancement.

"I want to talk to you about a few things," she said. "I've been getting a lot of feedback about your complaints, and I want you to know my point of view. I am trying to prepare you to stand on your own two feet when you leave here. People can grow so dependent on us that they don't know how to handle their lives after they leave, and what I am trying to do is really in your best interest. You are already too dependent on the FBI, and they continue to foster it."

"I'll be happy to stand on my own two feet as soon as you get me a car and some money," I countered. "I did not just run away from a tourist delegation, you know. I lived in this country for three years, and although there are obviously some things I don't know, driving a car and grocery shopping do not fall into that category."

"We have our policies," she said. "You'll have a car when the time comes."

"I can understand that," I said. "But then perhaps we'd better leave the building of my self-reliance until such time when I have the physical means of being self-reliant."

I could see that she disagreed, but it was pointless to continue the conversation. Somebody else, apparently, disagreed with her as well, because a week later I had a car and a weekly allowance of $100 to spend as I saw fit. I was asked to exercise discretion, but other than that I was free to go where I wanted.

Barbara continued doing her job, and I went on with the debriefings. A couple of times a pleasant young man came to give me IQ and job aptitude tests. Having come from a social sciences background myself, I was interested in the testing procedures, and we had a lively discussion about the methods used in both countries. A week later he came back with the results.

"Congratulations," he said. "You did extremely well. You certainly have very high aptitude for managerial jobs, although you also have a very good potential for jobs related to dealing with people." He named a few possibilities: credit manager, teacher, customer service. "You told me you were planning to go to a business school," he said. "I think it's a very good idea."

Encouraged, I brought up the topic with Paul. "We will probably be all done in a month or so," I said. "I have plenty of time in the evenings, and I would like to start getting ready for the exams.

Barbara told me there is a Graduate Management Aptitude Test I need to take in order to apply to a graduate school, and if I get to it fast, I may be able to start in the winter semester."

"We'll get you together with a specialist on graduate schools who will suggest some schools suitable for you," Paul said. "Meanwhile I'll arrange for GMAT materials to be brought to you."

"I know where I want to go," I said. "I want to go to Wharton." Against the rules, I had talked to one of my old acquaintances on the phone and had asked her for the names of some good business schools. The Wharton School of Business at the University of Pennsylvania had been one of them, and, unlike Stanford and Harvard, the other two schools she had mentioned, it was within driving distance of Washington. That factor was important—the prospect of being all alone in a strange city scared me, and I knew I would feel better if I could get to my friends in Washington within hours if I needed to.

"Well, that's just one possibility," he said. "I still think you should talk to our consultant. He may suggest some other schools you have not thought about."

I had nothing against talking to a specialist; meanwhile the materials arrived and I started studying. I immediately realized that it would take awhile: there were many math questions, and I had had no math since high school. There was nothing beyond my comprehension in the test, but I needed to refresh my memory and to practice a lot. The debriefings were tedious, but did not require a tremendous mental effort, and I was glad I had something interesting to do.

———

Everything was going smoothly for a couple of weeks until an ugly incident blew my quiet life apart.

One day Barbara asked me if I would mind talking to a couple of social scientists who were particularly interested in Soviet psychology. Although I was never involved in a pure psychological research, sociology is closely related to social psychology, and a talk with colleagues was a welcome and pleasant diversion from the monotony of my life.

Next day she arrived with a man. Apparently they'd come in separate cars and just met outside, because they did not seem to know each other. That was not unusual—Barbara was in charge of scheduling my time, and sometimes she arranged for meetings with people from different departments whom she did not know personally.

"Where is the other person?" I asked.

She seemed to be confused. "You said there would be a man and a woman," I reminded her.

"Oh, yes," she said. "The other person is not coming. Well, I am going to leave you alone so you can chat." And she left.

We sat down at the coffee table. I offered the man a drink, which he refused. He also refused tea and coffee.

"I am a Mormon," he said, looking disapprovingly as I poured myself a cup of coffee and lit a cigarette. Seeing my incomprehension, he explained that his religion did not permit drinking anything that contained addictive substances and did not approve of smoking.

"Well, as long as you are not personally allergic to smoking, I will smoke," I said. "If the smoke bothers you, I can move to another side of the table."

He said he did not mind and started asking me questions and scribbling his notes in a notepad. As we progressed with our interview, I was getting more and more puzzled by his questions. They were all personal: Did I love my mother? Did I ever feel an urge to compete with my mother? Whom did I love more: my mother or my father? Did I ever resent it that my father paid more attention to my mother than to me, and did I feel that he did not love me enough because of that? Finally I interrupted him.

"I don't understand what my feelings about my parents have to do with the state of Soviet psychology. Whose business is it whether I ever tried to compete with my mother, anyway?"

Now it was his turn to look puzzled. "It *is* my business," he said. "I am a psychiatrist."

"But," I said, "Barbara told me that you were my colleague interested in Soviet psychological research."

"I don't know what she told you. I met her for the first time outside of this door. But a psychiatric evaluation of defectors is a standard agency procedure, and that's what I was sent to do."

"Well, you are going to have a short working day today. The interview is over."

He left without saying goodbye, and I went straight to the phone and dialed Larry's number. "I am not going to take any more of this," I said flatly. "What did you get me into?"

"Wait a minute, cool down," he said. "What happened?"

Almost in tears, I explained what had happened. "Look, I've always cooperated with all requests. If there is such a procedure, then it has to be done. I just don't want to be treated like a child. Why does she always have to do things behind my back? Why can't she stop lying and level with me?"

He listened patiently to my outburst. "She is just an inexperienced and not very bright woman," he finally said. "I was not very happy with that choice to begin with."

"I don't want to be her training ground for gaining experience. Let her experiment on somebody else. Why doesn't she go back to shuffling papers where she can't hurt anybody? Anyway, if she walks in here again, I'll walk out."

"Now, don't be silly," Larry said. "I know you are upset, but things can be worked out. The agency is doing a good job, and you cannot blame the mistakes of one person on the entire organization."

I knew he was right. The other people from the agency were mostly nice and helpful. It's just that Barbara was the one who held the most control over my day-to-day life.

"I'll call you later," Larry said.

I did not see Barbara for three weeks. George stopped by a couple of times to get my signature on some papers and to verify the translation of my diploma. Anna continued her work with me. Then Barbara reappeared, but not alone. With her was a man who would almost singlehandedly change the course of my life.

———

Ian was a godsend. He was an easygoing man, about my age, with a mop of curly hair and quicksilver dark eyes, and seemed constantly to be in motion. He had been asked to give Barbara a hand, he explained, because she was swamped with paperwork and he had more time now than she did. Within days he set things in motion. A long promised consultation with an educational specialist suddenly materialized, a date for a GMAT was set. He spent a couple of days with me going over some difficult math problems that were still a stumbling block because I did not have any textbooks, and went through several dry runs of the GMAT with me. He also got permission to invite me to his home to meet his family. It was the end of October, and I was invited to bring the children for trick-or-treating. I had no idea what Halloween was, but jumped at the opportunity to go out. It was the first time I had spent an evening outside of the safe house.

We had a wonderful time. Ian's son, Mark, was about Kitty's age and spoke a little Russian he had learned from his father. Ian's own Russian was a bit rusty but passable; he explained that he had not used it for several years. Mark and Kitty got along immediately. Konstantin was still too young to go out, and Ian, dressed as Dracula, took Mark and Kitty—for whom we improvised a costume on the spot—for a long walk, while I stayed in the house with Konstantin and Ian's wife, Charlotte. When Ian showed up with the children an hour later, Charlotte and I were still engrossed in a conversation about movies; she was an even greater movie buff than I. But most important was the feeling of warmth in their house; of how welcome we were to participate in their family activities and family fun. I no longer felt isolated from the rest of the world; I was becoming a part of it.

It was years before I found out how Ian had gotten to work on my case and how much influence he had exerted over my future. He was not even a part of the relocation office, but dropped in there once in a while because of his interest in people and to break away from his other duties. On one of those visits he'd happened to pass Barbara's desk and seen the psychiatrist's evaluation of me, ready to be sent to other officials in the office.

He'd never met me, although he knew about my existence. It was not my name that attracted him to the report, but a few sentences that caught his attention. After turning the page, he picked up the report and went to George. "Something's wrong here," he said. "Nobody's *that* bad." The report described me as a mentally disturbed self-absorbed narcissist, almost a sociopath. George explained the tricky situation that had developed between me and Barbara, and Ian volunteered to take over the case.

Even now, so many years later, I tremble when I think what would have happened if Ian had not stopped by that desk at that particular time. I'd like to think that sooner or later common sense would have prevailed and somebody would have ordered a reevaluation, but even under the best of circumstances it would have been at the cost of tremendous mental anguish to me. Under the worst circumstances, somebody could have used that report as a basis for future action, and I would have been finished.

Even with Ian's interference, the reverberations from the report apparently reached some quarters. In the middle of October, Paul and George arrived to have a meeting with me. After about an hour of general chitchat, Paul got to the point.

"Your debriefing is over," he said, "and it's time to move on to your own life. We have carefully considered your tests; you did quite well, and all the tests show a high degree of aptitude for executive positions. Therefore we decided to send you to a good secretarial school. You can start in January, and in two years we'll find you a nice job as an executive secretary and you'll be on your own."

I was too stunned to speak. Finally, just to say something, I forced out, "Making what?"

"Oh, sixteen, maybe eighteen thousand," Paul said. "Of course we will supplement your income so you will have a decent standard of living."

Finally they left. I sat at the table where they left me, and suddenly started to cry so violently that Kitty ran over to me, scared. The darkest of thoughts went through my mind. All these months of danger; of walking away from my comfortable life with the silly notion that I could be something on my own, shape my own life; of leaving my mother without a chance of seeing her grandchildren ever again; all of that—and for what? To learn typing and to stay on government welfare for the rest of my life?

Suddenly I wished I had never run away from the embassy. I wanted to be back in Moscow, among my friends, with the people who loved me.

No, that was all wrong. I *had* friends here. They could not, would not, let me down.

I looked at my watch. It was not yet six. I picked up the phone and dialed Larry's number. He was still in the office. He listened silently to my recital and then said, "I'll call you tomorrow."

Somehow I had to get through the night. I busied myself with the children and then, about an hour later, I heard a knock on the door. It was Linda.

"Guess what?" she said. "My boyfriend is out of town and I developed this sudden craving for Chinese food, so I took a carry-out and invite you to be my guest for dinner tonight. By the way, do you mind if I stay overnight?"

Before ten the next morning, Larry called me. It was the shortest conversation of my life.

"Forget what happened yesterday," he said. "You are going to Wharton."

Larry had simply taken the matter to his boss in the Washington field office.

"Our credibility is at stake," he'd said. "The business school is the only thing Elena asked for, and we promised her that. She is the first defector from the Soviet Embassy here in forty years. If we go back on our word now, we won't see another defector coming out of there for another forty years."

Apparently his boss had agreed and had taken some immediate action, so Larry had felt confident enough to call me with the news. Not that the CIA decision about me had been adopted unanimously, either. There had been dissent on the committee that discussed my future, Ian being the most vocal opponent of the secretarial school. The basic argument of the proponents had been that with two toddlers on my hands I would never make it through the masters program. Barbara had openly called me "the FBI pet" and contended that my abilities were grossly overrated.

"At least let her try," argued Ian. "She's got better scores on the tests than any other defector that's come out of the Eastern Bloc in the past fifteen years. That school is almost an obsession with her, and she is a very determined woman. If she fails, we can always send her to secretarial school, and by then she'll agree with us."

My supporters had been overruled, but by a small margin, and the pressure from the FBI had tilted the scale in my favor.

The problem was, it was already November. Within a week my documents were prepared and sent to Philadelphia and two weeks later, I went there to see the school. I also visited Temple and Drexel universities as possible alternatives. I did not like Temple. Though Drexel was impressive, it required that all undergraduate courses be taken before enrollment in the masters program. Only some of the courses I'd taken in Leningrad could be credited toward the program. Simple arithmetic showed that I would need two years to complete an undergraduate program before I could even start working on my masters degree.

I went to see the dean of admissions at Wharton with trepidation. If Drexel had presented such a problem, what would they tell me in one of the top three business schools in the country? To my surprise the dean said that I could be accepted.

"We have a different approach here at Wharton," he said. "Our masters program is very concentrated, but it is designed for people who don't have an undergraduate education in business. Two-thirds of our students have liberal arts or technical background, and most come to us after years of experience in the industry. We are also proud to be a truly international school. Although we do not have an official student exchange with the Soviet Union, your background will complement well our student body." I'd already noticed the gallery of national flags on the ground floor; I'd tried to count them while waiting for the interview, but lost count after thirty. The Soviet flag had not been among them.

He went on to say that although my GMAT score was slightly below the cutoff score necessary for acceptance, my background and the essays I had written for admission were impressive, and they would gladly accept me. It was too late for the winter semester, though—they enrolled only about a hundred students in the winter and all the vacancies were filled. I could start the school next September. Meanwhile, he suggested, I could take two mandatory noncredit courses, calculus and computer programming, during the winter semester, to ease the burden later in the fall. He also suggested that a beginning accounting class in the undergraduate school would be helpful.

Walking on air, I returned to Washington after spending two more days in Philadelphia finding an apartment. There wasn't much to do now. The CIA had finished the debriefing and left me alone. Nobody came to my townhouse anymore except for an occasional visit from Anna, Ian, or the Bunch. I decided to visit my friends from "the previous life" before I'd left Washington—it was unlikely that the embassy was still actively looking for me, at least to the point of watching my friends' houses. There were two people I wanted to visit. One was Ben, an American publisher with whom we had done a lot of business and in whose home we had spent many weekends. His office had been in the same building as ours, and we were very close friends. The other was Sunny, a statuesque Chinese lady whom I had met at a diplomatic reception a couple of years before and with whom I had become very friendly. She'd given me a baby shower when I was expecting Konstantin—a custom I did not know about—and was always very helpful and understanding. I told Larry about my plans.

"I have bad news for you," he said. "Ben does not want to see you. His business depends too much on good relations with VAAP and he does not want to take any chances. As for Sunny, I don't trust her."

"Why?"

"Because she refused to cooperate with us."

"Good," I said. "That means she is really my friend. I am going."

The news about Ben was a blow. I could understand his reasons, but it was still a great disappointment. He and his wife had been very close to us while we were at the embassy, and I'd been hoping that they would be among the very few friends I had left in starting my new life. I also had a foreboding that he would not be the only

American who would find my background unsuitable for future relationships. To check my suspicions, I called another publisher in New York who'd also had substantial dealings with the Soviet Union. His wife was Russian; she'd been in a labor camp in Germany when the war ended in 1945, and, thinking that her family in Russia had perished, had moved to America instead of returning home. A conversation with Robert made me feel better.

"They can take their business and —— it for all I care," he said. "We are losing money on it, anyway. You did a great thing, and both Marina and I are very proud of you. We want to see you in New York, and if you need anything, just call."

He also told me that the reaction in the publishing community had been muted. Most people with whom we had dealt regularly knew about Lev's abrupt departure and the closing of the VAAP office, but he had not heard any comments. The representative of International Book had temporarily taken over our duties. I knew better than that. Anyone who replaced Lev would be an intelligence operative. With his cover blown, he would be useless here. In fact, VAAP never reopened its office in Washington.

The last two weeks in Washington were mostly spent going through the final formalities with the CIA. My legend—my new "personal history"—was worked out. To keep it simple, I was to tell everybody I was an emigré from the Soviet Union. The agency also provided a previous address for reference and inquiries, and a business card with an address and the telephone number in California to account for the three years of my previous job experience, should anybody want to check my background. I was also told that my living allowance would be twelve thousand dollars a year. The agency would also pay for the school, day care for the children, and my medical insurance.

The amount was less than I had thought. Ian had told me the living allowance was usually based on the person's previous standard of living, and I had expected something between twenty-five and thirty thousand a year. He could not figure it out himself. The only explanation, he suggested, was that the agency had started with that amount and then deducted the cost of my school and day care from it. Anyway, money was the last thing I wanted to argue about; I was too happy about going to school, and I had some small savings which I could use in an emergency.

I spent my first American Christmas with Ian and his family. Russians do not celebrate Christmas, but they celebrate the New Year's in much the same manner: there is a Yule tree, Father Frost—who looks remarkably close to Santa—and gifts under the tree. All embassy people had trees for the New Year, but we never had to pay for them. Since the important date was New Year's Eve, we usually went to the tree lots late on Christmas Eve or on Christmas Day. By then the lots were closed and we could pick up the unsold trees for nothing.

We had a big farewell party the day before New Year's Eve. All the members of the Bunch were there, as well as the CIA people who had worked closely with me. I offered to cook Russian specialties, but Barbara said that with all the packing I had to do, it would be easier to arrange for some deli salads and platters. I did not argue; I had already cooked quite a few dinners for the Bunch and did not have to prove myself as a chef again.

Close to the end of the party, Barbara told me she wanted to talk to me. We went to the bedroom where we could be alone.

"I want to tell you that despite some misunderstandings, I do not have any hard feelings and I wish you all the best," she said. She went through some of the incidents we'd had, reiterating her point of view. "Although you did not like the way I did things, one day you will understand that I was right," she continued. "People like you come here with exaggerated expectations, and since your FBI friends preferred to keep you happy, it was my task to bring you closer to reality. You think you know enough about living in this country, but you do not. You still have a lot to learn, even such simple things as how to keep a house in an American way. For instance, last time you cooked dinner for your FBI friends, Larry got so sick that he missed a day at work. They did not tell you about it because they did not want to disappoint you, but somebody has to tell you the truth."

So that's why she'd insisted on the deli takeout!

I knew about the incident. The dinner in question had consisted of specialty foods from Soviet Georgia. Its cuisine is close to the

Mediterranean, and rather spicy. Larry, a basic meat-and-potatoes man, had gotten an upset stomach, which had been reported to me the very next day. Nobody else had gotten sick, but since then I'd tried to avoid exotic dishes when entertaining my friends.

"I appreciate your advice," I said. "And since you are honest with me, I will level with you, too. It is true that there are many things here that I still have to learn. But you don't teach adult people by treating them like children. If you'd treated me as another adult, there probably would be no need for this conversation now. I hope you will keep it in mind when you start working on a new case. Meanwhile I wish you well, too."

Neither of us knew at that time that there would be no new cases for her to work on. She was transferred from the relocation office back to her previous duties.

I returned to the party, which continued well past midnight. Three days later Larry and Jim drove me to Philadelphia: a new person with a new name and a new life.

CHAPTER 14

*B*ARBARA was right about at least one thing—I had a distorted view of American reality. My life at the embassy had been more sheltered than I had realized. I had not had to deal with such major issues as health care, insurance, and taxes. I also had not learned how to live on a shoestring.

The first realization that I would not make it financially came with the first check. About 20 percent had been withheld for taxes. I sat there, staring at the check—the amount was only thirty dollars more than Lev and I had been paid together, with the rent, the car, and medical care already taken care of by the embassy. Now I had to pay for everything myself and still manage to feed and clothe myself and the children.

I'd rented an apartment in the suburbs because accommodations on the campus were far more expensive, and because I was scared to live in the city. I had visions of street crime and filth, and I knew I would not dare let the children out on the street. The apartment complex where I lived was in Devon, about twenty miles from Philadelphia. There were large lawn areas between the buildings, where children could play, and although the apartment was not as good as the one I had had in Arlington, let alone Chevy

Chase, it was well maintained. What I saved on rent, though, was nullified by increased transportation expenses because of the commuting distance. It did not take me long to discover that I had about three hundred dollars left in the budget after rent, utilities, and car expenses were paid. For the first time I regretted that I had sold so many of my clothes trying to raise money in Moscow: it did not look like I would have an opportunity to replenish my wardrobe for some time to come. I did not even have a winter coat.

There were still two weeks left before the start of classes. I found a day-care center that was on my way to the city. Actually, I did not have much choice—almost all the centers I called did not accept children under three, and Konstantin was only two—but even if I had had a choice, I probably would have chosen this one. It was located on the grounds of a large Catholic monastery, but was not affiliated with the Church. The school had an excellent reputation, and the children were well cared for.

I also followed Sunny's advice and got myself a life insurance policy. Given my precarious past and uncertain future, it seemed a prudent thing to do. The rental office gave me the name of an insurance agent. I did not know that I could get term life—the first-year payment on a vested life policy and the minimal furnishings I had to buy for the apartment took almost all my savings, leaving me without any emergency reserve.

Getting the insurance was the first in a series of incidents that showed me what a sloppy job someone in the CIA had done with my paperwork. Several days after I filled out the application, the agent came to see me.

"I have a problem," he said. "I have to verify your income, but no matter how I tried, I cannot find a trace of the company in California for which you worked. The income verification form I sent to them was returned by the post office, and the phone number you gave me does not answer. Perhaps you gave me a wrong number by mistake. I wanted to talk to you before I turned your application down."

"I'll try to get in touch with them myself," I said. "I'll call you later. Thank you for the trouble you took to come here and tell me about it."

I called Al, my CIA contact in Philadelphia, and told him about the incident. A week later he told me that everything was straightened out. I called the agent and asked him to mail another form. This time it came back properly filled out and I got my insurance.

My next problem was the medical insurance. The children developed a cold, and I took them to a doctor. When I sent the bill for reimbursement to the insurance company, it was promptly returned to me with a letter pointing out that my policy had a rider that excluded office visits from coverage. This time my call to Al was not so polite.

"What am I supposed to do with this policy? All I have with children of this age is office visits. Or was it purchased just to cover my hospital stay when I get a heart attack discovering your little surprises?"

Again he had to contact Washington. Nothing could be resolved in the Philadelphia office; Al had to forward a request about even minor things to George and his people and wait for a reply.

The icing on the cake came, however, when I went on my first date. The young man was delighted to hear that I was from Russia; he'd met some other people who had recently emigrated from the Soviet Union and found their tales fascinating.

"Which relocation center did you go through, Vienna or Rome?" he asked.

I did not know what to answer. Nobody in Washington had briefed me on the emigration procedures people who leave the Soviet Union normally had to go through. I had no idea even what a relocation center was. So much for my legend.

I pleaded a headache and went home. Was there anything the CIA had prepared for me that I could rely on? So far nothing had worked. I decided to devise my own legend. I was going to tell people that I had married an American scholar in Moscow on a scientific exchange. I had had some friends in Moscow who'd married foreigners, and I knew that they did not have to go through normal emigration channels. Then we'd separated, the story would go, and he was now living in Europe. I could explain Kitty's shaky English by saying that as long as my husband had been here, we'd spoken Russian in the family. It was still shaky, but would satisfy cursory curiosity.

The problem persisted, however. Because of my accent, total strangers opened conversations with me with the question, "Where are you from?" The moment I said I was from Russia, the response almost invariably was, "Oh, really? I never met anybody from Russia before. How did you get here?" A few times I pointed out that, in a way, an accent was a handicap, and would they walk up to someone in a wheelchair and ask how the person lost a leg? This just left people with hurt feelings, though, and mumbling, "I just wanted to be friendly!" In other instances, people who knew other Russians immediately offered to introduce me to my former compatriots, assuming that I wanted to have the company of people who spoke my native tongue. I could not explain that a Russian emigré community, heavily infiltrated by the KGB, was the last place I wanted to be. For a while I resorted to joking by saying that I had swum across the ocean, but finally, exasperated, I decided that my only way out was to hide the fact that I was a Russian altogether. My accent was not typically Russian; only people trained in linguistics could identify it correctly. Perhaps it was because I had studied Norwegian and had been fluent in it before studying English.

In any case, for most people my accent was simply an accent. With my Spanish-sounding name and Mediterranean looks, which I had inherited from my Greek ancestors, I could easily pass for a Latin American. I did not speak Spanish, which ruled out naming a Spanish-speaking country as my point of origin—too many people had tried to speak Spanish to me already just because of my last name. Finally I hit the jackpot. I decided I would pass myself off as a Portuguese. A Portuguese accent is very different from Spanish, and is not unlike a Russian accent. More importantly, most people had no interest in Portugal, assuming they even knew where it was. The ploy worked—in all these years I have never met anybody who spoke Portuguese and could call my bluff, and the moment I said "Portugal," all further interest waned and there were no questions.

Studying in an American college was a fascinating experience totally unlike anything with which I had been familiar in Russia.

I was not enrolled in a regular program yet, and so did not have to cope with the phenomenon of actually getting to decide which courses to take and which instructors to choose—just dealing with midterm exams, partial credits, and the grading curve was baffling enough.

The Soviet system of higher education is entirely different from the American one. First of all, specialization is chosen at the time of enrollment. All the courses within that specialization are pre-determined, mandatory, and the schedule is preset for all five years of study. My major was in philology, with a concentration in the Norwegian language. General lectures required for all students— Marxist philosophy, history of the Communist Party, history of Western literature, and so forth—are spread over the first three years of study. They are conducted before the entire class of several hundred students and delivered as lectures, with very little or no class discussion at all. The only homework required is assigned reading, but if the student falls behind, nobody would know because it is not discussed in class. Many times I crash-studied for exams, reading the textbooks assigned for the whole year in the last three days before the exam. Language studies, of course, were different. Although common international languages such as English, French, and German had large enrollments and could have as many as twenty students in a group, in languages such as Norwegian the enrollment was limited to five students a year. In such a small group, the study was intensive and homework was assigned every day and had to be done on time.

Although courses that take more than one semester have a mid-term exam, it is not graded, does not affect the grade in a final exam, and basically serves as a checkpoint that the student is familiar with the material covered so far. The examination process is completely different. Practically all exams are oral, and no books are permitted; all material has to be memorized, including the quotes from the Marxist classics. There are always two instructors conducting an exam to prevent subjectivism and favoritism. Student lists are put on bulletin boards indicating on what day and approximately at what time they should show up for an exam. The students are called into an examination room in small groups, given several questions, usually covering a fairly large topic, plus paper and pencils, and about half an hour to prepare. Notes written during that preparation time may be used as an aid in an exam, and that's where the students resort to all kind of tricks to help themselves.

Since no books are permitted in the examination room, and the volume of material that must be memorized is immense, most students prepare little memos covering the important factual points of the material, such as dates and events. These memos, nicknamed "spurs," are written in dense handwriting on thin paper, folded or rolled together, and concealed somewhere in the clothing. Female students clearly have an advantage in that respect. Spurs can be hidden in the girdle, in sleeves, and even in a hairdo. Most Soviet classrooms use regular tables and chairs, and whatever is under the table is usually hidden from the instructor's view. It is also critical not to be among the first ones to enter the examination room. Once the instructors start the exam, the next batch of students ushered in for preparation have the advantage in that the instructors are busy interviewing the previous batch and are not able to watch the preparation tables closely.

After reading the questions and locating the necessary spur, all I had to do was to roll it out and place it under my stocking—pantyhose did not make its way to Russia until very recently, and for that purpose it would have been a clear disadvantage anyway. After that, everything was easy. While pretending to concentrate on writing my notes, all I had to do was pull up my skirt, read the spur firmly held in place by a transparent stocking, and copy the contents to the officially supplied note paper. In case the instructor got up and walked around the room, the skirt was pulled back in place, hiding the signs of the crime.

Some women were so bold that they brought entire textbooks in their girdles. Men had a harder time finding hiding places; their favorite ploy was to attach spurs to rubber bands pulled through their sleeves, much like mittens are attached to children's coats. The spur could be then pulled out of the sleeve for reading, and in case of unwelcome attention, let go and retract into the sleeve.

The grade for the exam in pronounced before the student leaves the room and is based on the completeness of the answers. No relative grading is done: either you know the material or you don't. Therefore, unlike the American system of percentiles, the entire class can have a grade of excellent or the entire class can conceivably fail.

It did not take me long to appreciate the American system that tested understanding of the subject rather than the memory of the student. During my first midterm I was very nervous. The multiple response system was easier to handle than the Soviet system of constructing the whole answer from your head, but I knew I did not answer some of the questions, and was very surprised when I got a good grade. That's when the instructor explained to me the system of grading on a curve.

Accounting presented no problems—I had done the bookkeeping for our VAAP office and was familiar with the principle of the double entry. It was the other two courses—calculus and computer programming—that seemed to present insurmountable obstacles.

I was good at math in high school; in fact, my math teacher was very disappointed that I chose to go into liberal arts, saying that it was a waste of my brain. However, although it was not unusual for a woman in the Soviet Union to go to an engineering college, it was considered "unfeminine" and I did not relish the prospect of ending up as a shift supervisor at some factory far away from Leningrad. Foreign languages had a certain glamour, and with such a rare specialty as Norwegian, I was almost guaranteed a job in a major city—in the tourist bureau, the airlines, the merchant marine, or possibly in broadcasting. However, although math teaching in the Soviet high schools is thorough, calculus is not a part of the curriculum until college.

With the help of several individual sessions with the instructor, I got on track in calculus. It was computer programming that left me completely baffled. No matter how hard I tried, the meaning of what I was doing seemed to evade me.

Both courses were noncredit prerequisites for the masters program, because calculus was necessary for the courses in economics, and computer programming was required in order to be able to do the classwork in many of the financial courses. The school had a DEC-20 mainframe computer, and the language we were required to learn was APL. I did not know until much later that even among the programmers APL was considered to be one of the most complex, symbolic high-level languages and was used only by professionals. It was not something you'd use on a home computer.

The course was driving me to distraction. I could not understand the concepts; I could not figure out why the programs I copied from the book worked, and why every command I typed seemed to elicit only question marks from the computer, or worse, a message along the lines of "What do you think you are doing?" The whiz kids at the computer center had programmed it to recognize the most common mistakes and to respond with the one-liners. After hours of futile attempts to get something out of that machine, I was desperate, and those messages only added insult to injury. Most of the time my overwhelming desire was to kick the terminal, yell "Why don't you shut up!" and walk out of there. It seemed I would never understand what was going on behind that screen.

That lasted almost eight weeks. I was the most frequent visitor to our instructor's after-class hours and became almost a fixture at his desk. And then something happened. I could not pinpoint an exact moment in time, or an exact event, but all of a sudden everything became absolutely clear to me. I understood the logic of computer thinking, and the most important law of dealing with them: you cannot make a computer think like a human being— you have to learn to think in its terms, which is nothing more or less than straightforward, ruthless logic. Like many people coming from a background in liberal arts, I had been trained in intuitive thinking, in dealing with concepts that could not always be defined, in taking into account the imprecise human side of events. All of that had to go. Computers do not tolerate ambiguity. In a way, they are like children: the fewer choices you give them, the better you can get them to obey you. It has nothing to do with math or the formulas, just logic.

It was a personal triumph when I wrote a short program that ran from beginning to end and actually produced the same result that I had calculated by hand. It was also then that I found the love of my life—the computer. Although I did not have to use it very often after I'd started the core masters program, my warm feeling for this beautiful machine stayed, and eventually I came back to it.

———

Other than the struggles and the little triumphs of my classwork, my life was not much to cheer about. My children were still very young—two and four. Outside of day care, I could not afford a babysitter, which effectively cut off my social life. I dropped the children off at their school in the morning and drove to my school. I scheduled my classes to fall between ten in the morning and four-thirty in the afternoon. By five-thirty, I picked up the children, came home, and stayed there. I had not made any friends in school yet and could not participate in the after-school activities because they usually started in the late afternoon when I always had to leave and rush home.

The students were basically divided into two groups: those who'd come right after college and those closer to my age. I simply did not fit with the first group: they were too young. The members of the second group had come to continue their education after years of working; most of them had families, and they went home after school, like myself. I also was constantly haunted by money problems. Even a small outing could make a large dent in my budget. I was beginning to look shabby—I had few clothes, constant wear was beginning to show, and replacement was out of the question.

The most important factor in my reluctance to go out and make friends, however, was that I did not have much to talk about. Being a defector is even worse than suffering from amnesia. You know what your past is, but you cannot talk about it; it is as if it doesn't exist. Following the legend meant constant lying and trying to remember what I said to whom; besides, I could not use it in school, where it was known that I was Russian. Until then I never realized how important the past is in our daily lives: when people meet, the common way to build a conversation is to find out where you grew up, where you went to school, what your life was like. Without that, what do you talk about—classwork? Discuss *The Wall Street Journal*? It worked in school, but not in my personal life. Very few people start conversation on a date by discussing the stock market. Ninety percent of all personal questions were ones I could not answer without sinking deeper into lies, and finally I stopped trying.

I hated to ask the CIA for more money, but finally I had to swallow my pride and presented Al with my budget which, even cut to the bone, could not possibly be covered by my monthly allowance. The first few months I supplemented it with whatever was left of my savings, but there wasn't anything left by now. Finally the agency agreed to increase my allowance by $200 a month, which brought my after-tax income to $960 a month. It was enough to cover the rent, the car, and food and clothes for the children.

Finally spring came. I passed all my exams—nothing spectacular, but at least I did not fail. Now I had a whole summer—and not much to do. I decided to take a job and make some money to supplement my income and to take care of emergencies should they arise.

Mindful of the snafu I had had with the insurance company, I decided not to take chances applying for a job by myself. Instead, I asked Al if he could help me. I needed a job with flexible hours and, most important, it had to be something I could continue to do on a part-time basis after school had started in the fall. I also wanted a job in which compensation was tied to results rather than a straight hourly rate. I figured that with some extra effort I could make money that way.

The obvious possibility was to find a sales job. The opportunity that presented itself exceeded all my expectations. Al's friend owned an Oldsmobile dealership about three blocks away from where I lived, and the sales manager there was looking for a salesperson. He specifically wanted a woman—"to add a special touch," he said. I was hired.

CHAPTER 15

I learned more about America that summer selling cars than in all the previous years I had lived here. This was real life, a real make-or-break situation, and I could finally find out whether my dream of becoming part of American business had any grounds to it—or was indeed a self-delusion.

I was incredibly lucky. If I had been specifically looking for something I wanted to do, I would have chosen this job. I had never sold anything; I'd been told before that I could be persuasive, but I knew that in order to succeed I had to believe in what I was saying—I doubt I could sell candy to a child if I did not think it was good. The Oldsmobile dealership was ideal for me: I was driving my third Olds by now, I loved the car, and I knew a lot about its features and how it compared with other makes. I also had at least some idea of how a dealership worked from my long talks with Derek.

It was a small but well-established business that catered to a Main Line clientele. It was not very price-competitive with other, large-volume dealerships, but it had an excellent service department and a good reputation. There were only three other sales-people. All of them were older than I and had worked there for years. As I'd found many times before, being a woman had its advantages—men feel less threatened by a woman and they tone down the normally competitive behavior they display toward other men—that is, until a woman becomes competent enough to compete with them as an equal. I was no threat to any of them—after so many years there, they all had their established client base and did a lot of repeat business. They also knew I was there only temporarily. All of that added up to a willingness to help, to teach me the ropes, and to accept me into their close-knit family without reservations. We became very friendly, and several times I was even invited to their homes after work.

I enjoyed the work itself immensely. I'd always liked working with people rather than with paper, and I liked the variety this people-oriented work presented. Each time was a different situation that required a different approach. There were some unpleasant surprises, of course. Sales is one profession that can undermine your belief in your fellow men. I always took what people said to me at face value. In sales it does not always work. Jack, the sales manager, gave me a few invaluable lessons in that respect.

"You're too naive," he often said. "You think that if people like you and they like the car, they will buy it from you. That's a wrong assumption. You let people walk away, counting on the fact that they'll come back. That will get you nothing but lost sales. Always get them to make a commitment. *Get a deposit.*"

"But it does not mean anything," I said. "If they change their mind, they can get the deposit back anyway."

"It does make a difference psychologically," he insisted. "It's the commitment they make in their minds that counts. Once they write a check, they feel that they have made their decision. Otherwise, human nature, being fickle as it is, the guy may be walking past another dealership tomorrow, see the car he likes, walk in, and buy it. Do you really think he will remember how nice you have been to him and how much time you spent showing him the car and convincing him that it was right for him? What happens is that you sell him on an idea that he needs this car, and then he goes and buys it somewhere else, and the other guy gets a sale without lifting a finger. Selling an idea is not enough; you have to get him to buy not just a car, but this *particular* car. Also, remember that most people lie. They tell you that this is the first place they've stopped, and it's probably the tenth. Salespeople are fair game; most people suspect you of lying anyway, and they think nothing about doing the same to you. The showroom is not a place to nourish your belief in the better side of human nature."

Much as I disliked his cynical approach, most of the time he was right. I lost a couple of sales to people who spent hours with me and firmly promised to come the next day to buy a car. When I called them, they said that they had bought a car—someplace else.

I did sell five cars in the first month, though, and I was getting paid for it. It was not bad for a beginner, and things looked bright. Even with the babysitting expenses—the agency was not paying for the child care since I was not in school—I could still breathe a little easier financially. That was when I fell victim to the common American affliction—I got my first credit card.

I am still suffering from this disease, although, with six MasterCards, five VISAs, a variety of other cards, and a staggering debt, I have finally started on a slow and painful road to recovery from the plastic plague. The way I got into it, however, to a large degree reflects the typical Russian attitude toward money management.

Although there are no credit cards in the Soviet Union, being in debt is a common way of life. Most people don't save money. When a major purchase is needed, money can always be borrowed from friends. It is done with the confidence that the debt can be repaid—almost no Russian is in fear of losing his or her job. There are exceptions, of course—political dissidents and people who apply for emigration find themselves without a job very quickly—but under normal circumstances it is almost impossible to get fired. Therefore, the attitude "spend today, pay tomorrow" is very prevalent in Russia, considerably aided by the fact that if you don't spend today, you may not find anything to spend your money on tomorrow.

It did not occur to me that I could lose my job. I was doing as well as could be expected, and I did not see any reason to fear for my future.

The future, however, came in the unexpected shape of an oil embargo, and by the middle of July 1979, allocation quotas were in effect, gas station lines stretched for blocks, and car sales slumped. GM had just introduced its small front-wheel-drive cars, but there had not been enough of them delivered to dealers to make up for lost sales in the staples of the Olds line—full-size Delta 88s and midsize Cutlasses. By the end of July the dealership could no longer afford to have four salespeople and I was let go.

It was a strange and unfamilar feeling—losing something through no fault of my own. The sales manager took special pains to explain to me that it was nothing personal, just a business necessity, and as soon as the sales improved they would take me back part-time, as promised. I understood that, of course, but still the feeling of personal failure persisted. That was the other side of the free-market economy—it does not take into account your personality or ability. If you are in the wrong place at the wrong time, the money imperative takes over and there is nothing you can do about it.

There was nothing else I could do for the month of August—with school starting in a month, it was too late to look for another job, and the whole economy was slowing down. On balance, however, I came out of the experience clearly on the positive side. Besides making a couple of thousand dollars, I learned a lot of valuable lessons about business, selling, and people in general. Another side benefit was that until the end of my stay in Pennsylvania I did not have to worry about the quality of repairs on my own car—whenever I brought it in, it was given immediate attention, and I could always count on a free loan car when I needed it.

In a way, the loss was less than I had thought. When I started school, it became clear that the workload was so great that it would have been unrealistic to think I could have stayed in the program, taken care of the children, and worked part-time.

And, at least one other thing became easier that summer. I finally established a regular correspondence with my mother.

CHAPTER 16

I had talked to my mother on the day of defection and given her some instructions about the disposition of money and things I had left in her care. I'd also told her that she could not write me for a while because I would not have an established address, and I hadn't wanted to write her myself until things settled down back there, which, I knew, would take several months.

I did manage to make a few calls. At that time the telephone connection with the Soviet Union was reasonably good and not very restricted. It was possible to place a telephone call and get connected within an hour. Since I could not call from the safe house, Barbara usually went with me to a hotel where we placed a call from the receptionist's desk, paid in advance, and then waited in a cafeteria until the call came through. That way, if the call were traced by the embassy, we were gone from the hotel long before anybody could find us. For obvious reasons I could not say much except the most innocent of things. The content was not important; all I needed was to let my mother know I was OK and to make sure that she was still there, at home, and that there had been no drastic changes in their lives.

Finally we managed to establish a postal exchange through an intermediary, though typically it took a month between the date the letter was mailed and the date it was received.

At first we were very careful and simply exchanged short notes. It was important just to establish the link. We both assumed that the letters were opened and read on the Soviet side, and wrote nothing that could cause them to be censored or simply disappear. Gradually my mother started to write more details, and the letters, with few exceptions, got through. I was naturally curious about what had happened back home after Lev had returned. I knew that both families were certain to go through a lot of discomfort and questioning, but did not know the extent. My mother wrote me a lot about Lev and herself, but most of the things concerning my father were fuzzy. Finally I got a letter from a Soviet emigré who'd recently gone to Israel. It had been mailed from there, and for the first time I learned the details of what my father had gone through.

Of all the people connected with me, he probably suffered the most. Not physically—he was not harmed or arrested—but he was my father, after all, and it had been his responsibility to raise me as a good citizen. Even Lev could say that he had gotten me "as is" and had not been aware of what was deep in my mind. My father did not have that excuse—he was supposed to be responsible for what had gone into my mind in the first place.

He did not lose his job, because he was already retired from the Air Force. I took that into account when trying to calculate the amount of damage my action would do to my relatives. He did have a part-time coaching job in the Air Force Academy, working with the marksmanship team, and from that part-time job he was fired. It did not make him destitute—his retirement pension remained intact and he could still live comfortably—but his pride was hurt.

The worst blow he suffered was the loss of his membership in the Communist Party. It may not seem much to a lot of people, but for my father it meant the greatest dishonor a man could suffer. He had been a member of the party for forty years; it was part of his life, part of his identity. He believed in everything the party said and always followed its dogma to the letter. He felt that the expulsion made him an outcast, that all his friends would turn away from him, and he would not give up without a fight. He appealed directly to the Central Committee in Moscow. In the process, of course, he had to denounce me as an enemy of the State—an understandable thing for which I never held a grudge against him. There was an investigation and endless questioning, of him and people who knew him. He was well liked and respected in the community, and, of course, he really had had no idea of what was in my head, because I had stopped discussing anything meaningful with him years before, knowing that we could never understand each other's point of view. To the credit of the people who conducted the investigation, the truth prevailed. After about a year his party membership was restored and he was completely cleared. He also found another well-paid coaching job, resumed his volunteer position as the chairman of a society of arms collectors, and was happy again.

Lev went through a similar process. He was in limbo for several months while he formally stayed on the VAAP payroll in Moscow. Finally he was cleared of any wrongdoing and resumed his job at the Institute of Philosophy. I had not been particularly worried about him. He was a survivor. Any man who had had the opportunity to leave the system that had killed his father but still went back to work for it would swim to the surface again.

It was the human side of the events that was so hard to read about: the way people reacted and behaved. Some of the reactions had been expected, some came as a surprise.

LETTERS FROM MY MOTHER

January 12, 1979

I hope you received our New Year wishes. And now we wish all three of you Happy Birthdays.

The New Year was a real joy: we received the photos of the children and then your letter on the beautiful paper with flowers. It answered a lot of our questions about you and the children.

As for Lev, I wrote to him as you requested and asked him to contact the embassy and ask to release your apartment in Washington; I also asked him to initiate divorce proceedings so your divorce there could be valid. I did not get a reply. Only when I called in December to wish Masha happy birthday, Tatiana told me that he got the letter. My relationship with him is normal, and if anything is warmer now than it has ever been; apparently I represent to him a part of you, as well as he is now a part of all of you for us. He even said several times that if he had known me better before, we would not have lost "our girl."

In any case, I am the only person with whom he can speak well of you, and sometimes he has that need. Everything is so mixed up and complicated. At the same time, he wants to be done with it all and forget everything. You know his theory that life consists of independent and self-contained stages. So now, when he finally got all his belongings and begins to build a new life, he does not want anything to remind him of the past. Children as such do not interest him without you. He *does not want* to know anything about you, at least for now. Don't write to him, don't disturb him, let him be.

He is not living alone. Sonya, of course, using Xenia as a shield, charged ahead and tried to restore the family, but to no avail. Tatiana, however, immediately brought forward her friend Natasha, who is about forty and has known Lev for some time. She moved in with him and takes care of all his needs. The rest I don't know—it's their personal business. Both Tatiana and your mother-in-law passionately hate both you and me. They think I knew and encouraged you. I don't care, let them think what they want.

I wish I could write you more about Lev, but I will wait until we establish a regular two-way correspondence. Right now the best you can do is to try not to think about him. I know it is difficult because he was the center of your life for so long, and you would miss him. For him—nobody will ever replace you. Perhaps you will still find what's missing in your life—love and understanding—but he will never have that. The reason is that you never had it yet; he did—and lost it. He understands now that no woman in the world would replace you for him, but . . . there is nothing he

can do about it. He should have thought about it earlier and conducted your relationship differently.

Best wishes from many of our friends.

March 8, 1979

Hope you received my letters where I describe how we cele-
brated your birthdays here. Until we have some certainty about
our correspondence, I am never sure what gets to you and what
doesn't. This is my eleventh letter. I would like to send you gifts,
especially for the children so they would have a real proof of the
existence of their grandparents. If I send something you do not
need, you can give it to your friends as gifts. Write me what you
need and do not worry about money. I finally convinced your father
that he cannot take all his money to the grave with him, and asked
for my share *now* so I can spend it on you and the children. He
agreed immediately.

Your last letter worries me. It tells me that your life is not easy.
Of course you are a very strong person, but even strong people
need to relax once in a while. It would be wonderful if you could
find a nice woman to live with you and help you. I live in constant
fear that you are there all alone, what if you get ill or disabled?
Who would help you with two young children? If only I could be
with you!

Your photos are the focal point of my life now. At night they
are on my night table; during the day I carry them in my purse. I
read your letters so many times that I know them by heart. I thank
the Lord that at least I have them. Konstantin looks exactly like
Lev; hope he will not take after his father in other respects.

I have no news of Lev and I do not try to contact him. He knows
I still have some of his minor belongings and will probably show
up sooner or later. I am not sending him any photos. If I see him
and if he wants them I will give them to him. I probably won't be
in Moscow until summer. I wish him well to the extent it is possible
for him, and I am the only person from whom he can get news
about you if he wants to. Sometimes he does need to talk about
you and needs a listener.

May 17, 1979

I have sent you two letters with your old photographs, as you asked me to. Had no success with the parcels yet—there are so many rules and regulations as to what could and what could not be sent. But I am learning.

Now that I know you are getting my letters I want to tell you everything that happened here last August in detail. It's a long story, and I will probably write it in several letters.

On the evening of August 9, Tatiana called me and repeated the news three times. She did not let me talk to Lev, who was sleeping, and asked me not to call later. Father left for our summer cottage that morning. I realized that we had to go to Moscow immediately; I called our friend Misha, got him out of bed, and asked him to take me to the cottage. You know, I always thought that when in the movies the weather becomes wild in critical moments, with storms and lightning, the director does it for special effects. But it was the same kind of weather in real life: there was a terrible storm and my clothes were soaking wet in the few moments it took me to get to Misha's car. The wind was so strong that the car almost overturned on the country roads. We also had to be careful not to scare your father to the point of a heart attack by our sudden appearance in the middle of the night. By three in the morning we were back in our apartment in Leningrad. You know your father well and can guess what his reaction was. I convinced him to go to Moscow alone. Lev called the next morning. He was less abrasive than usual and asked me to hold on until our meeting. He wanted me to come to Moscow, too, but I couldn't and promised to come later. Father stayed there half a day and returned home immediately. As Lev told me later, he spent practically all the time trying to quiet father down. Father came home hopping mad and hating Lev even more than before.

I could not get to Moscow for another week, but spoke to Lev on the phone several times every day. Sometimes he got angry and demanded that I come immediately, but I explained to him that I simply couldn't. Tatiana called once and poured out everything she felt, but I took it, understanding her state of mind. I think Lev reasoned with her after that, because when I came she was composed, served us coffee, and left us alone. But even before she left, we exchanged preliminary opinions: I suggested family problems, and he put forward the official version—that you fell for an American and ran away with him. I must confess that within minutes I felt sorry for him and I knew that no matter who was right and who was wrong, he was in trouble now and I had to do everything I could to help him. That decision became the basis of our discussions and future relationship. Throughout the day, he swung from one extreme to another when talking about you; when it was the worst, I kept silent; otherwise I tried to help him to sort things out. He talked about the intimate side of your relationship, asked about your former relationships, related the story of his marriage to Sonya and all the details of his romance with Irina. He looked terrible, twenty years older. It turned out that Irina had already called—"by accident." He asked me if he should see her, and I sincerely advised him to do so. He called while I was there and made a date for the next day.

Next morning the conversation was about Irina and you, intermittently. Finally she called and he asked her to meet him at the metro station, but I said I was going to make a trip to your apartment and give your renters a warning that they should move soon, and that he should bring Irina to Tatiana's place because the metro station was not a good place to discuss such serious matters. We agreed that I would call him in the evening. By two o'clock, however, he came after me and asked me to come back to Tatiana's apartment. I realized that he had a need to talk to me constantly, because he could say what he wanted to say only to me, and I listened sympathetically, while others would not let him talk well about you, and he needed exactly that.

The matter with Irina resolved itself quickly. He spent considerable time prepping for the date, trying different suits and asking me how he looked. And then—complete disappointment. He said that she had aged, had had two minor cardiac arrests, and was living now with a writer who occasionally beat her and brought other women into their apartment, and she took all that from him. "I do not want her the way she is now," he said.

I did not like his cynical attitude, but even more than that, I was sad that it did not work out. I wished we could "hand him over" quickly, because I knew that soon Tatiana would not have any time for him, and Irina appeared to be his long and lasting love. It was an attractive solution, but, unfortunately, it did not work.

As to Sonya, she did not figure in the picture yet. Jumping a bit ahead so as not to come back to it later, I must say that she behaved with dignity and diplomacy. Her plan was simple—use Xenia and appeal for a reunion. But he said it was utterly impossible and gave his reasons for that. And thank God! It would be sad and detrimental to him if he fell for that provocation, because we all knew Sonya's true colors and that she would not change.

He would not let me go back to your apartment. His mother was renting a summer cottage, as usual, and was there with Masha, so I could have her room. Sometimes he woke me up in the middle of the night, and I felt that he was not completely in control of himself, he needed to talk, to compare notes, to find things out. I could barely take it, but did my best. He asked what happened to your belongings, swore when he was unhappy about something, but then recoiled and became peaceful again.

I sent part of the money with your father and brought the rest myself; Lev was surprised at the sum, but asked me to take it back for now. He was planning to go on vacation and then come to Leningrad to take his belongings and to start getting his life in order.

I spent the last two days of that week in your apartment together with him. I got everything in order, cooked him enough food for several days, and did his grocery shopping. He did not drink much, but I felt he could barely restrain himself from drinking more.

He was very kind and gentle with me; for him, I was a personification of you. He kept saying that if he only knew, we would not have lost you, and now—it's too late, the goldfish swam away. A few times, when I felt he could take it, I did voice some disapproval of the way he had treated you so he would not think I was completely ignorant of your problems. I must say that he did admit some guilt and wished he could turn the time back so he could be different. But it does not happen, and we finally agreed that things probably would have stayed the way they were. When we did talk about practical things and I asked what he counted on, dumping all this burden in your lap and jerking you like a puppet on a string, he simply said that women *do not walk out on men like him: it does not happen.* "But, Lev, it did happen." "Yes, it did, and now me, with my ego, I have to be in the position of an abandoned husband. I will never forgive her for putting me in this situation!" And then: "Wouldn't it be wonderful if a miracle happened and she returned, I swear everything would be different. . . . Yes, I did not pay attention to her, did not love her enough"; and then again and again all of the same.

He brought all his baggage the day before I left. To avoid embarrassment, I asked him not to unpack it until I left. We agreed about most of the things. As to his relationship with your father, only time will show, and we can only hope for the best.

When I was leaving he said once again how much he appreciated my coming to his rescue, that he admired my courage and regretted that he never bothered to find out all these qualities before. I told him that I was simply taking your place in doing all this for him.

To be continued. God bless you and the children.

June 11, 1979

I finally got away from the city for a week. It is very hot there, and I needed rest. We finally managed to send you a large parcel with things for you and the children.

To continue about last August. Even when I was still in Moscow, Tatiana mentioned that she was going to bring Natasha to help Lev unpack and get his life going in practical terms. I was relieved to know that somebody would be there to help him and did not ask any further questions. I also understood that Tatiana had her hands full and could not take the hassle of caring for her brother on a day-to-day basis. With her usual temperament and acidity, she poured her soul out in regard to you, but it was also understandable.

I did not meet Lev's mother. It was Lev's decision. He said that she and I had different mentalities and would never agree even in minor things, and therefore it was better to avoid the meeting altogether. He was right, and for me it was a relief. A few days later your father was in Moscow; he had to see Lev immediately and ran into Natasha in your apartment. He got mad, but I explained to him that it was really for the better. I am glad that you agreed with my assessment in your last letter.

Several days later Lev came for one day; he needed to talk to me urgently. We greeted him as we used to in the old times; there was his favorite food and plenty to drink. He was so touched that he even hugged and kissed me while I was doing the dishes, and I realized that something had probably reminded him of you, the beginning of your romance here in Leningrad, and some sentimental part of his soul had reacted to it. And then, again, a million questions, answers, speculations. He is confused, gets mixed up about times and events, speaks ill of people who were your friends and used to help you both; in short, unfortunately, he did not show his best side. He drank everything we had, went out, got two more large bottles of wine, drank it all, refused to pack his belongings he'd come to collect, and fell asleep. In the evening when Father and I started packing at least something so he would not go back emptyhanded, he found a bottle of cognac, bringing the total for the day to three liters, and completely lost control of himself. I wanted to keep him for another day, but Father refused categorically—he could not take another day with Lev. Somehow we got Lev into the car, hoping that he would sober up somewhat on the way to the station, but all we got was that we could not get him out of the car. We exchanged the ticket and spent three more hours in the car waiting for the next train, on which we put Lev.

I was worried about him and his luggage and all the money he had with him, so I called next morning to find out if he was OK. I should not have done it. Tatiana called me later and poured out her wrath that I dared to "disturb" her mother with the news of her son's drinking. They are still angry at me just because I am your mother, and also because they still think that I knew about your intentions. Lev also asked me about it several times. I did say last time I saw him that I suspected but did not discuss it with you.

He came to Leningrad again two weeks later to take the rest of his belongings, and was surprised how much there was. It was then that I told him: "Today we need each other; tomorrow the need will diminish, and later you probably will not even want to remember, let alone see me." That was exactly what happened. He called once again, in November, thanked me for everything I'd done for him, wished me a happy New Year, and said he would not call anymore. I called in December on Masha's birthday. Tatiana was nice, confirmed that Lev had received my letter with your message about the Washington apartment. She also said that she was fed up with Lev's problems, she only knew that he worked in the same place. That was the last time I heard from them.

There is more to come, though.

August 21, 1979

I promised to tell you in this letter how we resolved the money issue. If you remember, when we thought your stay was extended and we rented the apartment out, I took many of your belongings to Leningrad, as you asked me to, for safekeeping. It was a difficult task, but we managed. I did leave many books in Moscow with trusted friends.

Then Lev came back. He knew that his relatives did not do much in terms of keeping an eye on your aparment, but Tatiana presented it in such a way as if I had taken the things behind their backs. He was rather careful, however, discussing it with me, since he understood that everything was in my hands. Even in the very first days, amidst all the emotional outbursts, he asked me several times what exactly he had. I already wrote to you that I sent part of the money the very first day when your father went to Moscow and brought the rest myself. I also brought a full account with me. The sum was much greater than he thought, and I also gave him the icon you left here so he could sell it. He did give me enough money to cover my expenses for my trips to Moscow. He was also questioned heavily about your activities during your last trip to Moscow, and I gave him all the receipts from the consignment stores that showed that there was nothing criminal: no large quantities, no duplicate items, and he felt better with these documents in hand.

I already told you on the phone that I was going to give him *everything*. I did not want to keep anything and be accused of cheating. You told me, however, that I should keep some household items and your personal belongings, and I did. If I were sharing it with Tatiana, it would have been different and I would have kept some money, but since he returned I felt it belonged to him.

Please do not worry about me. My needs are small and I have enough to live on. I prefer to have peace of mind knowing that Lev has no grounds of accusing me of foul play. The things you brought me on your trips brighten my apartment, and everything I touch that is beautiful reminds me of you. All the little things that make my life easier and more comfortable—they are all from you, and I think that if I add up all the personal and household things that I've had in the thirty-eight years of my married life, I've had less than I have now. I hope I will live long enough to enjoy them.

There were some rumors that you received royalties for Father's book, but I do not think it is true, because I heard from VAAP that the project was put on hold and the publisher even had to pay a penalty for halting production. So, I figure, how could you receive royalties for something that has not been published yet?

September 26, 1979

What a great joy—received two letters from you, full of photos. You look good, and the children are beautiful. Bless you for sending all these pictures, they are my only real link with all of you. I am glad that you received the things I sent you; right now I do not know whether I can send anything because some people say that in the winter, when the navigation season is over, anything sent by surface mail would have to wait till the spring. Can't get a definite answer from the post office whether it is true.

You write that Kitty is constantly asking to visit Grandma. Tell her something she can understand and accept, like that the planes from here can only take mail but not people. She must understand firmly the impossibility of my visit, at least for the next few years. I myself would have given anything for the opportunity to see you, to touch you! I cannot stop thinking about the constant stress in your life; with two children you cannot relax even for a moment, and I wish I could be there to help you. There isn't much hope, though. Rudolf Nureyev has been trying to get his mother out for eighteen years now. She is eighty years old, and many famous people petitioned on his behalf, but . . . no. So what can I hope for? And now, when you need me most, I am helpless to relieve your burden.

I will keep trying, though. Many people are leaving, although some have the good sense to stay. You should have seen those crazies! They behave as if there's an epidemic or an evacuation; without thinking, one goes and drags others behind. I've heard that they behave like savages when they get there, and that in Italy they no longer want to rent apartments to Soviet emigrés. Soon there will be a backlash and nobody will want to take them. None of our friends emigrated or have any intention to, except the Geibers. Their situation is terrible now. Petya, your childhood friend, wanted to leave; he would not listen to any reason. His mother tried to reason with him—he majored in English, what kind of a profession is it there? "Every street sweeper speaks English there better than you do," his mother told him. No use. He talked his wife into it, and she left the medical school, where she had been am honor student for six years, two weeks before graduation. They could not apply for emigration without their parents, though, and his father, a veteran and a university professor, finally gave in, left his job, resigned from the party, and signed the papers. And now that Petya made all his family give up everything they had, his father-in-law, a chief engineer of a major factory and a war hero, changed his mind and refused to sign the application. So now they are all left with nothing, and Petya is in hiding, trying to avoid the draft. I can hardly imagine what future they have here. And there are many other families torn apart like this. I may have to do it myself. I want to be with you more than anything else, but I cannot even apply unless I divorce your father first.

Have no news of Lev. Would like to see him but do not dare to go to Moscow. Tatiana's number changed, and he still does not have a phone.

December 12, 1979

Finally received a parcel from you that you sent three months ago. Thank you for all these wonderful things. Rubber gloves are a lifesaver for me, I have diabetes and my hands get chapped in the water instantly. Our gloves are hard to put on, they tear up and leak. Please fill out the declarations more carefully, though. I know from your letter that there were other things there, but whatever was not on a declaration was missing. Also, the mascara was filched and an empty container substituted for it, but I don't want to argue with the Customs about it.

I went to Moscow for a couple of days. I could not find out from anybody how Lev was doing. Katrina called me, but she did not know. I am not going to visit him unless he wants to see me, but I wrote to Alana that I was coming, and she said she would tell him. Although he did not suffer as many ill consequences as your father did, for Father things are back to normal, and I was hoping that Lev would put his life back together as well. Alana also told me that there are rumors circulating in Moscow that you married a millionaire, a director of an automobile company, and I wanted to meet your friends and tell them it is not so.

Lev did not come to Alana's apartment, although he knew when I would be there. I also learned that he was in Leningrad for a week, but he did not call us or any of your friends. Alana runs into him occasionally. Natasha does not live there anymore. I do not know who was at fault that she left, but he lives alone now. He drinks heavily, and also tells everybody that he was cheated of his money, borrows from his friends, and drinks it all away. The apartment stands as it was when he arrived; all the appliances you brought from America stand unused and unpacked, all the wallpaper is still in rolls. Alana told him that she had pictures of his children, but he did not want to know anything. Just said: "I have only one daughter, and she lives here, in Moscow."

I felt very sorry for him until I learned how dishonorably he behaved in regard to many people who were kind to you and how he got many of them into trouble. He is a smart man, but this drinking will eventually ruin him completely. I do not think I will go there again. When I got off the bus and looked at that building, at the windows where I saw the curtains I hung myself, and I thought of all the effort that you and I put into that apartment, I started crying. It was my dream to see you finally in your own home, not in a rented apartment, and I never lived to see that dream. Maybe someday you will still have a home of your own there in America, but I will not see it, either.

I am going to get a divorce and apply for permission to join you, but my hopes are not high. Still, I must at least try.

CHAPTER 17

*T*HE first year in school went fast. I made a few friends, most of them foreign students. I did not date anybody, but I had some company to go out with for a drink, or to have a barbecue at my place, or occasionally to go to New York for a Broadway show—at least until my summer earnings ran out. There was a reason why most of my friends were foreign. Being Russian in America does not win popularity contests; many people have preconceived notions about the Soviet Union, and that attitude can easily spill over into an attitude toward a particular person.

It could have been worse, of course. In the apartment upstairs lived an Iranian family; they had a child the same age as my son and we'd met on a playground. Reza was an American-educated health care management specialist and had taught in an American college before going back to Iran. Then, fleeing from the revolution, they returned to the States. When the hostage situation developed in Iran he was turned down at every job he applied for even though his qualifications were more than adequate. The fact that he had fled from the same regime that was holding the Americans hostage did not matter—he was turned down simply because he was from Iran. One college board told him they wanted to have him—he was the only qualified candidate for the job—but that they were afraid hiring him would cause student unrest and demonstrations,

I did make friends with a few people who lived in the same apartment complex. The Iranian couple was one; another was a Russian woman named Nellie, who was introduced to me by the rental manager, acting on the same mistaken assumption as everybody else—that I wanted to meet other Russians. Interestingly, Nellie was in no rush to meet me, either, until we finally ran into each other in the rental office. Our first couple of meeings were tense, neither of us willing to talk much about our past. Gradually, as we came to know each other, I learned that like myself Nellie was living under an assumed name and had reasons not to get too close to strangers.

She was not a defector, but a refugee from Afghanistan. She'd originally been from Azerbaidzhan, one of the predominantly Moslem Soviet republics close to the Iranian border. She'd majored in English, taught Russian to foreign students at the University of Baku, and eventually married one of them, an engineer from Afghanistan, and moved there to live with him. Her husband had been a wealthy and highly placed government official in his country, and for a while she'd enjoyed a nice life there. Then the Communist regime took over. Her husband, a technical specialist, had been welcome to stay and work for the new government, but she, never an admirer of the Communist system and very friendly with Americans living in Kabul, lost her job as a teacher. Gradually she started to suspect that the KGB was making trouble for her. Her trips to the Soviet Union, where she had regularly gone to see her family, were abruptly canceled; and finally, after an ugly automobile accident from which she barely escaped with her life but the culprit was never found, she decided that her life was in danger and managed to obtain a visa to the United States. There, since her English was excellent, she quickly found a job as a marketing manager; her husband stayed in Afghanistan for reasons not unlike those that had influenced Lev's decision—he was much older than Nellie, well established in his country, and although he would have been able to find a job here as a geological engineer, he would probably have had to start at a much lower position because his English was not very good. Because he could not transfer his holdings out of Afghanistan, he stood to lose a substantial fortune if he left.

I was struck by the many coincidences in Nellie's and my situation. The whole apartment complex seemed to be filled with people who had for some reason been displaced from their normal surroundings; the place had the eerie quality of a misfits colony—everyone had either rejected their own society or been thrown out by it. We were all used to better and different lives and to an entirely different social milieu. Everybody I met was there because of unfortunate circumstances and really belonged someplace else—Reza, a wealthy Iranian, could not get any of his money out of Iran and could not find a job here; Nellie used to live in a mansion and give parties to high society in Kabul, and was now supporting herself and her two teenage children on a small salary; Nancy, a troubled woman who drank heavily even while she spoke longingly about the house she used to have instead of her "crummy apartment." My own life, of course, was vastly different from what I used to know. Yet we all had hope and were struggling to get back to where we used to be. I hoped that my life would change after I finished school; Nellie was working on new skills and looking for a better job; and I knew that Reza, who refused to be defeated by rejection after rejection, would eventually find a job. In fact, he did, a teaching position at a New Jersey college.

What I did not realize at the time was that our transition was permanent; even though we could improve our life somewhat, none of us would rise back to the status and social position we'd had in our homeland. I did not figure it out by myself, at least not then. I was still full of hope for a bright future and too naive about the workings of this country. It was a Russian emigré I met in school who explained a few things about life here to me.

I met Aron by accident. It was the end of the second semester in school, and we were supposed to choose an area of specialization. Wharton has an unusual system of grading and academic credits. Nineteen courses must be taken in a two-year MBA program; each is a semester long and earns one credit; in addition, there are a few mandatory noncredit workshops such as oral and written communications. Nine courses constitute a mandatory core and must be taken by everybody; four courses must be taken in the area of specialization; and six are electives. There are only three grades—distinguished, high pass, and pass. Class rank is not calculated, probably on the assumption that just getting through the Wharton program is good enough.

Most of the students chose to specialize in finance—the subject on which the school's reputation has been built. Another popular major was strategic planning, which I chose. Some of its courses were taught at the Busch center, a research center that occupied an entire floor in the school building. Most of the students there were doing their PhD studies, but some courses were offered for MBA candidates as well.

I went to the center to talk to a prospective instructor and to find out what the course would involve. The instructor was away, and I was steered to one of the PhD students for information.

"You don't want to take courses here," he said. "Our philosophy here is different from what they teach you downstairs in the MBA program." He sounded snobbish and seemed to be trying to put me down. I thought that maybe he was not expressing himself well—he looked Middle Eastern and spoke accented English. From my own experience, I knew that the subtle nuances of the English language could easily give a wrong meaning to the most well-meant statement. I did notice that there were a lot of foreign-looking people in the center.

"Your courses are officially listed in the MBA program," I said. "I would like to take some in order to complete my major."

"What we teach here is opposite to what they teach you there," he persisted. "In the MBA program they teach you how to run corporations and to work for a capitalist society. Here, we try to learn how to feed the hungry people of the world and to change the rotten capitalist system that makes people suffer. Anybody who enrolls in the MBA program believes in capitalism and does not belong here."

I could not believe what I was hearing. For a moment I felt as if I were back in the Soviet Union.

"I do believe in what you call a rotten capitalist system," I said. "I lived under socialism long enough to know that it does not work. And I also do not believe that your personal philosophy is shared by everybody here in the center, or these courses would not be offered to MBAs. I think I'll wait till Professor Davis gets back and I will talk to him directly." The last thing I wanted to hear was Soviet propaganda, but I had a feeling this student was overstepping his authority.

"Where are you from?" he asked suddenly.

"I emigrated from the Soviet Union," I said. "So don't tell me about equality and the hungry people of the world—I've heard it all my life."

He suddenly smiled. "We have a Russian professor here," he said. "Come and meet him—I am sure you will find a lot of things to talk about."

I did not want to meet another Russian, but I agreed. I had no reason to refuse, and, at least, a professor would tell me about what was going on in this strange place.

The name on the door, Aron Kantsenelinboigen, sounded familiar. I was certain that I had heard it before. After we were introduced I recited my conversation with his student.

"Well, Murjab does tend to take things to the extreme." He smiled. "What he meant to say is that our approach may be a little unorthodox. We do welcome MBA students here because we think that a different perspective from a global point of view will give the MBAs a better understanding of how things fit together in a society, not just from the point of view of a single corporation, and we hope that a sense of social responsibility in our future industry leaders will eventually make our society a better place for all of us. We certainly do not advocate Communism here, and, being an emigré like yourself, I took my stand when I left the Soviet Union."

Gradually we got involved in a long conversation. I remembered now where I had heard his name—he used to work for the Institute of Econometrics in Moscow, which was located in the same building as Lev's institute, and I was certain I'd seen his name in scientific journals. We both knew a lot of people in the social sciences back in Moscow, and for a while I felt as if I were back home, talking about the situation and personnel moves in social research in the Soviet Union. He'd lived in the United States since 1973, but was well informed on the current news in the Soviet social sciences—from friends and fellow emigrés, he said.

I started to visit Aron frequently, dropping in whenever I had a couple of hours between classes. Conversations with him were refreshing and stimulating, bringing back memories of conversations with my embassy friends. He had the same Soviet-American perspective they had, in terms of knowing and understanding both sides though obviously he was far more critical of the Soviet system than my embassy friends had been. He did not reject it flatly, though.

Like many educated Russians, he could see both the good and bad sides of the socialist regime, and therefore could see clearly both the advantages and the shortcomings of the American system. He was interested in a wide variety of subjects and had interesting and often unusual theories about many social and economic issues. He was equally interested in my opinions and my knowledge of social research, since his concentration was mostly in economics and mathematical modeling, and we often spent hours discussing controversial matters, often disagreeing, but always respecting each other's opinion.

As time went by, we became very good friends. I met his wife, Zhenia, who taught Russian at the university's school of liberal arts, and his son, who was a student there. Yet sometimes I intercepted a puzzled look on his face. I knew what was causing it. In our conversations I often mentioned people in Moscow whom he knew. They were of his generation and held high positions in Moscow; I usually referred to them by their first names, and he was obviously trying to figure out how at my young age I had come to know all of them so intimately. In the end he probably decided that I was simply a name-dropper. I still did not dare to tell him about my past, and although that conclusion probably diminished his opinion of my credibility, I decided to let it be.

One day, however, he caught me off-guard. I came to visit him and noticed that his small office was almost filled up with cardboard boxes.

"A friend of mine is emigrating, and he sent all his books in advance," Aron said. "His name is Vladimir Shlyapentoch—did you know him?"

"Yes, of course," I said. "He was in the Institute of Sociology at the same time I was there." Aron smiled, and I thought it was sort of an impish smile but could not figure out why. We talked for a few minutes, when the door opened and a man came in. The moment I saw him I understood why Aron had smiled so strangely; he thought he had finally caught me redhanded, called my bluff, and would put an end to my name-dropping.

He was the only one smiling. His friend's jaw dropped in complete surprise, and I thought feverishly what to do next.

"Well, well, what do you know," Vladimir finally said. "Of all the people in the world, you are the last one I expected to see here. How is life on the CIA money—you must be doing quite well?" His expression was hostile.

"You two know each other?" Aron said in utter astonishment.

"Certainly do," said Vladimir. "So, tell me—did they buy you a house? How much is the CIA paying you?"

Aron still could not comprehend what was going on. He did not expect such a turn of conversation.

"I have a class," I said to Vladimir. "May I speak to you on my way downstairs?"

I almost dragged him to the hallway. "What do you think you are doing?" I said angrily. "Aron has no idea who I am. And what's all this talk about the CIA?" I explained briefly the story of my defection.

"I am sorry," he said. "Everybody in Moscow said that the CIA offered you a lot of money and you sold out, and everybody is angry that you ran away like that and stole Lev's children."

"Some day I'll tell you more about my family situation at that time," I said. "How is Lev?"

"He is doing well. They kept him in limbo for a few months but finally decided that he was clean. He's back in the institute as a department head. He's telling a lot of bad things about you in Moscow."

"I can understand that he is angry," I said, "but please do not believe everything you hear. And please try to smooth things out with Aron. He is a wonderful man and I'd hate to lose his friendship."

Vladimir promised to take care of that and not to tell Aron anything more about me. I went downstairs, although I did not have any classes. After some thought I decided I would have to tell Aron the truth. He'd heard enough to be very curious, and it was not fair to try to hide things from him. I valued his friendship immensely, and I also knew by now that I could trust him.

"I admit I had some misgivings," Aron said when I came to see him the next time and told him my story. "It just did not sound right—the things you were telling me and your age. Now, of course, I understand that all these people were Lev's friends and you knew them socially. And yes, I did think that Vladimir would walk in here and say that he'd never met you, although the timing was a coincidence."

Actually I was relieved that the truth had come out. It had been difficult for me to watch what I was saying and to filter out references to my past. It had brought strain to our conversations; there'd always been a certain barrier that prevented us from being true friends. Now that barrier was removed and I felt free to talk about whatever I liked.

My friendship with Aron and occasional trips to Washington were the only bright spots in my life outside of school. Even the trips were not as much joy as before. Larry had been promoted and was involved in sensitive work; he'd been advised that his superiors were not happy about his continuing to see me. Neither could I see John. I was no longer their official ward; from now on I was just another defector, and as such always under a cloud of suspicion: I might turn around once more, or, worse, have been a double agent from the beginning. There was no way to fight it. I did not want to do anything that could have negative effects on the people who had been so good to me, and much as I hated to lose contact with them, I accepted the fact that I could cause trouble for them. I did continue seeing Ian and Anna, who had apparently cleared it with the agency, and Jim and Linda, who did not have as high a position in the FBI as Larry did.

I told Aron about my feelings of being misplaced and the lack of intellectual companionship. "Americans are not interested in anything outside of their homes and their careers," I said. "I do not meet anybody who is interested in, or knows enough about, the arts, international politics—all the things that were so much a part of my world before the defection. The students in school do not read anything except the business section of *The New York Times* and *The Wall Street Journal*. They can recite the list of Fortune 500 companies, but do not have the slightest idea what is going on outside of the stock market, and I am afraid I am turning into a zombie."

His answer was profoundly true, and I wondered why I had not thought about it myself.

"There are people in this country who are exactly the kind of people you are longing to be with," he said, "but you no longer belong with them. We will never have the same position in this society as we had back home. When you finish school, it will be a little better, you will start work and start meeting people who will become your social circle. But you will never rise above being middle class. Maybe upper-middle class, but still middle class. In Moscow we were part of the upper class, the elite, and your behavior, your expectations, reflect that. You'll have to scale down your expectations. You will not be able to socialize with the upper-class, because here you either have to be born into an upper-class family or have an immense fortune to be accepted in high society. You have neither. Just because you have a good intellect, are an interesting person, and belonged to the elite in your home country does not give you access to the elite of this society."

I knew he was right. My old life was over, it was only a matter of mentally adjusting to the new one. Not that the adjustment was easy; I could get used to living on little money as long as the children were fed and healthy; there would be people like Aron to provide intellectual company, and the books would do the rest. It was the change of attitude on the part of other people that I found difficult to accept. Mothers of my children's playmates in school shunned me when they learned where we lived; they were not even "high society," but people of the same status and means as the Americans with whom I had normally socialized in Washington. It was my own status that had gone down. Especially disquieting was the change in my personal life. On the rare occasions when I went out, the men felt free to adopt a "your place or mine" attitude on the first date and were annoyed when I refused. I considered the possibility that it was a normal way of behavior that I simply had not encountered before in my position as a diplomat's wife, but the feeling persisted that if I were not living in low-income housing and were better dressed, they would not have dared to expect "reciprocation" in return for a dinner out. The pattern was so consistent that I finally simply stopped accepting invitations. This was definitely one area in which I had no intention of lowering my standards and reducing my expectations.

Part of my disenchantment was caused by reasons beyond my control, though. Philadelphia is not Washington, and I lived on the Main Line, which is a very conservative and well-established suburb with a rather closed local society. My obstetrician confirmed that when I mentioned my isolation.

"It's not you, it's just the wrong place for a foreigner." He laughed. "Look, I grew up in San Francisco and my wife is local. I've lived here for twenty years by now and I am still considered an outsider!"

Yet, the place was depressing. I hated Philadelphia and wanted to get back to Washington—its straight, planned streets, the open areas around the Mall, the river that reminded me so much of Leningrad, the scenic parkways that started my day with beautiful views. There was nothing to cheer me on my forty-minute drive from home to school, nothing to uplift my spirit, no beauty. Therefore, when the spring semester ended and most students took summer jobs, many of them with prospective future employers, I decided to forego the chance. Much as I would have welcomed an additional income from a summer job, I decided to stay for the summer semester and finish the school half a year earlier.

CHAPTER 18

*T*HE second year in school was easier than the first. My life fell into a fairly routine pattern. My time was divided between home and school—the rest was a vacuum.

I continued getting letters regularly from my mother, although I was too exhausted to write with the same regularity. It caused some hurt feelings and concern, and I tried to send at least a few words every couple of weeks just to let her know I was still alive and well. Not that she believed me—she knew that even if I had a problem I would not write her about it, knowing that she was unable to help me from there.

She went through a rather messy divorce with my father and was finally free to apply for emigration. She could not ask to join me—there was no way I could send her a formal invitation that would serve as a legal basis for her application. In order to do that, I would have had to deal directly with the Soviet consulate in Washington, fill out a variety of forms, and, among other things, disclose my whereabouts. That, of course, was out of the question.

Meanwhile, the emigration restrictions in the Soviet Union were tightening. Until 1979 people emigrated in large numbers, since it was enough just to be Jewish and have a relative, any relative, abroad who had put in a legal request for unification of the family and sponsorship papers. A lot of such requests were issued for people who were barely related, or even not related at all, and the Soviet government finally caught up with the fact. In addition, relations between the two countries were worsening. The greatest wave of emigration took place in the Nixon era, when Soviet-American relations were at their height. After the Carter administration took over, the number of permissions steadily declined. Linkage with trade and the grain embargo did not help, either— the Soviet Union may occasionally make a goodwill gesture toward the West, but it does not like to be cornered or treated like a disobedient child. Emigration dropped from about fifty thousand a year to less than two thousand.

I had always questioned the idea of linkage, because I knew how the life and intellectual atmosphere of the Soviet Union fluctuated almost in unison with the state of Soviet-American relations. It was not just a matter of human rights or Jewish emigration. When times were good, everybody felt it: books were published more freely, social research was less dogmatic, people felt better. Since worsening relations usually affected trade, goods became more scarce, and that in turn led to tightening of the ideological screws and more interference in personal lives in order to keep control of the population.

The grain embargo and the boycott of the Moscow Olympics brought disastrous results. Emigration, which had been on the increase before the Olympics, was restricted to direct relatives. It meant that uncles, aunts, and distantly related great-grandparents no longer counted as a family and therefore could not legally request reunification. Very few people had parents, children, or siblings in the West. By changing the eligibility rules, the Soviet government effectively brought emigration to a halt.

Other restrictions were introduced as well. When they'd been preparing for the Olympics, the Soviet Union had opened an additional number of international telephone lines, and for a while it had even been possible to dial there direct. Suddenly it became almost impossible to get through. Calls had to be placed a week in advance, and the number of calls that could go through on any single day was severely limited. For a while it was possible to call just after midnight and make a reservation. Then the telephone company changed the rules; they started accepting reservations at noon, and all reservations had to go through New York. International operators in other cities could not get through busy signals to New York operators, and within fifteen minutes all the calls for the day were reserved. I finally gave up trying and resorted to letters as the only means of communication.

It was in this atmosphere that my mother tried to get an exit visa. As I learned later from her letters, she found an ingenious way to deal with it. She said that her mother had confided in her before she died and revealed to her a family secret—that she'd had an illegitimate child before she married my grandfather, and that the child had been taken out of the country by his father shortly after the Revolution. The family had lived in Poland, Belgium, and eventually moved to Israel. Mother said that she had kept this secret on her conscience since 1966, because if she had told my father or me we would have been obliged to indicate it on our work applications, and it could have hurt our careers. That was true—there is a question on Soviet work applications about relatives abroad, and listing one can be a serious impediment to a person's career and, in my father's case, would have prevented him from having a security clearance.

Anyway, by a miraculous stroke of luck some friends had managed to locate my long-lost "uncle" in Israel, and my mother had gotten an official invitation to join him. She was elated. She was so certain she would succeed in her scheme that she started shipping some of her books to me in advance. I warned her not to raise her expectations too high. I had no way of knowing if the story was true. It was possible that she had kept it a secret, but it did seem a little farfetched even to me, and so it would, I knew, to a lot of other people. She could not produce any birth records on the Soviet side, but since the archives in Odessa had been completely destroyed, there was no proof that the event had *not* taken place, either. To prove it through "reverse logic," mother tried to get a copy of her own birth certificate. Her records had been destroyed as well, so she argued that the lack of records did

not prove anything. She even managed to get over the first hurdle—her application was accepted, and she was convinced the
people in the emigration office believed her story.

It was my father who put an end to it. Since his reinstatement
in the party, he had become particularly concerned about anything
remotely illegal that could mar his newly reacquired reputation.
He went to Moscow and made a formal statement that he was
aware of his ex-wife's application and that in his opinion the request
was fake and she did not have any brother abroad. The application
was turned down. Mother appealed several times, but his statement
was on file and her application was turned down every time. After
four times the emigration office in Leningrad refused even to talk
to her.

From the beginning, I had no hope. It did not matter if the
brother had been real or fake—the authorities certainly knew that
I was the primary reason she wanted to emigrate. My father's
statement only made it easier for them to refuse, but even without
it they would have found a way.

———

The fall semester started. For me it was the last semester, and
it was time to start thinking about graduation and a job. One
welcome change did take place in my environment: Al, my CIA
contact, retired and was replaced by George, who had been involved in my case back in Washington. George was far more energetic and involved in his job than Al ever was, and at that time
I needed agency help more than ever. The interviewing season
started in October. It was not as intense as the spring season, when
about six hundred students graduated at the same time, but even
a smaller winter class brought dozens of corporate recruiters to
school. I had my résumé printed and sent out, and was invited to
eight interviews—about average for any Wharton grad.

My immediate problem was that I had nothing suitable to wear
for interviews. We had been given substantial coaching in how to
"dress for success" and interviewing techniques, and besides the
fact that my clothes were old and showed merciless wear, nothing
in my wardrobe even resembled a business suit—in the embassy

I'd always worn dresses or velvet blazers and skirts. I could not afford to buy a new suit on my budget. George requested money from Washington, arguing that the job search was their responsibility and any expenses related to it should be covered. The agency paid for the suit.

The interviews did not bring any results, though. Some companies simply sent rejection letters—"Your specialization does not fit current requirements"—but one recruiter, a woman from General Foods, was kind enough to call me and gave me a hint of the problem.

"We cannot fit you anywhere," she said. "On the one hand, your degrees and age make you overqualified for entry-level positions. On the other hand, we cannot hire you into a middle-management position because you have no work experience in this country."

I had a feeling it was the same problem with all the other corporations with which I interviewed. My grades were good—in my calculation I was somewhere in the upper third of the class—I just did not fit anywhere. I wondered quietly if the fact that I was a single mother with two children, and a foreigner, had anything to do with it as well, but I just didn't know. The fact was, however, that of the entire graduating class, I was the only one without a job offer by the end of the recruiting season.

January came. I finished school, and still did not have a job. Finally, Paul, the boss of the Washington office, used some of his personal connections and got me a job with a management consulting company in Washington. The arrangement he made did not add much to my self-esteem. Only one person in the company—Paul's friend—knew my real story. The president of the company was told that I had independent means, but that because of my late entry into the job market I desperately needed a job, any job, to gain work experience. The pay was of no importance. He jumped at the opportunity—what other company could boast of having a Wharton graduate on the payroll for only $7800 a year, less than they paid a receptionist? The agency would continue my support at the same level as they had when I was in school.

I was grateful to Paul for taking the trouble and finding the job for me. I also knew I had no other options. I could not sit in Pennsylvania for five more months doing nothing; and there was no guarantee that the spring recruiting season would be any different for me. Still, I was unhappy. From the beginning the whole idea was that I would get my education and be self-sufficient. Now I was back on agency welfare for an indefinite time.

"Don't worry," Paul said. "It's a fair arrangement now because they had no plans for hiring anybody, and you are a totally unknown quantity. After a while, when you prove what you can do, they will increase your salary, and the agency share will gradually decrease. In a year you'll be completely on your own."

"But what will people there think? The information about my pay rate will not be limited to your friend or the company's president. Accounting will know, and soon so will everybody else. I cannot talk to everybody in person and explain our scheme."

"There will be no need. The payroll information is confidential."

I did like the people with whom I talked in Washington, and, of course, I wanted to return to Washington rather than move to any other city. After Philadelphia, Washington was a feast for the eyes; more important, it was the only place where I had friends I could rely on in case of emergency, and after two years of living in fear about what would happen to the children if I broke a leg or became seriously ill, it was a critical consideration.

I was hired as an associate, but without clearly defined duties because of my lack of specific experience. The idea was that although I would be formally attached to the department headed by Paul's friend, I would be on loan to other departments to work on specific projects, and that way would learn about different aspects of the company's multifaceted business: contracts with local governments for strategic planning and economic development; consultancies with associations; fund-raising for private schools; marketing strategies for colleges. There was certainly a lot to learn, and I awaited the beginning of my "real" work eagerly.

I was expected to start in the middle of February. As it happened, I had a bad car accident at the end of January and was stranded in Philadelphia while the car was being fixed and the insurance company processed my claim. Because of that I could not drive to Washington to look for a place to live. I had no choice but to do my apartment shopping with the help of the *Washington Post* and the telephone. A few calls made it clear that Chevy Chase was out of my reach—the rents had gone up drastically. Finally I found what sounded like a suitable apartment in Northern Virginia. A friend of mine in Washington went there to inspect the place and leave a deposit.

Meanwhile, my lease for the Philadelphia apartment was about to expire and I had to move. The car was still not ready; the accident had demolished the right fender, the hood, the grille, and the windshield, and the body shop had to wait for the parts to arrive.

As had happened many times before, and would happen many times later, help came from unexpected quarters. It was something I was beginning to learn about Americans; in normal circumstances they might be a little distant and slow to open up, but when real need arose, somebody always came forward and offered a helping hand.

In this case it was my classmate Carolyne, with whom I had become friendly in my last year in school. She and her husband had a house a few blocks from where I lived; their son was about the same age as Konstantin, and Carolyne's mother lived with them. We'd often spent time together during school breaks, and I visited them in their house a few times, but it was not a close, intimate friendship of the type I'd had in Russia. However, when Carolyne heard about my problem, she immediately asked me to move in with them until my car was ready. I gratefully accepted, put most of my belongings in storage, and moved out of my apartment.

The starting date of my new job was approaching, and my car finally was ready, but I still had not received a check from the insurance company. It turned out that it had been sent to Carolyne's address, as I had requested, but because the envelope had been addressed to me, it had been returned by the post office. Meanwhile, I was getting nervous, and once again, Carolyne helped me out. She offered to lend me the money to cover the cost of the car repair until the insurance check came. The next day, with two days remaining till the start of my job, I left for Washington.

I had been lucky in my telephone hunt. The apartment turned out to be nice. I had never been in that particular area of Virginia before, but I liked it instantly. I spent the remaining day making arrangements for Kitty's school—she was already in the first grade—and day care for both children. On February 17, nervous and full of expectations, I started my first real job in this country.

CHAPTER **19**

MY first month on the job was confusing—both for me and, I think, for my employers. Nobody seemed to know what to do with me.

After two or three days of shuffling and rearranging files related to school fund-raising, I was requested by the economic development department to do some work on input-output analysis. The impressive name turned out to be a simple recalculation of percentages on huge economic data tables—a fifth-grade student could have done it easily. The work was tedious, and after a few days my wrist ached from the endless punching of buttons on a calculator. There had to be a better way of doing it.

Full of enthusiasm and the desire to do something productive for the company, I requested a meeting with the president. The request was granted: it was a medium-size company, about seventy employees, everybody was on a first-name basis, and the president, a charming, quick-minded man always on the go, encouraged the open exchange of opinions and made himself accessible to employees.

"How do you like your new job?" he asked.

"I do not know yet. I haven't done anything that a high school kid couldn't have done."

"Well," he said, "it takes awhile in the beginning, and there are always dull parts of the job. Somebody has to do it."

"Jerry, this is the kind of job people should not do at all. It is a job for a computer, and you do have one. Why isn't there a program that would do these recalculations? From what I hear, this kind of work needs to be done on practically every project the economic development department does."

"Our computer is a turnkey system," he said. "It only does accounting, nothing else."

"There must be a way to program it to do other things," I insisted. "There is no such thing as a computer that only does accounting."

"Frankly, I don't know. All our programming and maintenance is done by an outside firm. Their programmers come here once every two weeks. Why don't you get in touch with them and find out? If it can be done, I'll authorize your training. It might be a good idea to have this capability in-house."

Encouraged, I contacted the programmer. Yes, the computer had the capability to be programmed in modified BASIC. The language was on the machine. Within two days the programmer came in, reserved a separate space on the disk for my work, brought three thick manuals, and set up a schedule for my training.

It took me a week of training and two more weeks of the same nightmare I had gone through in school trying to learn a computer language; however, it was a far less painful process. BASIC was radically different from APL, but in many respects it was also easier and less sophisticated in its capabilities. I had not used the computer very much in school after completing the course, but the main lesson of my first confrontation with it had not been forgotten—always use logic—and soon the machine was obeying my commands. An additional terminal was installed for me in the back room, outside the accounting department, and after the first month I was kept very busy indeed. The input-output analysis was followed by modifications to the accounting system itself, which was even more fun; I could finally apply the knowledge of accounting I had learned at Wharton, and I got more and more involved in it.

Gradually I started doing work for other departments as well.

The association department did quite a few surveys in the course of their work, and the data processing was always contracted out. Emboldened by my initial success, I went to see Jerry again.

"We can do this data processing in-house and save a lot of money," I said. "But our computer is completely inadequate for statistical calculations. I can investigate other possibilities if you want me to."

"Go ahead," he said. "I'm beginning to trust your judgment. Your first idea worked out well."

I was grateful to Jerry for going along with all this. I also realized that, in a way, the strange arrangement Paul had made for me was working in my favor. There was no way Jerry could have afforded to let me spend so much time learning new things if my salary had cost the company more.

By the summer, my hands were full. I spent most of the time at the computer terminal, and I was asked to do other odd jobs. Paul's prediction that the information about my pay rate would not go beyond the accounting department's walls was wrong. Each project director got profit-and-loss statements that showed labor expenditures. Soon everybody knew that using me on a project did not add much to the cost. I was requested for all kinds of work for which even a department secretary's labor was too expensive. Even computer work began to seem repetitive and boring—I was tied to the terminal by what seemed to be an umbilical cord, unable to move to actual project work. It was a dead end, a grave I had dug for myself.

I called Paul and reminded him of the initial arrangement.

"I think I deserve a higher rate now," I said. "I've done a lot of things for the company and become more valuable to them than when I started. Changing my rate would make project directors think twice before asking me to do secretarial work."

He called his friend. After some discussions, the answer came back; everybody was happy with the status quo, no change.

I could understand that. What company president in his right mind would pay more for something he already had for less?

However, I needed more money. The cost of living in Washington was higher than in Pennsylvania; the day-care costs were high; I needed decent clothing; and my car required more and more repairs to keep it going. I started looking for a part-time job to supplement my income.

———

The logical choice for a part-time job was to find something in sales, something I could do in the evenings or on weekends and earn commission. I scanned the classified ads and, after ruling out a number of possibilities, finally settled on selling the *Encyclopaedia Britannica*.

I immediately ran into the same problem as in the car dealership—prospecting. I simply could not do it. I had not been brought up that way. I could not call complete strangers in their homes, uninvited, and start talking to them, or, even worse, make repeated calls. I believed that if people liked the product and had a need for it, they would buy it. Pushing them into buying something they did not want went against my grain. I knew it was an acceptable sales method, and salespeople were almost expected to be pushy. It just wasn't for me.

For a while, however, I did work from the booths Britannica had set up in major shopping malls. The booths are not used to make actual sales, but to make an initial contact and an appointment for a home presentation. That resolved my prospecting problem, and I started working for Britannica on Saturdays and, occasionally, Sundays. With the full-time job at the company and occasional evenings spent on sales presentations, however, I was constantly tired. Sometimes I dreamed of having a couple of days off just to give the apartment a thorough cleaning and to mend the children's clothes that were piling up in the box. I also felt guilty about not spending enough time with the children. The only day I usually had free of work was Sunday, and then I tried to catch up on housework and get some rest. Most of the time I did not have enough energy to take them out for a walk or to a museum. I did establish a routine of taking them out to eat every Friday; I tried to keep it up as much as possible and to spend that time talking to them and listening to their news about school.

In January I tried to bring up the question of my raise again.

I'd worked for the company for almost a year by then and felt the request was justified. It was turned down again.

Unhappy, I started to look for another job. I was mostly interested in finding something that would let me program computers. The more I worked with the computer, the more I became convinced that I'd finally found something I wanted to do all my life; I had not discovered it earlier simply because I had never had the opportunity. The newspaper was filled with ads for computer jobs; I sent out dozens of résumés, contacted personnel search companies, and went to several interviews. I did not get a job, though. It was the story of my interviews at Wharton all over again—too much education, too little actual computer experience. Some companies offered entry-level positions with training, but the starting pay was just too low.

I finally came to the conclusion that if I was too old to start at the bottom or even at the middle of the career ladder, then my only way to the top was to start my own business. Only my naïveté about the American business world and my inexperience could have brought me to that conclusion, but at the time I was convinced I could make it.

"You're making a mistake," Jerry said when I came to talk to him about my decision. "It takes time to develop business. What kind of business are you planning to have and what are you going to live on?"

"I'll do survey data processing," I said. "You used to subcontract that kind of work to outside companies until we started doing it in-house. There are very few companies that do this kind of work, and I can compete with them in price because I'll have very low overhead. I hope you'll continue giving me survey work after I leave here."

"That's no problem," he said. "But our surveys depend on the type of projects we get, and you cannot count on them to be a regular source of income."

"I'll get other work as well."

"I still think your decision is premature. But I wish you luck. If you change your mind, come back."

If he'd offered me more money at that time, I would have stayed.

But he didn't. I handed in my two-weeks' notice and started making plans for my business. I figured that between the agency support and a couple of surveys that were already in the works at the company, I would have the necessary income floor to get by until I developed more business.

During February I wrote the text of my company brochure, had it printed, along with the stationery and business cards, made the silly step of incorporating the company on the premise that businesses felt more comfortable working with incorporated enterprises, and got an association directory. I carefully selected the names of associations that had enough of a membership and budget to be interested in a survey, but a small enough staff to suggest that they did not have their own data-processing department. Then I rented an electronic-memory typewriter and produced 1500 personalized letters announcing my services to the world.

The mailing did bring results. I received seven replies: four were "just shopping" for a possible future survey; one required bidding, and I suspected that without a track record I would not stand a chance; and two were actually planning to do a survey and were realistic prospects. Both were located in New York.

What I did not take into account was the way associations work. All decisions are made by their boards of directors, which meet infrequently and practically never make decisions on the spot. I went to New York to meet with the executive directors of both associations; both said that they needed a proposal which they would then submit to their boards. I sent the proposals and settled down to wait.

By June it became clear I was running out of money. The start-up costs of the business had been higher than I expected; my previous employer did not expect any survey work for the next several months; and the CIA money did not cover my monthly budget. My first crack at my own business had been a dismal failure. I had to find a job.

One day at the end of June, when I had just run through my bills trying to figure out which default would hurt me the least, my phone rang. It was the manager of a Radio Shack computer center where I had interviewed in January. At that time he'd had no openings.

"I have an opening now," he said. "If you want the job, it's yours."

Doug was a maverick manager. His motto was that people could learn about computers, and could be taught the basics of selling, provided they had the brains and enough education to do it. As a result, he hired people with no experience in sales, but with interesting backgrounds and the desire to make it.

The people who worked at the store were an interesting bunch. There were five of us. One had a PhD in economics, another was a former professor of African studies, and a third had a master's degree in psychology. The base pay was low, but with good sales, people could make twenty-five thousand dollars or more a year. With consistently good sales, there was an almost certain prospect of getting to manage a computer department within a year, and then to progress to be a center manager.

Another thing that attracted me to Radio Shack was that I could work from the store itself. The problem of prospecting, or "cold-calling," still plagued me. It was the main reason I had stopped working for Britannica after only a few months. Although Radio Shack also required prospecting, I explained to Doug from the very beginning that it was something I could not do, and he agreed to let me try to work solely from the floor and promised not to bother me with prospecting as long as the results were good.

Armed with a stack of manuals, I spent four days in the back room in front of a computer, working my way through the store's programs; they were not difficult to learn, and soon I was on the floor. I did need more help as I started getting into actual selling situations, but everybody was ready to give me a hand. It took me about a month to really get going; by the end of the probationary three months my sales were well over the quota.

I liked my new job. The store was like family—there were only seven of us, including Doug and the customer support representative. There was plenty of opportunity to learn as much about computers as I cared to. There was always enough time for an hour or two at the computer, working with the programs, setting up demonstrations, or just learning new things. Soon I became proficient enough to be able to help my customers with the inevitable problems people enountered after buying their first computer, and they often called me for help. The customer support representative was always busy, handling several telephone calls at a time, and I preferred to take time from sales activities to help my customers rather than make them wait for hours until customer support could return their calls.

An additional factor in my enjoyment was that I had gotten this job all by myself. I'd found an ad in the paper, gone to an interview, and been hired on my own merit. Whatever I was making was my own doing. I was still getting money from the agency, though, and this dependence became almost an obsession with me. I wanted to terminate it as quickly as possible. Three months after I started working for Radio Shack, I called my Washington contact, Ken, and told him they could cut my allowance in half, hoping that within a year I would be able to terminate it entirely.

By November I was number three in sales in the Central Atlantic region. Then, in January, the store's sales slumped, and the regional marketing manager came to visit the store.

My conversation with him was stormy.

"You are not doing any marketing," he said. "I looked through your book and there is no record of you making twenty cold calls a day as the company requires."

I explained that my own methods worked best for me, and that I had an agreement with Doug about cold calls. He disagreed. We argued for almost an hour, and the conversation became more and more heated. I vented all the frustrations the other salespeople shared, adding a good deal of what Wharton had taught me to think about the best way to run a company.

"This was all very illuminating," he said finally. "But as long as you work for this company, you will follow company policy, and I will personally check your log in two weeks to see that you made twenty calls a day."

It was useless to continue the conversation. I walked out of the office, went to my desk, and five minutes later handed Doug my resignation.

My decision to quit my job was not entirely impulsive. In a way, the marketing manager had provided me with an excuse, and I jumped on it. I had gradually gotten fed up with sales—although most customers were nice, some treated the salespeople like pariahs.

I thought that by now I had a good chance to find something better. I felt that I had learned enough about computers to find a more professional job, either with a company that sold more serious business systems and provided a better environment for its account reps, or as a free-lance consultant. I knew from my customers that they often used consultants to help them set up the programs and train personnel. Some of these consultants were good, but quite a few were not, and I knew I could do a better job. I hoped that my former customers who had come to rely on me for help and support would hire me to do the same for them after I left Radio Shack.

Another reason I decided to jump was the terrible time crunch I was in. One of the contracts I had started to negotiate in New York long before had finally materialized. I had started work on the survey at the end of November, and now the questionnaires were coming back and the bulk of the work needed to be done. I simply could not keep up with it in the evenings and weekends. I was determined to do a good job and to complete the project on time because it was a start in my own business. I had not abandoned the idea, just put it aside for a while. The survey would also provide some income for the next couple of months, and I hoped that by then I would either have found a job or developed enough of a consulting practice.

As it happened in my first attempt at self-employment, I grossly miscalculated. The first couple of months I was very busy catching up on the work with the survey project. But nobody wanted to hire me as a consultant. The same people who'd spent hours with me at the store, resolving their software problems or learning how to operate their computers, hired "professional" consultants when they had work that needed to be done. I was good for them in the store because it was free of charge, but when it came to paying for services, they wanted something more. Nor could I find any decent job—six months of retail sales did not count for much in companies that were selling equipment worth tens of thousands of dollars.

There was also another problem. I had not thought about it at first, but many of these companies sold computer equipment to the government. Some required US citizenship, which I did not have, but even without it I did not want to work in a company that had any kind of dealings with the government. I had read enough and talked to enough people to be afraid that as a defector I would not be trusted. Although the Agency told me that I was free to choose any job I wanted and they would give me a clean bill of health, I did not want to take a chance. There would always be people who would suspect me. Therefore, I preferred to work with small private businesses or associations; they constituted the bulk of Radio Shack customers, but very few of them had enough computer work to justify a full-time position. Part-time consulting was the only chance, and with that I was getting nowhere.

I still had enough to live on, thanks to the New York project, but I was beginning to worry what would happen after it ended. The agency support had been cut in half at my own request; I did not know whether it could be reversed, but I was determined not to ask for it unless I faced the real prospect of starvation. Fortunately, as it had often happened in the past, an opportunity came along almost by accident.

I was in my old store buying additional equipment for my own computer. I often stopped there, anyway, because although I did not particularly miss my job, I did miss the other salespeople with whom I had become very friendly. Doug saw me at the counter and came out of his office.

"Our customer support rep is leaving," he said. "Want to come back as a CSR?"

I thought about it for a moment. It was not a bad idea. Being a CSR would shield me from the hassles of sales. It was a technical job that required constant learning and a very detailed knowledge of both computers and the programs. Building my technical expertise and my reputation in technical support rather than sales could be very useful in the future if I decided to try consulting again.

Doug was happy to have me back, and even the marketing manager who'd been the cause of my first resignation did not object. To my surprise, it was the district manager, with whom I always had a good relationship, who had reservations about my return.

"You won't stay long," he said. "You'll quit again. You are too independent. You'll never conform to our policies to stay with this company for long. It is too structured for you, but that is the way we work, and you will be unhappy again. How many times can I rehire you?"

Finally we worked out an agreement that I would stay for at least one year. I made arrangements with the babysitter to pick up the children from school in case I was delayed downtown in an emergency, called my old car pool members, and offered them a one-way morning ride downtown, which was gladly accepted, and went back to work.

Returning to Radio Shack as a customer support representative was probably the smartest move I'd made since I'd left school. My main duties were to help customers with whatever problems they may have had running their computers. Most of the problems were easy, caused by lack of knowledge, negligence, and, most often, a stubborn refusal to read the instructions and to take proper care of their equipment. Some were interesting and challenging and required in-depth knowledge of programs. It was a hectic job—the phone rang incessantly, customers walked in with their diskettes and questions. Not every Radio Shack center had a CSR—the center had to achieve a certain level of sales and maintain it for several months before the CSR position could be opened. In fact, at that time there were only four of us for some twenty computer centers and departments, and I often took calls from

the other stores; my name was becoming well known among customers. More important, I could take any time I needed, or wanted,
to study the new programs, without worrying about my income.
Other people did the selling; my job was to know as much as
possible.

All of that continued happily for about a year, and then I started
feeling the familiar itch again. I was overworked, money was tight
again, business was going down. It was time to move on.

This time I was more confident, not only because my knowledge
of computers and practical work experience was greater now. There
was something else. I'd finally become convinced that "the land
of opportunity" was not an empty phrase. This was the third time
in four years that I was contemplating changing jobs, but I was
not afraid to do it. Every time I'd done it in the past, things may
have looked bleak for a while, but eventually something had come
up. I simply could not believe that with all the possibilities open
to me, I would not land something better than what I was doing
now. This country had so much to offer; it was up to me to find
it.

I quickly landed several interviews; most were along the same
line—technical support—but one offered a unique opportunity. It
was with the House Information Services—a quasigovernmental
organization that provided computer services to the House of Representatives. It was not part of Civil Service, therefore I would not
formally work for the government—something I continued to avoid.
The position did not even require US citizenship, although the fact
that my papers were already going through INS was a bonus. The
management was looking for a programmer to put together a user
data base that would keep track of the usage of their computer
system. The task was extremely challenging; there was a brand
new computer with nothing on it, the data base had to be designed
and programmed and put into operation within a matter of months;
the person who would do it would have practically the sole responsibility for the project. The people who interviewed me were
eager to go ahead; after weeks of newspaper advertising I was the
only suitable candidate they had.

I was still concerned about my background. I called the agency and was told that they had no objections and that they would talk to the personnel department to clear whatever information I could not supply on the application when the time came. Still, I did not have much hope. I'd run into this strange attitude toward Russians before; the basic idea seemed to be that it was safer not to have them around. I felt it was only fair to share my concerns with Rick, the project manager who was planning to hire me.

"Don't worry," he reassured me. "Although we have to submit it for approval to a House committee, we've never had our decision overruled yet. We make our own personnel decisions here, and we have enough clout to push them through. It may take a couple of weeks, but you are as good as hired."

Well, I wasn't. Rick called and said that the application had been turned down in the House committee. He was angry and frustrated.

"I don't believe it," he said. "We go there and tell them that we need you urgently, that there is nobody else, and what do we hear? That they cannot hire a Russian in an election year—what if the press finds out? They told us to come back after the elections and there would be no problem."

"I told you it would not work. Don't worry. To tell you the truth, I hadn't really counted on it."

"We cannot wait till the elections. We must have the system operational by then or we'll lose our appropriations. We'll have to keep looking, I guess."

I assured him that there were no hard feelings. It was just politics, I said. I found it rather amusing that he was more upset about it than I was, although it was my prospective job that had been denied to me. For me, it was just another confirmation that my background and origin would forever remain a handicap in the job market. I'd suspected it all along. Now I had proof.

That my past was a handicap I had no doubts, and not just in the job market. It backfired seriously in a couple of more personal situations as well.

I met Jacques in my car pool while I was still working for the management consulting company. It was not really a car pool—I was afraid to be caught downtown without any means of getting home in case of emergency; I did all the driving, but we shared the expenses of gas and parking. We spent almost two hours every day commuting, and people in car pools usually get to know each other rather well. There were five of us, and every day we exchanged news about our families, discussed the recent events, or just chatted the time away. Jacques worked for an international organization in Washington, and, being a foreigner, had quite a few gripes about life in the United States—the quality of life, the cost of medical care, not enough social services. I used to tease him about being the kind of flaming liberal that comes only from being the spoiled offspring of a rich family, which he was, and would argue in favor of a free-market system. Our arguments often kept the whole car pool amused and busy during the trips.

I did not realize, however, that at the same time he was developing a crush on me. The thought of anything personal did not even occur to me—he was ten years younger—but eventually we did start seeing each other, and he began talking about marriage and commitment "for the rest of your life."

Jacques was separated from his wife, Arlene, but it had not been a mutual decision. He had left her—and she still wanted him back. The fact that I had entered the picture only made things more complicated for her. She enrolled the help of her father, who held a high position in a government agency, he called a few of his contacts, and soon Arlene had a trump card in her hand. Then she called Jacques.

"Your girlfriend has a rather interesting background," she said. "I'll give you a choice of several options: I will call your organization and tell them that you are involved with a Soviet defector, which will undoubtedly ruin your career because they are rigorously trying to stay above politics; or I can make a quick call to the Soviet embassy, which, I assume, will be very happy to learn her whereabouts; or you can come back and I will forget I ever knew her."

He went back. I was furious. Not at him—he did not have much choice—nor at her—she'd simply been fighting for what she considered her property. I was furious because I'd been told that my file was buried under seven locks at the INS and there was no way anybody could get access to it, not even for the purpose of a security check. I did not know whether Arlene's father had friends at the agency or whether my INS file had been dug up—the only relevant fact was that it had not taken long for her to find everything she needed to know about me.

Another incident took place a few years later, but was equally disturbing. I'd known Ron for several years—we'd dated for a while when I'd begun my first attempt in the business. Then we'd drifted apart, he'd gotten married. We remained friendly, though, and ran into each other occasionally, being more or less in the same business—the community of computer professionals is not that big. On one such occasion he said that his marriage had not worked out and he was separated. We started dating again, and it was getting rather serious this time, until one night the dreaded question came up.

"You know," he said, "you never really told me much about yourself. I only know that you went to school here and what you were doing thereafter. How did you come to be here in the first place?"

I told him. He listened with interest about my adventures and asked a lot of questions. One question bothered me, though.

"Is the CIA still keeping an eye on you?"

"You mean, like tapping my phone and things like that? No, I don't think so. I don't even think they were doing it while I was still in Pennsylvania. It certainly would be a waste of money and time if they did."

"You did have a problem with the House Information Services," he persisted. "Do you think the agency called there behind your back and told them not to hire you?"

"I have no reason to think so. They certainly told me that there was no problem with me taking that job. I think what Rick told me was true—it was a politically tense situation, and I was not a US citizen then. Why are you so concerned? You don't work for the government."

"I am undergoing a security clearance right now," he confessed. "I am bidding on a large RCA contract, and they are heavily involved in defense research. In order to do my own work for them, I must have a 'need-to-know' clearance."

"How long will it take? If you think your relationship with me might be a problem, we can keep it quiet for a while." Not that we advertised it anyway. He was still separated and waiting for his final divorce, and I did not want to start rumors that could reach his wife. Although he said that the divorce was amicable, I was not certain his wife felt the same way.

"Oh, three to six months," he said. "No, I don't think our relationship would be a problem. After all, they must have checked and rechecked everything when they gave you citizenship, because it qualifies you to apply for government jobs."

We switched to another topic, but I had a feeling that the news disturbed him. Several days later he abruptly canceled a dinner we had planned. I never heard from him again.

The incident brought forward again my years-long debate—was I right in hiding my past? I still tended not to tell people about my background right away. In personal relationships, such as the one I had had with Ron, it had obviously backfired—the longer I hid my past, the more time the relationship had to develop to the point where breaking it up would be emotionally difficult. Yet, I preferred to take that chance—or even stop dating—rather than be completely open with strangers.

Some of my friends knew about my background, of course. Just like with Aron in Philadelphia, I found it very difficult to build a true friendship with somebody when I constantly had to watch what I said about my past. My confession never brought any adverse reaction; on the contrary, my friends appreciated the difficulties I had gone through and admired my action. But they were few, trusted friends, and I was not ready to make my background public knowledge. I still feared that the embassy might want to get back at me.

Fortunately the feeling was not as acute as it had been during the first two years. Then it had been a nightmare. I hadn't been able to get a quick divorce because Pennsylvania was one of the last holdouts of the old divorce laws. I'd been afraid that Lev, or the Soviet government on his behalf, would go to court to get the children back. I'd been fairly certain he would not do it on his own—he did not want the children—but the government could have asked him to sign the papers. Another possibility was a case like the one that had recently happened in Chicago. A twelve-year-old boy named Walter Polovchak had refused to return home with his parents, Soviet emigrés who had changed their minds. Walter had been given asylum by the US government, but the ACLU had brought a case in court that his parents' rights had been violated, and demanded his return. It was beyond my understanding that an American organization would do something like that, but it was the other side of being a free country. Although the action would have ruined the boy's future forever had he returned to the Soviet Union, there was nothing to stop the ACLU from acting the way it did.

Finally, no-fault divorce law was passed in Pennsylvania in the middle of 1979, and I immediately got my divorce. It was a relief to have the formal custody of the children, established by the court and not easy to challenge. Still, I had to be careful. Although I had renounced my Soviet citizenship, I had no way of knowing whether the Soviet government had accepted it. Technically, my children and myself could still be subject to Soviet law, in the eyes of which, of course, I was a criminal. My only hope was to get my American citizenship, but I had to wait five years for it from the moment my residence permit was granted. I was lucky that I had never been a member of the Communist Party—in that case the wait would have been ten years. The citizenship would resolve the problem once and for all—unlike other countries, such as Italy, which permit people to hold dual citizenship, American law is unequivocal: an American citizen cannot be a citizen of another country. With the citizenship I would be much better protected.

Now at last my citizenship was finally in the works. It was 1984, five years had passed, and the agency initiated the proceedings. I knew it would take several months because of the backlog at INS, and waited eagerly for the moment. It signified so much to me—finally, the ultimate freedom, I would truly become a part of this country which I had come to love and admire so much.

I also hoped that with citizenship I would have more opportunity to try to help my mother. I still did not believe that she would be let out of the country. The policy of the Soviet Union in regard to defectors' families remained unchanged, but at least I could formally try. Mother has always been a sick woman and even drew a disability pension, because after two spinal surgeries she could not spend too much time sitting up. That precluded any desk job, or practically any job at all. Her health was deteriorating. After the divorce she'd moved to the southern republic of Soviet Georgia, but soon realized that the climate was worsening her asthma and had had to move again to a better climate. I thought wishfully of how much I could do for her here. Every time I saw newspaper accounts of people getting out of the Soviet Union, I thought that if I were free to act, maybe I could get enough support from the US government to get my mother's release. Some cases were so odd that they defied reason. One Soviet emigré, Eduard Lozansky, even secured the release of his ex-wife whom he had divorced before he left the Soviet Union. It had been illogical to expect any results—as an ex-husband he had no claim under the Soviet law— but he'd rallied enough public support and even gotten two US senators to stand by him at his proxy wedding in Washington. Finally, as a gesture of goodwill, the Soviet government had let his ex-wife go. Things like that happened occasionally and depended solely on the state of Soviet-American relations. There was always a possibility that another case could slip through the net.

The problem was that I could not go out and lobby for it. I did get in touch with Robert Kaiser at the *Washington Post*. I had read his book, admired his knowledge of the Soviet Union, and decided he would be the right person to ask for advice. He was intrigued by my story and promised to keep our meeting off the record. He was not very optimistic about the chances of getting my mother out, however.

"We cannot lobby for you," he said. "We can run a front page story and attract enough attention to your case, but then you would have to take over. Such an undertaking requires a sustained effort, sometimes months or years of lobbying, and nobody can see it through except yourself. If you are not ready to go public—which, by the way, is a mistake, because publicity could be your best protection—there is nothing anybody can do to help your mother."

I knew he was right, and I was grateful for his advice, but until

I got my citizenship the issue was moot. He did get in touch with me again when there was another attempt to escape from the embassy and he needed some background information. Another woman, the wife of a second secretary at the embassy, had defected, but broke down during the meeting at the State Department and gone back to the embassy in tears. I was happy to help him, and, true to his word, he kept my name out of print.

I did call Jim, who was still with the FBI office, about the incident with this woman, a Mrs. Mamedova. I was sad to learn that she had not been successful in her attempt. I knew all too well how hard it must have been for her to make that decision, and how much support she needed in the first few days after defection.

"You know," I said, "I wish you'd remembered that I am still here. When you have a situation like that, it may be helpful to let the person talk to me and get some reassurance."

"Could be," he said, "although in this particular case she was beyond salvation. She did it on an impulse and was immediately overcome with regrets and guilt. She broke down completely at the meeting. We could see it coming, and I think that a meeting with you could only have jeopardized you and not done any good for her."

"All the same," I said, "you know you can count on me if you need me."

"We will."

By the end of November my papers had started moving through INS channels. Ken, my agency contact, called me and said that they had set a date for my interview—a few questions on US history and political organization, nothing to worry about. The paperwork was all taken care of, and the supervisor of the INS office was apprised of my situation, so there would be no questions of a personal nature I could not answer.

I should have known better than that. The interview went smoothly; after a short wait I was called to sign some papers, when suddenly the clerk noticed that the spelling of my first name on my driver's license and my application for citizenship was slightly different—Yelena and Elena.

"We need a copy of a court decision about your name change," she said. "We cannot process your papers without it. If you don't have it, you will have to rewrite an application with the correct spelling and resubmit it for reprocessing."

I knew that my name had been legally changed at the same time I had gotten my divorce, but I did not have any papers—the agency had kept them.

"Your office was supposed to be notified about this case," I said. "Perhaps your supervisor is better informed."

She went to see the supervisor, came back, invited me in, and left me with the supervisor. I started to explain why I did not have any relevant papers and referred to my conversation with Ken. Her eyes showed total incomprehension.

"I had no notification from anybody," she said. "I have no idea what you are talking about." She was experienced enough, though, to figure out that she had an unusual case here. "Why don't you give me the phone number of this man who handled your paperwork and I will contact him myself. Call me two days from now."

I left, quietly swearing. Nothing had changed. I knew it was not Ken's fault—he had not handled the liaison with INS himself. Somebody else in another department had assured him that everything was done, and that's what he had told me. It took several days to sort things out, and finally I was told to go for another interview. This time there were no questions, and the official date in court was set for December 20, just in time for Christmas.

The big event turned out to be almost an anticlimax. It was official and dry. There were about a hundred other people in the courthouse receiving their citizenship the same day. We stood in line for almost an hour. Then we were shepherded into the courtroom, assigned our seats, and told to remember our seat number as a reference for the rest of the proceeding. There was a roll call; I was the only Russian. Most of the others were from the Middle East or Asia. The judge made a speech, followed by a speech from an elderly lady who represented the Daughters of the American Revolution. I expected an uplifting event—after all, for all of us there it was the culmination of our dreams—but there was nothing uplifting there, just bureaucratic procedures and head counting.

"At least they could play the national anthem for us," whispered the man standing next to me. "They play it at every football game. Don't you think this is a bit more important?"

I agreed. Most of the people in the room would go home and celebrate this event with their families and friends. It was a tremendously important turning point in their lives, an event that was very symbolic, the end of a long struggle. Many had risked their lives coming to this country. Couldn't we be welcomed a little more warmly as its new citizens? Even a high school graduation ceremony carried more emotional impact.

A year and a half had passed since I'd left the Radio Shack. My life seemed to have settled into a manageable pattern. The gamble had paid off—as soon as I'd left, the customers followed me. Gradually I switched from support and training to systems development, specializing in accounting systems for small businesses, where my Wharton background and programming capabilities combined to my advantage. After two aborted attempts, I was finally running my own business. I learned what it meant to be your own boss—if anything goes wrong or the work is not done on time, there is nobody to cover for you. Weekends ceased to exist for the most part—there was too much work to be done— but I did not mind. This was what I had always wanted—to make my own decisions, to do my work the way I saw it. I'd paid dearly for this privilege, and I was not going to complain. This was what this country was about, and I loved it.

The children were doing equally well. Kitty finally stopped asking questions about her father and was old enough to understand when I explained to her our family history. She and Konstantin became typical American kids—Barbies, Transformers, McDonald's and pizza. Both did well in school, and it finally assuaged my guilt about not giving them enough of my time in the process of chasing the American dream. They did not speak Russian at all, but developed some interest in Russia, which I encouraged— there are already too many people in America completely ignorant about the Soviet Union, and there is no need to increase their ranks. And I had changed, too.

"I must be getting old," I complained jokingly to one of my clients while working on the computer in her office. "Why else would I trade my comfortable Oldsmobile for that sporty thing where my knees touch the steering wheel? Subconsciously, I must be trying to jazz up my image." My old reliable car had finally required so many repairs that I could no longer afford it. To my own surprise, and almost on an impulse, I bought a sporty turbo four-seater. My children laughed for two days watching me try to tame a manual shift after so many years of driving an automatic.

"I don't think so." She laughed. "More likely you always wanted a sports car but did not feel secure enough to let yourself admit it."

There was truth in that. Success in business had undoubtedly brought me more security and confidence. I even gave good old "Dress for Success" to Goodwill and stopped wearing conservatively tailored business suits. I felt that my reputation had become well enough established to afford a little more flair.

The past would not go away, though. It got back at me in ways that were unpredictable and could not be foreseen or avoided. Once, I met a Russian emigré at a party at Anna's house. He was actually from Soviet Georgia, and his Russian was not very good, but it was still better than his English.

We went out, and I quickly found myself forced to speak about Russia and life in Moscow.

Merab was very apprehensive about his halting English and because of that did not socialize much with Americans. His life was between his job, in which he was surrounded by his former compatriots, and his apartment, in a building where his colleagues lived. He had little knowledge about events outside of his transplanted native world, and the only topic of conversation we could maintain for more than a couple of minutes was about the old life back there. In addition, I switched to Russian to make it easier for him. It took me half an hour to get back my fluency in Russian— I had not spoken the language practically since I had left the embassy. Even with Aron, who'd constantly jumped from Russian to English, I'd always spoken English.

It was a mistake. Later that night I had a nightmare, the worst

I could recall in many years. I dreamed that I was in Moscow, surrounded by Russians, speaking Russian. For some reason my mother was not there. I was searching for my children—the State had taken them away and given them to Lev, but he did not want them and had sent them to an orphanage. The last thing I remembered of my dream was myself, standing on my knees on the pavement of a snow-covered street, begging my mother-in-law to tell me where my children had been sent so I could at least go and see them from afar.

I woke up in the middle of the night. The dream was still vivid in my mind, and I could not fall asleep again. I'd never analyzed why I avoided seeing Russians and speaking Russian. My rationalization was always that the Russian community was supposed to be so infiltrated by the KGB that it was not safe for me to be seen there. As for the language, I simply found it easier to speak English. I did notice that I had no problems speaking about Russia with my American friends, in English. It was as if English provided an impersonal touch to the conversation; I could talk about "life there" as if it were somebody else's life.

Now it seemed that there was a deeper reason for my reluctance to speak Russian. Sometimes our bodies know better than we what the stress points are, the danger signals, and they try to protect the mind by shutting certain things off. It was the combination of speaking about Russia *in Russian* that broke that carefully constructed safeguard and brought the nightmare out of the deepest freeze of my memories. There must have been something still lurking there—fear of reprisals? Guilt? Fear of rejection? I brought the question up with a very good friend whose opinion and common sense I highly valued. The end of my affair with Ron was still fresh on my mind, and the nagging question remained: had he disappeared because he was afraid that his security clearance was in jeopardy, or was it because he disapproved of what I had done?

"I do not see it as a question of your morality," she said. "Perhaps it is because I am an American, and we grow up with a sense that personal freedom is the main value of human life, and whatever people do to achieve it is morally justified. My only reaction, when you told me about your past, was an immense pride that you took such a risk to do what you thought was right for you and your children, and I doubt very much that any American would interpret it in any other way."

Still, I was not convinced. I loved Russia. I felt bitter about the system that forced people to choose between their motherland and the desire to be in charge of their own life, and I still felt guilty about leaving. If only I could have both! All I wanted was to have my own business—a normal thing for anybody here, but what a price I had to pay for it!

Or maybe Bob Kaiser had been right that by hiding I created my own problems, opened myself to blackmail, and exacerbated my inner doubts. What was there to hide after all this time? It was unlikely that the embassy would undertake anything against me now—I was formally divorced from Lev, and both I and my children were citizens of this country. I remembered a book I had read recently, a memoir of another Soviet defector, Vladimir Sakharov, a former KGB officer who had defected to the United States years before. He'd gone through many tribulations here, but finally made his own life. After years of hiding, he'd come out into the open and was now giving lectures and consulting with the American business community on their dealings with the Soviets. I'd seen an interview with him on television, and he'd said he was sick of pretending to be somebody else, and even though he knew he was taking a risk by revealing his identity, it was the first time in many years that he finally felt free, just by being himself again.

Still, I was not ready. I knew that unpleasant surprises, such as Ron's sudden departure from my life, would continue to happen as long as I continued to live this lie. All I could bring myself to do was start telling my acquaintances about my past a bit sooner before I really got involved—at least the disappointment would not be so great later.

And so I continued to live my life in the shadows of my past until a sudden and unexpected event forced me to make a decision and helped me to take that final step.

CHAPTER **20**

*I*N early September 1985 a small article in the newspaper caught my attention. It said that Vitaly Yurchenko, a high-level KGB official, had defected while on a trip to Italy and was now in the hands of American intelligence in Washington.

I read it twice. I could not believe my eyes. Vitaly Yurchenko, the embassy security officer who'd given us such a stern lecture about the dangers of American recruiting attempts at that women's meeting at the embassy? Could it be the same person?

A few days later the press reported that he had been attached to the embassy in Washington during the late seventies. There was no question—it was the same man. It still did not make much sense. The papers reported that he had been the number-five man in the KGB and had run all the North American spy networks. I did not know much about KGB operations, but I did know what his duties had been at the embassy—counterintelligence, internal security, keeping an eye on us. How he had managed to transit from such a relatively low-level job to being number five in active operations was beyond me. Maybe security was just his side assignment as a senior KGB officer? But he wasn't even senior among other KGB people in the embassy.

The fact was, however, that he had defected. It was an interesting twist of fate. Maybe that was exactly what the FBI had been trying to accomplish with my own defection—to show other people at the embassy that it could be done. I often wondered why nobody had followed, except for the one misguided attempt by Mrs. Mamedova. The obvious reason of course was that nobody had been unhappy enough to contemplate such a drastic step. There was also the possibility that the security had been tightened after my departure. A fairly steady stream of defections, most of them KGB people, had been taking place in other countries; only recently one high-ranking officer had defected in Greece and another in London. Well, maybe I had underestimated Vitaly. I'd never known him well, and after that memorable meeting I had avoided him like the plague. But he couldn't have been such a bad guy, after all, if he decided to take such a risk. He must have had a reason for it. I called Jim.

"Do you think you could arrange for me to meet with Yurchenko? After all, we are old colleagues. Seriously," I added, "I've been there. There are some reports coming out that he is having a difficult time with the debriefing. Maybe I could give him a helping hand. I know there is life after debriefing, but he may not. Besides, I am dying to know what happened in the embassy after I left."

"Might not be a bad idea," Jim said. "He did mention that he started thinking about it while he was still in Washington in the aftermath of your defection. Let me sound it out—you know he is out of our hands by now."

I knew that. The CIA would have him by now, and that was exactly what worried me. I did not want a repetition of Mrs. Mamedova's story. I did not want the fame of being a lone star, the only person who had defected from the Soviet Embassy in fifty years. I wanted company.

Jim called back a few days later.

"The guys here generally think it's a good idea," he said cautiously. "We have to put it through channels, though. See if you can talk to Anna's husband about it—he can try to pull some strings unofficially through his old buddies in the agency, and it may work faster. It will take awhile for us to put it through."

I called Anna. She no longer worked for the agency. Her husband, formerly a high CIA official, had retired from the agency a long time ago and had been in a private consulting practice for many years, but he still had tremendous connections. He supported the idea enthusiastically. Both he and Anna knew many other Soviet defectors and knew only too well how many things could go wrong. By now even I knew the official statistics—almost 50 percent of all defectors go back. It was a staggering, and sobering, figure.

I could only wait, though. Yurchenko was certainly being kept in the safe house. I knew there would be objections about taking me there—for both his security reasons and my own. The CIA does not encourage defectors to get to know each other; it is a prudent measure—if one goes back, the others could be jeopardized. The recent return of Svetlana Alliluyeva to the Soviet Union showed only too clearly that even after many years people can still get homesick and run back.

The papers continued to publish reports on Yurchenko. He was apparently providing interesting information. The FBI made at least one arrest and was searching for another man whom Yurchenko had ostensibly pointed out. There were also reports that he was not as high ranking in the KGB as had initially been suggested. The speculations abounded about his true status and knowledge. There was still no word from the FBI or Anna's husband.

I did not even know why I was so concerned about it. He was not my friend. The best explanation I could think of was that strange feeling of fraternity that people sometimes develop after they have gone through a disaster or a life-threatening situation together. It is the knowledge of something that other people who have not been through it cannot understand; emotions that cannot be explained but only understood by somebody who has been there. It was one of the reasons I still had such warm feelings about the FBI people who had been with me at that time. They did not need any explanations; they knew. I only knew that I wanted to see Vitaly; he was somebody like me. Nobody could get through this experience without scars. If he had the same kind of feelings I did when I was cooped up in the safe house, he needed somebody like me—to listen and to understand what he was going through.

I finally put it out of my head. Thinking about all the things that could go wrong with Vitaly stirred too many old memories. I could only hope that Jim would prevail and the permission would be granted.

It all came to a conclusion on November 5. I was driving home from downtown Washington, where I'd spent all afternoon doing computer work. It was raining and as usual Washington traffic was crawling. Rain and snow always create traffic jams in Washington—it is a city of fair weather.

I was listening to my favorite radio station. It played the music I liked—the classics of the big band era—and my radio was always tuned to it. The six o'clock news break started. The first item was Yurchenko.

"Vitaly Yurchenko, the highest-ranking KGB official ever to defect to the United States, is back at the Soviet Embassy tonight," said the announcer. "We are awaiting more information from the news conference scheduled by the embassy for six o'clock tonight.

I immediately switched to an all-news station. More news was coming in. Apparently Yurchenko had been having dinner with one of the CIA people in a Georgetown restaurant, only a few blocks away from the new Soviet Embassy compound, when he'd left on the pretext of going to the restroom and never returned. There were no speculations yet about his being a double agent— that would surface later. Right now everybody waited for the press conference.

What went wrong? I could only guess. He was a KGB officer, after all, and his debriefing would have been much more intense. If by any chance he'd overbilled himself in regard to his rank or knowledge, he would have had a hard time on cross-examination. It was only human to try to evade certain questions when personal friends were concerned. It is one thing to walk out on the system, and another to point a finger at personal friends, knowing that it could endanger their lives, and especially so for a Russian who places personal friendship so high on his priority list.

Had he just become homesick? Possibly. Even after many years here, I sometimes thought longingly about going to Leningrad, just for a few days, to see that majestic city, to touch the granite of its columns and embankments. I sorely missed long nights with my friends, the endless stream of coffee or something stronger, and endless talking. And of course I missed my mother. It was November 5—two days before the biggest national holiday in the Soviet Union. It is of course the kind of official holiday I've described before, but there are no unofficial holidays in Russia, and it is an occasion for parties, for friends and families to get together and celebrate. Had it made his homesickness worse? I could guess forever and never know the truth. Whatever it was must have been serious, because going back was suicide. The KGB does not forgive its own. He might be able to save his neck by providing information about the American debriefing procedures, and even some intelligence information gathered from the questions he was asked, but he would never work again. Under the best circumstances he would fade into the obscurity of an early retirement; under the worst— I did not want to think about it.

Why did he do it? He could have been a plant, of course—but if he were, he would have stayed. Or maybe he'd realized, just as I had after a while, that he would always be suspected of being a double agent. There were precedents—the most notorious was the case of Yury Nosenko in the early sixties. He'd spent three years in solitary confinement at a military base while the CIA tried to decide whether he was a genuine defector or not. He'd finally been released and now worked as a consultant for the CIA, cleared of all suspicions. Had Vitaly seen the same fate for himself? If he had, it was not difficult to see how he had decided to exchange one prison for another. At least in the other one they spoke Russian.

The problem of trust is a sore point for many defectors, and, truthfully, cannot be resolved. The Soviet Union does indeed occasionally send a plant to identify CIA personnel involved in debriefing, to learn about changes in procedures, or, in the longer term, to infiltrate American society. It takes time to establish who is a genuine defector and who is not. On the other hand, those who truly defect often do it for ideological reasons. Being taken care of financially is not a very important factor—they want to contribute their share in the fight against the system they left, and having their motives distrusted can hurt them badly.

It was 6:45 when I finally got home. I rushed to the TV set to catch the evening news. They televised part of the news conference. Vitaly looked somewhat drained, but otherwise perfectly composed and even smiling. He read a prepared statement that said that he had been kidnapped while in Italy, kept under drugs, and brought to the United States against his will, and that he had escaped at the first opportunity. I did not believe a word of it. I'd heard it too many times from every defector who returned, and I'd seen many, even when I was still there. They all said, with slight variations, that they had been abducted by hostile intelligence services and kept under lock—a month, a year, whatever time period it took them to decide to go back. I'd met two such people in Leningrad. One was a former graduate student of philosophy, in England under a student exchange program; another was a former professor of Marxist history. I could never believe that the "hostile" service would go to such trouble as to kidnap them. For what purpose? To start classes in Marxism? The fact was that after their return both existed on handouts from friends or occasional translation work their friends got for them without mentioning who would actually do the work.

I did not know then any of the other circumstances surrounding Vitaly's stay here. They would surface in the press later: stories about an involvement with a woman attached to the Soviet Embassy in Canada, who refused to defect with him, after which he became difficult and uncooperative. There were also reports that he had been planning to disappear in Italy so nobody would ever suspect that he had defected and his wife and family would not be punished, and had been very frustrated about leaks to the press. Both interpretations were plausible. Even I had gone through considerable planning before actually defecting; he was an experienced officer and must have worked out what he thought to be a foolproof plan, only to see it blown apart by political expediency. I could not dismiss the possibility that his reunion with the woman he loved had not gone smoothly; it was not inconceivable that by the time the CIA had gotten him to Canada, the KGB had been there ahead of him and coerced her into refusal.

All of that I did not know yet, however, and even afterward I could only speculate, just like everybody else. And even if I had known, it probably would not have overshadowed what I felt—that the main problem had been his inability to adjust to being a defector. I remembered all too vividly my own loneliness, the debriefings, the despair that almost had made me think about suicide when things had not gone as I expected, the guilt and the second thoughts I had had. Victor Belenko had had a CIA contact on whose door he could knock at three in the morning before turning himself in to the Soviet Embassy as he intended to do; I had my FBI friends who pulled me through the darkest moments. Did Vitaly have somebody he could *really* talk to, or had he been surrounded by the male equivalents of Barbara? Vitaly's depression would have been a normal stage in the defection process, but somebody should have seen it coming; there should have been somebody with him who could see him through this crisis, to tell him that it was all right, he'd done the right thing, and all these feelings would pass; that he could be happy in this country, happy with his life again. *It did not have to end like this!*

I went to the phone. There was no question in my mind where to call.

"What city, please?" said an impersonal voice on the other end.

"Washington, DC," I said. *"ABC Nightline."*

———————

At that moment I still did not think of myself as going out into the open. All I wanted to do was share with somebody the frustration I felt that a man like Vitaly, a man of immense value to this country, had been lost, possibly because of bureaucratic ineptitude, and the conviction that something should be done to prevent it from happening in the future. I needed somebody who would tell it to other people for me, who would be able to explain it to the world so the rest of the people would understand.

Nightline was a logical choice. It covered its subjects in greater depth than the regular evening news; at the same time it always got to major events quickly, and I was certain they would be doing a program on Yurchenko, possibly the very same day.

To the woman who answered the *Nightline* phone, I probably sounded incoherent. My accent always becomes stronger when I am upset; in addition, I wasn't really sure what I wanted to say, and I was still afraid to say too much about myself. It was a miracle that she did not dismiss me as another crank call; instead, she did what any good professional journalist would have done in her place—she kept me talking on the phone until I was able to collect my thoughts and say that I had been a member of the embassy here, had defected some years back, had gone through the same process as Yurchenko had, and that I felt that something might have gone wrong in his debriefing process. They were planning to have a program on Yurchenko the very next day, and she would not let me go until I'd promised I would call them and talk to the producer myself.

The next day I was more calm and rational. I called Bob Kaiser at the *Washington Post;* I felt that after knowing him for several years I owed him a chance on this story. He said he had the same feeling—something must have gone wrong there—and asked if I was willing to talk to one of his reporters. Since he was now in charge of national news for the newspaper, he was not involved in interviewing himself.

I did not want to disclose my present identity—the fear was still there. I told Bob to use my old name—Yelena Mitrokhina. It was also the name I gave to the *Nightline* producer, Tara, when I reached her shortly before noon. My call was expected—the woman to whom I had talked the previous evening had told her in detail about our conversation. Tara was elated; within an hour she reached Ted Koppel in Philadelphia. When I called back a couple of hours later, she asked me to appear on the broadcast.

I agreed to go on the air. I still had my blond wig from years back, and I knew that coupled with dark glasses it would make me practically unrecognizable. I did not have to disclose the name I was currently using. I felt that the issue of how a defector was handled was important enough to speak out, but I still thought it would be just one appearance and one interview. After that I would go back to living my life quietly, as before.

I spent three hours with the *Post* reporter, had my picture taken, still with the wig and sunglasses, went home, and returned downtown later for the broadcast. It was easier than I had thought; Ted

Koppel was easy to talk to. His voice sounded so nice and reassuring in my earphones that I almost forgot I was sitting in front of a camera that was sending my image to millions of homes. I talked about the stress and anxiety all defectors went through, and the critical need for support from people who are with the defector at that time, and how many things can go wrong if those people are not right for the job. After the broadcast we shook hands and I went home. It was an interesting day. Tomorrow I would go back to my regular routine, being Alex Costa again. No one would know that it was me up on the screen. The children would go to school; I had several appointments with clients whose computers needed my immediate attention. My frustration subsided—I had done what I could to bring the problem to the public, and that was all I could, or wanted, to do.

Little did I know that fate had other plans for me. I'd started a chain of events that I could not control.

I was making breakfast for the children when my phone rang at eight in the morning. It was my best friend, whom I had told the day before about the broadcast and the newspaper interview.

"Did you see the paper yet?" she asked.

"No," I said. The children had gone to bed late because they had gone with me to the ABC studio, and I was in a hurry to get them out to school on time.

"Go and look. I'll talk to you later."

I went to the porch and picked up the paper. One glance told me what she meant.

My own picture looked at me from the front page. Everything was as I expected—the blond wig, the dark glasses. Except for one little detail—the caption said that my name was Alexandra Costa, and the text of the article specifically emphasized that it was the name I had adopted after defection.

The next fifteen minutes were hazy. I got the children up, gave them breakfast, and practically pushed them out the door. Then I ran to the phone and called Patrick Tyler, the *Post* reporter with whom I had spoken the day before.

"Have you seen the paper yet?" I almost yelled.

"No," came back a sleepy voice. "Hold on."

In a couple of minutes he came back. "What's wrong?" he said. "I do not see any problem."

"It's the name that's wrong. I thought we had an agreement."

Gradually we both realized the misunderstanding. It had been a long interview, and I had given Pat both names, one to use in publication and the other in case he needed to reach me to get more details later that day. Because I knew that Bob Kaiser was aware of my intention to use the old name, I assumed he had told it to Pat, and I had not emphasized it clearly enough during the interview. Pat, in turn, had assumed that I did not want to jeopardize my family back in Russia, and kept my old name out of print. Had he not been so tired in the evening, he would have watched *Nightline* and would have realized the mistake, but he had not stayed up that late. Had I stayed in the ABC studio for a few more minutes, I would have seen the early edition of the *Post* and would have called Pat in time to stop the presses, but I had been tired and the children had to be taken home as quickly as possible.

Pat was desolate, but I was not angry at him. It was an honest error, his assumption had been logical, and if it was anybody's fault, it was my own. I should have made it clear beyond any doubt which name I wanted to be used in print.

I thought feverishly. Now the embassy had the name I was currently using, and it would only be a matter of time until they knew my address. My phone number was unlisted, but the phone company had the records—difficult to get, but not impossible. Another source would be the Department of Motor Vehicles. Both would not give out the address without a court order, but bribes have been known to work miracles.

At least I could make it a little more difficult. I called the telephone company and changed my billing address from my home to a post office box I used for correspondence with my mother. Then I called Ken at the CIA.

He sounded upset and wanted to know why I had jumped into it in the first place. He was also genuinely concerned about possible repercussions. I explained my motives for going ahead with the media. "As for repercussions," I concluded, "you tell me—what do you think will happen?"

"We don't know. But we think it would be prudent to change your name again and move you to another city. We cannot guarantee your security if you stay here."

"I don't want to move. I've already thought about it and I don't think the embassy would really go after me after all this time. My situation is different now; I am much better protected from a legal point of view, and I don't see what they would gain by going after me except a lot of bad publicity. Besides, they have more important defectors to chase—I am not at the top of their list. It took me four years to build my business, and it has been built on my name and my reputation; if I move to another city I would have to start from zero, and the last thing I want to do is go back on agency welfare."

I did promise to keep my eyes open and let him know at the first sign of anything unusual. I also asked him what I should do with the media—by then Tara had already called me with a list of people who called *Nightline* and wanted to talk to me. I had taken down the numbers—*Time* magazine, Cable News Network, UPI— but had not returned any calls yet.

"Return the calls," Ken said. "Since you don't want to move, right now publicity is your best protection."

It made sense. It was the same thing Bob Kaiser had told me years ago. I could also see it working—Arkady Shevchenko, whose defection had been politically far more important than mine, had chosen never to hide and had not even changed his name. He was a public figure now, and it had apparently worked for him.

But what about my business? How would my clients react? Was the disaster with the House Information Services and my breakup with Ron indicative of what was to come, or was my friend right in saying that for most Americans it was a natural assumption that people should seek freedom in any way they could? Right now the damage was limited to one broadcast and one newspaper article. I fervently hoped that most of my clients were early risers who went to bed by ten. There was less hope, though, that they would overlook the front page of the *Post*.

The issue resolved itself quickly. I began receiving call after call. Some people had seen *Nightline*. Most had not recognized me in disguise—until the moment I had started to talk. My voice and accent were instantly recognizable by anybody who knew me well enough.

Even more people saw the *Post*. They were the ones who were genuinely puzzled—if I had decided to print my name, why the wig? After I explained the mistake, the reaction was the same: is it safe for you now?

Nobody was apprehensive; nobody canceled my appointments. Their sentiments could be summarized in a few words: "We are concerned about your safety. And we hope that being a celebrity will not prevent you from continuing to work for us. We need you."

The morning that had started with panic was becoming a celebration. It was as if the burden had suddenly been lifted from my shoulders. All the fears disappeared. For seven years I'd been living on my star, silent and lonely, afraid to set foot outside of my little private domain. I'd stepped down from it and found the world ready to greet me with open arms and a smile.

My throat was beginning to hurt from nonstop talking. I went to the kitchen and made myself a cup of an old Russian remedy—half tea, half milk, with a dash of baking soda. The day was not over. I had a long list of calls to return.